The Sterling Bonds and Fixed Income Handbook

A practical guide for investors and advisers

By Mark Glowrey

Hh

HARRIMAN HOUSE LTD

3A Penns Road
Petersfield
Hampshire
GU32 2EW
GREAT BRITAIN

Tel: +44 (0)1730 233870
Email: enquiries@harriman-house.com
Website: www.harriman-house.com

First published in Great Britain in 2013

9780857190420

British Library Cataloguing in Publication Data
A CIP catalogue record for this book can be obtained from the British Library.

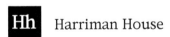

Contents

Acknowledgements

I would like to thank my publisher, Harriman House, for their patience in waiting for this much-delayed book.

A debt of gratitude also goes to Michael Dyson, then working at Barclays Capital, and Anthony "Bonzo" Lorenzo of Winterflood Securities who stepped up to the plate in 2006 to provide the initial sponsorship for the **www.fixedincomeinvestor.co.uk** website. This sponsorship in turn was generously continued by the bond teams at BARCAP (Will Hall & Gurnaik Johal) and Wins (Oliver Brown and Stacey Parsons), and in due course by my own employer Canaccord Genuity. I would also like to thank Chris Martin and the eCube technology team for creating the website.

Finally, thank you to Barry, Oliver, Mike and all the contributors to this book, and of course my wife Corina, without whose support it would not have been possible.

eBook edition

As a buyer of the print edition of *The Sterling Bonds and Fixed Income Handbook* you can now download the eBook edition free of charge to read on an eBook reader, your smartphone or your computer. Simply go to:

http://ebooks.harriman-house.com/sterlingbonds

or point your smartphone at the QRC below.

You can then register and download your eBook copy of the book.

Harriman House

About the Author

Mark Glowrey is Head of Retail Bond Sales at Canaccord Genuity. Prior to this, he spent over a decade as a director of Stockcube Research Limited, a leading independent analysis company. Mark has over twenty-five years' experience of trading securities and advising institutional customers, starting his career as a dealer on the floor of the London Stock Exchange in the early 1980s before moving on to specialise in fixed income securities and treasury products. In 2005, he launched Fixed Income Investor (**www.fixedincomeinvestor.co.uk**), a resource for private investors in the sterling fixed income market. Mark has also contributed to many well-known investment websites and publications over the years including the *Investors Chronicle*.

In his spare time, he can generally be found on the water, up a hill or occasionally under a paraglider.

The views and opinions expressed in this book are those of the author, and not those of his employers.

Foreword by Dr Stephen Barber

This is a timely book. Bonds have been rather overlooked by investors in recent years but this is changing as portfolio strategies adapt to our evolving needs and the rapid alterations in global markets. Like many readers, I have accumulated a fair collection of investment books on my shelves but none of them offer a thorough guide to bonds and fixed income instruments. I suppose they have not been seen as particularly sexy: after all, notwithstanding the Eurozone sovereign debt crisis, it is the equity markets which tend to make the news with their "thrills and spills" as the author puts it. And yet, increasingly, bonds are once again playing a crucial role in our investment planning, whatever our objectives might be.

Almost all portfolios can find a place for fixed income, if only as an alternative to cash. After all, returns are usually better, risk can be managed and it is possible to buy liquid bonds which can be sold when funds are required. But there is no need to stop there. Traditional asset allocation is all about balancing equities with bonds and the inclusion of fixed income is a tried and tested way of reducing portfolio volatility. With so much emphasis on equity returns, reducing volatility has been the primary function of fixed income. This is the *life stages* approach to investment management where we accept greater risk when younger but attempt to reduce volatility, and therefore uncertainty, as retirement approaches. As such, those with a longer investment horizon have been attracted primarily to shares. Portfolios must always be adaptable and over time this changes. During the decade or so prior to retirement, a rebalancing should take place which re-allocates assets away from equities and towards the dependability of bonds. During such an investment stage, and beyond into retirement, the predictability of bonds provide for precisely the sort of returns that are demanded. It is old advice but good advice.

There is, however, much more to bonds than simply managing portfolio volatility. Mark Glowrey will surprise many readers of this book when he demonstrates that in historical analysis, the performance of bonds compares really rather favourably to equities. Even pedestrian British government bonds, gilts, have outperformed UK shares over the first decade of this new century. It is the sort of statistic to make all investors reappraise the merits of fixed income. Bonds are not only about lowering risk, they can also be about long term growth and even speculative investments.

Profits are, not unreasonably, what most investors are interested in. But profit has come to mean capital gains. However, even when it comes to shares, most of our longer term returns will actually derive from income rather than capital growth. As such it is one of those mindsets as investors we must learn to shake. Total returns of income combined with capital are what count and this is what bonds and fixed income can offer. For the longer term, more passive investor, income is perhaps more readily available from these products than great capital gains. Also, depending on one's tax position, this can be eaten up by income tax. But it is worth considering that you are not liable for capital gains tax on profits from gilts and increasingly tax efficient wrappers are being employed to manage taxation.

The combination of Individual Savings Accounts (ISAs) and Self invested Personal Pensions (SIPPs) have helped to make investment portfolios as tax efficient as possible. Within these wrappers, investment choice is relatively free, profits can be taken CGT free and no additional income tax is due. This makes the selection of bonds and other fixed income products an even more attractive proposition and means that investors need not distinguish between income and capital returns.

Not only is this book timely, I cannot think of a bond expert more trusted or more in tune with the needs of private and professional investors than Mark Glowrey. His analysis is always insightful and always makes for better investment decisions. Those skills are brought to bear in this book and it makes for a dependable volume of which I for one will take full advantage.

I am sure that a new era of bond investing is upon us and that portfolios of every type and size will be all the more successful for the inclusion of fixed income. You have picked up this book and that means that you see the potential of this asset class to help fulfil your objectives. I'm convinced that readers of this guide will build better portfolios.

Dr Stephen Barber

Preface

Who this book is for

This book is intended to fill a gap in the plethora of investment guides available for self-directed investors in the UK. Any number of books covering equities, leveraged trading, funds, ETFs and even alternative investments such as collectables are available, but to date the coverage of the gilt and corporate bond market has been slim. Of course, there are numerous works intended for investment professionals in this field, but these are highly specialised publications which typically focus on one aspect of the fixed income market, for instance credit derivatives or portfolio immunization – subjects that are likely to be of little practical use to an investor who wishes to build a small to medium size portfolio in the gilt and fixed income markets.

The professional investor also typically has distinct mandates to follow. These will usually be to achieve superior performance to his peers or an index, or to match future liabilities. Such investors will manage their portfolios accordingly. The private investor will typically have more straightforward criteria; to get a good return on his capital whilst avoiding unacceptable levels of risk. expense or complexity. This absolute return approach will frequently mean that the private investor's selection of individual bonds, and the resulting portfolio may look quite different from that of the private investor.

The book aims to be a practical guide for UK investors and their advisors, enabling those with perhaps £10,000 and up, or a few £100,000s to put their money profitably to work in this rewarding and often overlooked asset class. The book is intended to be first and foremost a practical guide and covers both bond theory and the more mundane but important subjects of dealing, settlement and day-to-day portfolio operation.

I hope that Sterling Bonds and Fixed Income for the Private Investor will find a ready home on the bookshelves of investors, private-client stockbrokers, wealth managers, trustees and even a few fund managers. Company treasurers and investment bankers, particularly those employed in origination and new issues, may also find it a useful read, if only to remind them that there is demand from the man on the street, and how best that demand might be met.

What this book covers

This book covers the theory and the practicalities of investing in the UK government bond (gilt) and sterling corporate bond markets.

Virtually all categories of debt within this subset are dealt with over the following chapters: straight or vanilla bonds (the most common type) through to convertible, floating rate notes and index-linked issues. Both domestic and Eurosterling corporate bonds are covered – investment-grade and sub-investment grade alike. There is also coverage of the subordinated sector including permanent interest bearing shares (PIBS) and enhanced capital notes (ECNs), an asset class that already has a strong following amongst the UK private investor community.

Whilst the book is primarily intended for those investors who wish to put their money directly to work in the bond market, chapter 14 also covers bond funds and ETFs (exchange traded funds), comparing these popular investment vehicles with the do-it-yourself approach.

It is also worth considering what this book does not cover. As the title suggests, the book is intended as guide for UK investors, who will typically have sterling savings to put to work. Whilst chapter 12 deals with overseas and foreign currency bonds, this section will serve primarily to contextualize the more in-depth study of sterling bonds. The subject of overseas bonds is too great to be fully covered in one handy-sized volume. In particular, it would not be possible to cover the huge US domestic market and its subsets of tax-deductible, municipal and mortgage-backed debt.

Note: the book is illustrated with numerous examples of bonds trading the markets over the 2010-2011 period. Prices and interest rates will reflect those in force at that time.

Introduction

My initiation into the bond market was in the mid 80s at a very junior level as a London Stock Exchange clerk. I stood by one of the gilt jobber's pitches whilst a very serious man in a pin-striped suit fired off a rapid string of coupons, maturity dates and prices denominated in complex fractions. It was a process seemingly designed to exclude the ordinary investor. By the early 90s I found myself still dealing in bonds, this time on the Euromarkets and in a wider range of currencies. Again, the industry was an exclusive club, trading huge blocks between financial institutions.

It struck me as strange that whilst I, and indeed many of my colleagues, made their living by selling and buying these instruments, most of us had never personally owned a bond. This was in considerable contrast to the frantic personal account dealing seen in the equity departments of most banks and brokerages. So I decided to give it a go, and by the mid 90s I was dipping my toe into the world of bonds with my modest savings. I soon discovered that investing your own money was a very different game to advising treasurers or fund managers – but more of that later.

The turn of the millennium saw me move into the world of independent research. Here I was able to pick up on the subject of bonds and the private investor in more detail, launching the **www.fixedincomeinvestor.co.uk** website and advising directly on a range of bond portfolios. It was a good time to be in the bond markets, which continued to outperform the turbulent equity markets of that decade.

Timing, of course, is everything. When I was investing in bonds back in the late 1990s there was an underlying bull market in the asset class, combined with enough volatility to make investing interesting; at times very interesting! But a reader today may ask: is now the time to be involved in bonds? I would suggest that, yes, it is.

Indeed, any serious investor should always be involved in bonds to some degree if he or she is to maintain a balanced portfolio. There are other, more immediate reasons to be involved in investing in bonds. The ultra-low interest rates that central banks have put in place look set to hold force until the middle of this decade, and income seekers are hard pressed to find returns.

Whilst yields may be low on gilts, corporate bonds provide more substantial coupons. Sensible returns are available from respectable issuers and risks for investors lower than the equity market.

There are other practical reasons to get involved in bonds. The rapid growth of low-cost ISA and SIPP accounts has meant that every person can have their own personal tax shelter. Investors can keep and, importantly, re-invest, the interest they receive from bonds. Finally, the growth of the LSE ORB market has meant greatly improved access for private investors in the bond markets, a move that has been strongly supported by the UK's private client brokers and wealth managers.

This book aims to help the average investor find his way into the bond market. I sincerely hope that bonds will soon become a permanent feature in your portfolio.

Mark Glowrey

PART I:
The Basics

Chapter 1
What's a bond? Some key concepts

E verybody knows what shares are – buy a share and you own a small stake in a company. If the company does well and makes a profit, this may be distributed to shareholders as dividends. If the company continues to do well, these dividends will rise. Meanwhile, the capital value of your share, driven by other investors in the market, will likely rise.

That's the plan.

But as most investors will tell you, it doesn't always work out like that. Dividends may be conspicuous by their absence. Even reliable blue chips such as BP (or indeed most of the world's banks) can be knocked for six by disaster, and dividends withheld for many years.

Bonds are different. A bond holder does not own the company – he or she is lending it money, and that loan comes with the usual package of conditions: a fixed annual or semi-annual coupon and agreed date of repayment. In a nutshell, a bond is this; a tradable security with a fixed interest payment and (usually) a pre-determined repayment date. The key point is this: the forward cash flows of the investment are known.

What is more, in the majority of situations the company does not have the option to withhold such payment and the bondholder has a prior claim on the issuer's assets in liquidation.

Bonds can be issued by a government, company or many other types of organisations. Effectively they are marketable loans, or IOUs, issued by these entities and bought by investors such as banks, insurance companies and fund managers.

> **Tip:** It is worth mentioning at this point that there are numerous retail-targeted investment products marketed as "bonds". These include fixed term (typically 2, 3 or 5 year fixed term deposits from banks and building societies) and packaged equity-linked products from life insurers etc, again often with a fixed life. This is sloppy nomenclature on the part of the financial service industry and I, for one, would like to see the term "bond" reserved exclusively for fixed income securities.

Investors are often heard to say "I don't understand bonds", but the truth is that these instruments are much simpler than equities.

Key features

The key features can be broken down as follows:

Feature	Description
Issuer	This is the entity which is borrowing the money. For instance, £500 million will be borrowed, and £500 million of securities will be issued. Typically these will be sold at "par" or 100p in the pound. Thus, for every 100p invested, 100p will be repaid at a pre-determined point in the future.
Coupon	The issuer commits to pay a rate of interest of X% per year. This coupon will generally be a fixed amount and is paid annually or semi-annually. The rate will be determined by the investment bank advising the issuer, who will assess demand in the market at the time of issue – the variables being a combination of current and future interest rate expectations combined with an appropriate risk premium for the issuer.
Maturity	A date is set for the repayment of the money. This is known as the redemption date. The bonds will be redeemed at "par" or 100p in the pound (with some rare exceptions).

At launch, bonds are sold to investors (typically institutional) via an investment bank or broker. This is known as the primary market. Gilt issues are also offered directly to the general public. After this primary phase, bonds are then free to trade between investors and/or market counterparties. However, unlike equities that trade through a centralised stock exchange, bonds generally trade on a peer-to-peer basis from one institution (such as an investment bank) to another (such as broker).

This global market in bonds is enormous. Figures released by the International Monetary Authority in 2002 estimated the total amount of debt securities as around 43 trillion US Dollars. At the time this was nearly twice the total of the world's stock market capitalisation. The number of bonds in circulation is considerable, and a large and regular issuer such as the European Investment Bank or General Electric may have several hundred issues trading at any one time. These bonds will be issued in a variety of currencies and may differ greatly from each other in terms of coupon or coupon type, date of maturity and other features such as imbedded puts and calls.

This book is primarily concerned with the sterling bond market, and even in this relatively small subset of the international bond markets, a quick check on my Bloomberg Terminal reveals over 6,000 issues outstanding. Bear in mind that this number is constantly changing (bonds are issued and redeemed all the time).

Although the bond market is considerable in size, one point to bear in mind is that the secondary market is less consistent than that seen in equities. Many bonds are bought on a buy and hold basis as new issues, and this investor behaviour has a tendency to reduce secondary market turnover. Government bonds remain highly tradable with very tight bid-offer spreads for large size deals. However, the liquidity situation in corporate bonds is variable with only a proportion of the huge number of new issues that are readily tradable in the secondary market or accessible at any given time. The skills required to deal with this variable liquidity picture make bond dealing a slightly more complex art compared to the highly transparent equity market, and I address this issue over the course of the book.

Chapter 2

Why buy bonds? The risks and rewards of investing in bonds

The last four decades have seen the emergence, growth and eventually the almost total domination of equity investing. Prior to this, pension funds had invested mainly in bonds, the view being that fixed income securities were a logical and safe home for the money. All this was to change in the 1950s, in a move largely credited to the then fund manager of Imperial Tobacco, George Ross Goobey. Mr Goobey, an actuary by profession, reached the conclusion that equities were undervalued and started switching the fund into the then unfashionable stock market.

He was right. Over the coming decades, inflation destroyed the real return from fixed income securities and equities proved the place to be. This view, sometimes known as the "cult of the equity" is now almost a universal belief with equities widely considered to be the first choice for investment.

But is this the whole story?

When an investment approach is almost universally adopted, it's often time to worry. Certainly, the bear market in the early 2000s eroded the longer-term outperformance of stocks against bonds; undermining the theory that bonds are simply an antiquated asset class, suitable for only the most unadventurous or complacent investors.

At the time of publication of this book, the argument for equities looks somewhat weaker than usual. The highly respected *2011 Barclays Equity-Gilt study* (now in its 56th year of publication) shows that UK Government bonds have outperformed equities over a ten year period and are virtually level-pegging over a twenty-year period.

The figures shown below are "annual real returns" (i.e. inflation adjusted). Income is assumed to be re-invested.

Table 2.1: comparative performance of UK equities and gilts

Asset	2010	10 years	20 years
UK Equities	8.9%	0.6%	6%
Gilts	4.4%	2.4%	5.8%

What is more, the performance that bonds have provided over the last couple of decades has been delivered with far fewer heart-stopping moments than the thrills and spills experienced by equity holders over the 1987 crash, the millennium technology boom and bust, the flash crash of 2010 etc. (I could go on!)

Consider also that a balanced portfolio with a mixture of equity and bond holdings will show lower volatility than a pure equity portfolio.

Of course, past performance does not dictate future performance but these statistics somewhat undermine the theory that bonds are simply an antiquated asset class, suitable for only the most unadventurous or complacent investors.

The rewards

Before we move on to consider the potential risks and rewards of different types of bonds, here are seven good reasons why every portfolio should contain bonds:

1. Security

Government bonds have historically offered the investor unparalleled security. Even in the current credit crisis, the risk of the UK or other major governments being unable to repay their debts is comparatively low. Of course, we live in a changing world, and the Greek financial crisis and growing indebtedness of the Western world means that investors should not be complacent. An asset class that has been historically safe may not be safe in the future. Nevertheless, higher-quality government bonds should theoretically be considered superior in credit quality to a bank deposit. Why? Basically because governments have the power to levy taxation in order to service their debt.

High-grade, multi-national government agencies (such as the World Bank) also offer an extremely safe home for the investor holding bonds to maturity. Of course, not all bonds are issued by governments or their agencies. Many bonds are issued by companies and other organisations whose ability to service the debt may be less certain. However, even corporate debt can be considered a safer investment than the company's equity. In the event of bankruptcy, bondholders are ranked above shareholders in their claim on the company's assets.

2 Return of capital

Bonds also differ from equities in one other very important aspect. In order to realise your profit (or loss) on a share, you are wholly dependent on the ability to sell the instrument back to the market. When an investor buys a bond, the redemption date is fixed in advance, reducing the investor's reliance on the uncertainties of future market sentiment or liquidity.

3 Income

With an ageing population in most developed countries, income becomes an increasingly valuable aspect for any portfolio. Income available from bonds is generally higher than that available from equities. Also, future income payments are a known quantity, unlike dividends from equities, which may be reduced or withheld entirely in times of low profitability. This makes bonds ideal for investors who wish to secure future income over a defined period of time. With bonds paying annually, semi-annually or sometimes quarterly, a carefully chosen bond portfolio with six or more holdings can produce a reliable monthly income.

Also, most bonds pay their coupons gross, without withholding tax. Investors can take advantage of this by holding qualifying bonds within an ISA, producing a tax free income for life, hopefully rolling up the full £10,000 allowance year after year to build up a meaningful sum.

4. Capital growth

Bonds are associated with income, and understandably so. But, a stream of income, if received gross and re-invested can be a powerful tool for capital growth. With the advent of low-cost and easily available tax-efficient ISA and SIPP accounts, this is now a workable strategy for the UK investor.

> **Tip**: Seven is the magic number. A 7% income, if re-invested, will double a sum of money over a decade.

5. Diversification

A well managed portfolio should contain a variety of different assets classes; equities, government bonds, index-linked bonds, corporate bonds, property and alternative assets all have their role to play. This simple approach, also known as "not keeping all your eggs in one basket" is one of the most effective strategies for reducing risk in a portfolio. In certain economic scenarios, such as a recession, bonds will generally show an inverse correlation in price movements to equities. Note that in the 2000-2003 period, when the FTSE100 declined by nearly half from the millennium highs, longer-dated gilts saw prices rise over the same period (as can be seen in the following chart).

Figure 2.1: long-dated gilts v. FTSE 100 (2000-2003)

6. Benefit from falling interest rates

When an investor buys a fixed coupon bond, he or she locks in interest rates for a defined period. Because of this, falling interest rates will cause the market value of the bond to rise. Investors who buy bonds in falling interest rate scenarios will receive the double benefit of a secure income and capital appreciation of their asset.

7. Speculation

Many financial instruments offer the potential to speculate on future price movements, and bonds are no exception. Liquid government bonds are often used by traders speculating on future interest rates while corporate bonds can see sharp price movements from changes in the perceived credit quality of the issuer.

To summarise, bonds as an asset class are about income investing. This is not to say that such a strategy can not produce capital growth – the power of a re-invested stream of coupons is a powerful tool.

Historically, UK investment has been about chasing capital gains. This is perhaps due to the history and the memory of post-war inflation and the relatively (I stress *relatively*) lenient tax treatment of capital gains. Income gained on investments has historically gone straight on to the investor's top rate of marginal tax.

The development and now wide acceptance of ISA and SIPP account allow bonds, and indeed other income-producing assets to be held within a simple, legal inexpensive tax shelter. This has been a game changer for the approach of many investors, and I would venture the opinion that this development has further to run over the next few decades.

The risks

All investments involve risk, and bonds are no exception. Indeed, as some savers with the Icelandic banks and their subsidiaries discovered in 2008, not even bank deposits are truly risk free. Before we go on to consider the relative risk of the fixed income and equity asset classes, it is worth taking a moment to consider the different types of risk that an investor might face. Investment risk can be broken down into roughly five categories as follows:

1. Risk of default

The risk that the issuer may be unable to return all or some of the money advanced to them. In the bond markets this is known as a *default* and in the unlikely event that the issuer defaults or goes bankrupt, you may lose some, or all, of your investment.

2. Market risk

The investor buys a bond at a price. This price will then fluctuate from day to day according to interest rate expectations and credit rating changes, creating a paper profit or loss. Thus, if the investor needs to sell the asset to raise funds, they face a risk of capital loss.

3. Issue-specific risk

Many bonds are issued with imbedded features such as calls, which enable the issuer to repay the debt ahead of schedule. This can be disadvantageous to the holder. However, such features are clearly laid out in the bond prospectus, so careful investors can either avoid such issues, or make contingency plans.

4. Event and operational risks

Operational risk encompasses a variety of hazards such as brokerage charges, slippage or a shift to an unfavourable or punitive tax treatment. These types of risk can be reduced through careful planning and monitoring. An example of event risk would be the issuer of the bond becoming the target of a leveraged buyout, increasing the degree of risk of lending money to the company.

5. Inflation

We can also add to this list the risk of inflation, which can reduce the real value of any asset or portfolio over time. Bonds, with their fixed interest and redemption payments are particularly vulnerable to this risk.

Chapter 3
The players in the bond markets

A market is both created by, and exists to service, the needs of its users. In this aspect the bond market is little different from any other; and understanding the types of participants and the roles that they play is key to understanding how a market operates.

At the most basic level, the market consists of bond issuers – effectively the sellers of bonds – who need to raise capital. Set against this supply are the buyers – a wide variety of investors seeking a return on their capital. Between these two shades of black and white are many shades of grey. This chapter takes a look at the main players.

Issuers

If organisations did not need to borrow money, there would be no bond market. Thus Polonius' oft-quoted advice from Shakespeare's Hamlet[1] to "Never a borrower or a lender be" holds little sway in the industry. Major borrows have huge and repeating funding needs and tap the deep and liquid bonds markets on a regular basis.

Issuers range from sovereign governments, through huge multinationals such as BP or Unilever down to the medium size companies – FTSE 250 midcaps such as GKN or Enterprise Inns. All are seeking competitive sources of medium-to-long term capital. Issue size will vary from around £10 million (perhaps the smallest size possible) through to a typical £100-250 million issue and up to £500 million or £1 billion. Such block-busters are known as *benchmark issues*, generally liquid and transparent and useful points of reference for establishing relative value in the market.

Smaller companies are generally underrepresented in the corporate bond markets. The minimum practical deal size and the associated costs make the market unsuitable for such borrowers, whose needs are better matched by venture capital or bank lending.

---

[1] Often attributed to Charles Dickens' Mr Micawber, who should have heeded it.

Common sterling bond issuers

Well-known issuers in the sterling bonds markets include the following organisations. Bond investors should familiarise themselves with these borrowers. The issues of these organisations often become the benchmarks – large, liquid and well-known bonds against which other, possibly more interesting, bonds are valued.

The European Investment Bank

Europe's state-owned development bank, the EIB, was established in 1958 after the Treaty of Rome and was the first of the European Union's financing institutions. Its shareholders are the 27 Member States of the Union, which have jointly subscribed its capital. The EIB's Board of Governors is composed of the Finance Ministers of these States. The EIB's role is to provide long-term finance in support of investment projects.

The EIB is a regular participant in the sterling bond market, issuing a range of maturities, effectively shadowing the structure of the gilt market with a range of bonds offered across different maturities.

Kreditanstalt für Wiederaufbau

The German government-owned development bank, KFW, is based in Frankfurt and was formed after WWII as part of the Marshall Plan to rebuild the then shattered Germany. Effectively a German state credit. The bonds are AAA-rated and trade tightly to gilts. As with all large financial organisations, KFW raises finance across the international financial markets, including the sterling bond market in order to better diversify its funding base.

UK banks & building societies

Banks are typically the largest users of the bonds markets both as issuers and as investors. Banks raise different types of capital and funding in the markets. This results in a variety of different types of bank debt, ranging from senior (ordinary) through to subordinated bonds (a higher risk and higher yielding type of debt – more on this later). The sterling market is notable for the high number of subordinated issues from these issuers.

Some investors, notably the banks themselves, have historically viewed bank debt as the "next best" credit after government and government agency debt.

This perception of the quality of bank debt has weakened considerably following the events of the credit crunch, with investors preferring bonds issued by other sectors. It remains to be seen if the conventional pecking order will be restored.

> **Tip**: When buying bank or building society bonds, double check the seniority of the issue. Subordinated bonds are a less secure form of debt. These have their place, but are a somewhat different kettle of fish to senior debt – higher risk, subject to coupon deferral and much more volatile. Risk is fine, but as investors we will expect to see a higher return to compensate.

General Electric

The giant US engineering and financial services conglomerate. Often judged to be a financial sector company rather than a true corporate (the company derives around half its revenue from financial services). GE has a balance sheet the size of Jupiter and the company's bonds typically show correlation to bank debt. GE has a systematic program of issuance into the sterling bond markets and they have bonds trading at a wide range of maturities.

Utilities

Utilities such as National Grid and Severn Trent are frequent issuers into the UK market. The low-risk nature of the utility business makes such issuers a popular choice for the typically risk-adverse bond investor.

Tesco

One of the UK's biggest companies and a frequent issuer on the GBP (and other) bond markets. In 2011 Tesco Bank (a subsidiary) issued a sterling bond into the retail market and has a pipeline of such issues planned.

The above examples are simply some of the most well-known issuers of sterling bonds. Further research will yield a list of hundreds of other issuers and their bonds. Often, the less well-known the issuer, the more interesting (and potentially undervalued) the bond.

> **Tip**: keep an eye open for bond market debutantes. Bond issues from new or unknown issuers often have to be priced to sell – great for "stags".

You can find a table of popular sterling bonds in the appendix at the back of this book. Please note, this represents only a sample of a wider market. Liquidity and transparency are moveable feasts and this, combined with the inevitable process of redemption and new issues will make the list look quite different a few years down the road.

Investment banks

It is fair to say that investment banks (IBs) are the bond market. The reverse is also true; the bond market consists of investment banks. A study of the results of the major players such as Goldman Sachs, or the late Salomon Brothers or even our own domestic operators such Barclays Capital, show that it is in bonds and their associated derivatives that the greatest returns are to be achieved and the largest positions found. Not surprisingly, it is also where the greatest losses appear from time to time. Why? Because bond markets are scaleable and open to bulk trading, enabling the highly aggressive and ambitious IBs to put on trades by the billions.

Standing aside from the proprietary trading activities of the investment banks, these organisations have two important roles to fulfil. The first is issuance. New bond issues, sometimes known as the *primary market,* is the meat and drink of the investment banking industry. Major borrowers need to issue large amounts of bonds, and to do so regularly. This business is fee-generating for the IBs, and repeatable. In addition to the fees charged by the IBs (perhaps 0.4% of the sum raised on a ten year bond), there is a considerable amount of additional revenue that can be generated from offering hedging or related swap contracts, both to the issuer and the buyers of the bonds.

The bankers will constantly be scanning the financial markets looking for opportunities, and pitching deals to their client base. Primary bond market activity is one of the most hotly contested activities in the financial world and the league table of issuance is closely followed each year. Here's how 2010's league table for the sterling market panned out, according to Bloomberg.

Table 3.1: ranking of investment banks in sterling bond market (2010)

Bank	Deals arranged (£bn)
HSBC Bank	13.5
RBS	12.9
Barclays Capital	11.2
Deutsche Bank	8.6
RBC Capital markets	6.6
UBS	4.5
Goldman Sachs	4.3
Nomura	4.2
JP Morgan	4.1
Lloyds TSB Corporate Markets	3.6

It is worth pointing out that the sterling market is a relatively small pond. The top underwriter in Euro-denominated bonds issued a volume of EUR79 billion.

Euroclear

Custody is not a subject that receives much attention in the financial press, but you might be surprised how often the subject arises amongst market professionals.

When an investor buys a bond, his broker will need to settle the transaction. Domestic bond markets, such as gilts, have settlement systems that were in many cases established before the dawn of time. However, the majority of corporate bonds, including sterling corporate bonds, are *Eurobonds* – a type of instrument that has a distinct structure and settlement systems.

The history of the development of the Eurobond market (in the late 1960s) is based on bearer bonds. As the market developed, it became clear that some form of centralised custody system would be needed to enable the speedy transfer of ownership without the need to physically move piles of bearer certificates from one vault to another.

To meet the custody and settlement needs of the growing Eurobond market, JP Morgan established Euroclear in Belgium in 1968. The system proved to be an enormous success and Euroclear remains the hub of the international bond markets and turned over a remarkable EUR451 trillion in 2006.

The Euroclear system has come a long way from its Eurobond roots in the sixties, and now provides a settlement system for numerous classes of securities. However, it is with Eurobonds that most people associate the system.

The system works on a delivery vs cash basis. All bonds are lodged centrally. Nowadays the bonds are typically represented by a single certificate and most investors and their brokers will never actually see or lay hands on a physical certificate.

Banks, brokers and custodians will then hold accounts with Euroclear. When a trade is to be settled (typically between one and three days after the trade), each counterparty will place his or her instructions, either to deliver the bonds or to pay the cash consideration. On the relevant settlement date, Euroclear will then debit the respective cash and custody accounts accordingly.

UK investors may also encounter their bonds being delivered into the UK's Crest system. We will deal with this in more detail in chapter 15.

Tip: all bonds are held by professional custodians – in Euroclear, via Crest or in the US DTC system. If you are ever approached by anyone offering you bonds, or claiming to hold bonds, outside of these systems, give them a very wide berth.

Brokers & intermediaries

The majority of bonds are dealt on a peer-to-peer basis. That means that one principal (typically an investment bank) will sell a block of bonds on to a customer, perhaps a fund manager or a bank or building society treasury. In the equity market, there is a fairly clear differentiation between the *buy side* companies (fund managers such as Fidelity, Legal and General etc.) and the *market* (i.e. brokers and traders grouped around the stock exchange or other trading platforms). Not so the bond market, where many shades of grey exist.

Operating within this multi-layered world of banks, proprietary traders, insurance companies, money market funds and investment banks exist numerous bond brokers – often operating in specialised fields. In the manner of a Victorian naturalist, I have attempted to break down the taxonomy as follows:

- **Investment banks**
  The top of the tree amongst the numerous bond market intermediaries. The investment banks are the main players and will issue bonds on behalf of the borrowers. The IB's hold positions in bonds, make secondary markets and sell to brokers and institutional investors. They will also be active in buying bonds and repackaging the debt through the use of swaps, derivatives and other financial engineering.

- **Bond brokers**
  These deal in bonds but do not take positions in the bonds. Unlike stockbrokers, who act as agents on pre-agreed commission rates for their client, bond brokers usually take a turn; introducing a margin between buy and sell orders. Usually, bond brokers (sometime known as agency brokers) will sit between the street, as the collection of market makers is known, and the client, who will hopefully be fund manager or other end-investor.

- **Inter-dealer brokers**
  As above, but specialised wholesale brokers who work on shifting large blocks of bonds and other instruments between major players (mainly investment banks).

- **Broker-dealer**
  A broker who will take some positions, either to facilitate a trade or for speculation.

- **Stockbrokers**
  Retail-facing organisations offering private investors access to the financial markets. Stockbrokers vary from low cost online execution-only platforms to high-end discretionary wealth managers. As the name suggests, stockbrokers are typically focused on stocks, and to some degree funds. However, many stockbrokers are now responding to client demand and offering direct trading in bonds. It is through a stockbroker that most private investors will gain access to the markets.

- **IFAs (Independent Financial Advisors)**

  The typical UK IFA deals with packaged funds and has comparatively little involvement with direct investment into the financial markets.

A day in the life of a broker-dealer

I asked Oliver Butt, a partner in the illiquid and distressed debt specialists, City & Continental, to describe a typical day at their offices on Lombard Street in the City:

"Most of my customers and also ourselves, for our own book, are interested in bonds with high returns or a good chance of substantial capital gain. These bonds require more thinking about than the run of the mill 'safe' corporate bonds.

Therefore I begin the day by trawling through messages I get from the market – and by this I mean the bond dealing desks of banks, investment banks and other brokers.

I receive maybe 200 such messages a day in the form of email or the Bloomberg message system (effectively an electronic message system for securities professionals), to see if there is anything interesting on offer, and I check for prices or news on bonds I am following. Another good source of ideas is to ask, when I ring up a trader to close a trade, if there is anything else he particularly thinks is a good idea or if he has something illiquid on his books he doesn't want that is going cheap. It is always good to keep probing, not because the traders are trying to hide anything but because frequently people forget what they have on their books or erroneously assume you will not be interested, so don't mention it.

Then, particularly if the security I am looking at is a financial sector bond, I will tend to read or at least skip through the prospectus. It is very important to work out if and under what circumstances a bond can stop paying interest without going into default. Are there any other nasty clauses that could get you? Forcible equity conversions or write downs under certain circumstances, for instance. Even though you may know the category of debt into which a given bond falls you have to look at the small print. Generally older issues are more kind to investors.

I then also consult the news to see if there is anything relevant to do with the issuer. Sometimes you are investing in the eye of the storm where you have to accept there are plenty of unknowns and a fair degree of random outcome but it may be alright on the night. Other times it is an old story or problem and in this case you have more time to consider and there will fewer guesses to make. Investing in speculative-grade bonds can be as much an art as a science and you have to try and work out what will happen if things go pear-shaped – i.e. will bond holders lose money? Is it the sort of corporate with a good business which will be recapitalised by shareholders without pain to bond holders or what degree of government support could there be? Can you trust the government to play fair (probably not if they can help it)? Or will there been some sort of arbitrary, inequitable and retrospective outcome as they choose to over-rule the prospectus you have spent so much time combing through? On the one hand if the authorities are in trouble you may well be too as they seek to play to the public gallery. But, on the other hand the bond market is collectively very powerful and the government have to make sure they don't bring the house tumbling down on their heads if they lose all trust.

Sometimes there are opportunities when the bond has already gone over the edge and into default. As long as the expected recovery is greater than the current price you can be on to a winner. Also could there be a debt for equity swap? It can be good if you enter at the right moment. For example, British Nuclear Energy went bust, bonds traded down to 25%, there was a debt for equity swap and the price zoomed up to 200%. For this it is best to get hold of an analyst at an investment bank who has gone through the story in detail. For these types of situations the analyst, and it can involve leg work to track down the right person, is the person you want to speak to and will know much more than the trader who is really only there to trade the flows. Research having been done, occasionally you ask a trader why a bond is trading so cheaply and you get the answer "Don't ask me mate! That is just where I got hit by someone clearing out an old position." Then you know the odds are in your favour – he makes a turn but you have superior information.

And then it is on to the phones."

Investors

There are probably just two types of investor in the equity markets: funds and private investors. The world of bonds has many more types of end user, all of whom may have marginally different reasons for buying a bond. Below is a list of the various types of fixed income investors that I have encountered over my years in bond sales:

Table 3.2: classification of investors in bonds

Investor	Description
Bond funds	Obvious buyers of bonds, but by no means the largest class of buyer. Often specialised by currency, type of credit etc.
Banks	All banks (and building societies) run liquidity portfolios – assets that can be easily bought or sold. Fixed rate bonds are often swapped back into floating rate cash flows to match liabilities. Banks are significant buyers of bonds.
Supranational (the World Bank etc.) and government agencies	Often have considerable sums to invest, mostly in government and quasi-government bonds.
Central banks	Many central banks hold foreign currency reserves. These are invested in high-quality fixed income, typically government bonds and their short-term relations, government bills.
Life insurance companies	Buy bonds to match long-term liabilities from life policies, savings plans and endowments.
General insurance companies	Buy bonds (usually short-dated) to hold in the gap between receipt of premium and payment of claims. It is said in the industry that this cash-flow based investment is the main area of profitability.
Investment banks	A surprisingly large amount of bonds are held by the industry that helps issue them, either as market-making inventory or for speculative/trading purposes.
Corporates	Some, but not all, companies are cash rich. Microsoft, for instance, is said to have a $40 billion cash reserve. That money has to go somewhere.
Wealth managers and private bankers	Effectively an upmarket breed of stockbroker, but more likely to be active in the bond markets than the average broker.
Private investors	The single smallest class of buyers of bonds in the UK (but growing). Typically dealing via UK stockbroker or execution-only platforms.

Chapter 4

The life cycle of a bond

The timeline of a new issue

Corporates and other bodies have funding programs, dictated by both their future capital requirements and the need to roll or re-finance expiring and maturing sources of funding. With this in mind, chief financial officers (CFOs) will be constantly in touch with the primary issuance, or debt origination, departments of investment banks.

The CFO's primary duty is to obtain the funding the business needs, with the right maturity profile and at the right price. In addition to this, a good CFO will consider factors such as funding diversity, in order to make sure that the company is not over-reliant on one type of investor.

The bond market, and its participants, operates internationally. Frequently, a UK borrower will opt to issue into non-sterling markets if there is sufficient price advantage, swapping the proceeds back into its own base currency to match assets against liability. The same is true for the sterling markets, overseas operators will issue bonds denominated in pounds as and when the price is right – this will be influenced by numerous complex factors including local interest rates and yield curves, the degree of domestic demand for the individual credit and the complex and ever-changing market of cross-currency interest rate and basis swaps.

The lead managers and the selling group

Turning to the gilt market first, new issues are handled by the government's Debt Management Office (DMO). There is a straightforward issuance procedure for gilts where the market makers and members of the approved group may bid for the new bonds and auctions are held on a scheduled basis with the calendar determined just after the budget in March.

The process of launching new corporate bonds is somewhat different. A Eurosterling corporate bond will usually be launched through the route of a *lead manager* (usually a large investment bank) and one or more *co-leads,co-managers* or syndicate members. The lead manager will take on most of the risk and the workload of bringing the new issue to market. The co-managers and syndicate members will help ensure that the bond is distributed across a wide range of investors, and also provide a buffer of liquidity in the first days or weeks of the distribution process with syndicate members taking the bonds onto their own books for a few days or weeks to smooth the process of selling large blocks of bonds to investors.

Primary issuance is a profitable business for investment banks. The fees charged by the various members of the issuance syndicate vary, but a UK corporate might pay 0.35-0.45p in the pound to issue a ten year bond. Retail-targeted bonds are typically smaller in size and thus fees will be higher in percentage terms. Here the fees may be around 1% of the total (and in some cases higher). These fees will be shared with a distributing group of brokers, with 0.25%-0.5% being a typical distribution.

Above and beyond these fees will be the profit (or loss) booked on the trading books during the syndication process. This will be a factor of the bank's decisions in selecting the right issues to participate in and the skills of the trader in hedging and trading the positions over the distribution period.

Note – The new issue process in bonds is intended for professional investors and moves quickly. For instance, exploratory talks between the issuer, the investment bank and key investors on pricing etc. may be held on the Wednesday. By the following Monday the outline pricing and terms of the new issue will be announced on the screens. This announcement will take the form *of;*

> *Acme Corporation to issue seven-year sterling straight, guidance is 160-170bp over gilts. Co-leads Barclays Capital and RBS.*

This means that Acme will be issuing a conventional fixed coupon bond with a seven year maturity. The term *pricing* basically means the yield and is a combination of the level of coupon and the discount/premium to par. In this case, it is expected to be an equivalent to yield equating to 1.7% (170bp) more than gilts of an equivalent maturity.

By Tuesday morning the issue will have been priced – i.e. the final margin over gilts or LIBOR/Swaps set and the bonds sold at a fixed price. By eleven o'clock the entire issue may well have been placed. This rate of progress makes it hard for private investors to get in at an early stage.

An exception to this is the new *retail targeted* bonds that we are now seeing in the UK. The issuance procedure here is set over one or two weeks in order to allow private investors (and their brokers!) time to react. Typically, the broker will not charge commission to his client for purchasing such new issues. The broker will receive a selling commission from the issuance group by way of recompense as detailed above.

Tip: pricing on retail bonds is set at launch. Over the 1-2 week offering period, the underlying gilt and credit market may move, making the issues relatively cheap or expensive by the time the issue launches. Speculative traders, take note. "Stagging" is not just for equities!

The life cycle of a bond

Below is a typical timeline of an imaginary seven-year bond's life cycle.

Date	Description
Issuance	An investment-grade corporate issues a seven-year bond offering a yield of 0.7% (known as 70 basis points) greater than gilts of an equivalent maturity. This incremental margin of yield is known as the spread. Demand is good for the sector and the company's debt and the majority of the issue is placed with UK fixed income fund managers. A smaller amount is placed with trading accounts and held on the books of the issuing group.
A month after launch	The bond continues to trade tightly and in good size in the secondary market. Continuing demand from the fund managers pulls in the spread (i.e. the incremental yield margin over gilts). The bond's price is now equivalent to 62bp over gilts.
A year after launch	Turnover in the secondary market has decreased considerably.
Two years after launch	A credit event sees the bond's rating slip from AA to A+. Nervous fund managers sell their positions, accepting a price equivalent to 80bp over gilts. Secondary market volumes increase and asset-swappers move in, buying up the debt and swapping out the cash flows to floating or foreign currency proceeds before passing the debt on to a new set of investors.

Four years after launch	The double-A credit is restored. Spreads, and buyers, move in again. Liquidity is somewhat diminished by the number of bonds that have been locked up by the swap deals two years ago (which typically run to maturity).
18 months to maturity	The bond is now becoming of interest to cash fund managers and treasurers. With a new set of buyers on the block, spreads tighten in to gilts +50bp. The higher prices flush out some sellers from amongst the original buyers, who then go on to re-invest the proceeds in new longer-dated issues.
Maturity	The capital is repaid to the bond holders. Meanwhile, the company is refinancing.

Note – in the equity markets *spread* refers to the bid-offer spread – the difference between the buying and selling price. This is also true for the bond market, although the term is more usually employed to describe the incremental yield of a corporate bond when compared to a gilt of equivalent maturity or other benchmark interest rate.

Chapter 5

What happens if interest rates move?

Investors will generally buy a bond for two reasons. The first is to lock-in a known future income stream. The second is to attempt to benefit from rising bond prices. *But what would cause the value of a bond to rise?*

As with all traded assets, it will be down to our old friends, supply and demand. There are two main variables affecting the price of bonds

1. interest rates, and

2. the perceived credit quality or risk of default for the bond.

We'll consider the effect of the former on bond prices in this chapter, and we'll look at credit quality in the next chapter.

As interest rates fall, a bond paying a fixed rate of interest every year will become increasingly sought after by investors and therefore the price of the bond will rise. Conversely, rising interest rates, perhaps accompanied by inflation, will make the fixed income stream unattractive to investors and the market price of the bond will fall. This relationship between price and yield is the key to understanding the factors moving the fixed income markets.

Price & yield

The key to understanding the return on all fixed income instruments is to view a bond as a series of discounted cashflows. Understanding discounted cashflows is the key to all investment analysis. The core concept is the current value of a future sum of money, after allowing for interest, capital growth and/or inflation.

With equities, these future cashflows are unknown, but the accurate calculations can be performed for bonds. Consider that at the start of the investment, the investor pays out cash to purchase the bond. Over the course of the bond's life, the investor will then receive several payments, usually one or two a year from interest payments, known as coupons, and a final repayment at the end of the bond's life-span, known as redemption.

Given that the future cashflows are known quantities, the relationship between the price of a bond and the yield received by an investor is governed by mathematical formulae. We are going to look at three methods of analysing a bond's yield:

1. income yield

2. simple yield

3. yield to maturity (YTM).

1. Income (or running) yield

Let's take an example of a gilt, the UK Treasury 5% 2014. This bond pays a 5% coupon (divided into two semi-annual payment) and matures on the 7th September 2014. Thus, if we were able to buy the bond at the face value of 100% (or *par*), we know that we would receive an income 5% per annum on our investment until maturity.

But what would happen if we paid less than par for the bond? Let us assume that we purchase the bond for 95% of face value. Our income (or *running*) yield would be:

par/purchase price * coupon = running yield

Or

100/95 * 5% = 5.26% per annum

In this example, the UK Treasury 5% 2014 is trading at a price of 110. This premium to par has the effect of reducing the bond's income yield as follows:

100/110 * 5 = 4.5% per annum

The income or running yield (sometimes also known as the *flat yield* or *current yield*) does not take into account any profit or loss made by holding the bond to redemption, and simply assumes that the investor will be able to sell the bond at the same price that he or she purchased it for.

For a more accurate measure of yield, we must turn to the *yield to maturity* – the standard calculation employed by market professionals (also sometimes known as the *redemption yield*).

Before we turn to the more complex *yield to maturity*, it is worth considering the *simple yield*. This is a good rough guide to the return available on a bond, and can often be worked out in one's head.

2. Simple yield

Let us take a theoretical bond with one year left to run until redemption. The bond has a 4% coupon and we have purchased it in the market for 97%. Our return will consist of two factors, the running yield over the 12-month period and the profit made on maturity. Let us assume that we invest £1,000. Thus, for our initial investment of £970, we will receive the following:

£40 coupon payment (our running yield)

£30 profit on redemption (£1000 – £970)

Our return over the twelve month period is £70 on £970, or 7.2%. From the point of view of many investors, this type of calculation is perfectly adequate for assessing the return on a bond. Known as the *simple yield*, the formula can be expressed as follows:

simple yield   = running yield + (annualised) profit on redemption

               = (coupon/bond price) + (100 – bond price)/(bond price x years to redemption)

or, expressed mathematically:

simple yield = (C/P) + ((100-P)/P x t))

where,

C = coupon

P = current bond price

t = life to maturity of bond (years)

For longer-dated bonds, the same theory holds true. Let us take the Goldman Sachs 5.25% 15 December 2015. In June 2011 the bond had four-and-a-half years left to maturity and was trading at a price of 106.

Common sense dictates that a bond with a price standing at over par will yield less than the coupon. Let's see what our simple yield approach throws out:

Again, we can start with the running yield. The 5.25% coupon will be diminished by the over par market price as follows:

running yield = 5.25% x 100/106 = 4.95%

now, the profit (or, in this case, loss) on redemption:

profit on redemption = (100-106)/106 = -5.66%

annualised over the four and a half years holding period:

profit on redemption (annualised) = -5.66%/4.5 = -1.26%

finally, adding the two (the running yield and profit to redemption) together gives:

simple yield = 4.95% -1.26% = 3.69%

Thus, our simple yield on the bond is 3.69%

The simple yield is a useful quick and dirty calculation, but it does not account for the time value of money for the cash received at different times over the life of the bond. This is particularly significant for longer-dated bonds where the premium or discount paid for a bond may be many years away from the final redemption payment. For this, we need to turn to a more complex calculation – the yield to maturity.

3. Yield to maturity (YTM)

With longer dated bonds, the same methodology as above (for the simple yield) applies; but to gain a more accurate measure we must discount each future cash flow according to when it will be paid. The formula used to calculate this is known as the *yield to maturity* (YTM) and is effectively the internal rate of return on the investment, allowing for each and every cash flow). The calculation assumes that the interest payments received on the bond can be re-invested at the same rate, although this may not be the case in real life.

The formula for this calculation is somewhat of a handful, and certainly not one for mental arithmetic. It can be expressed as:

price = coupon * 1/r [1 -1/(1+r)^n] + redemption/(1+r)^n

where **r** is the YTM

Mathematicians will be interested to note that working out the YTM from the price is an iterative process.

Note – for more on yield calculation see the appendix.

Bond calculators

I would not recommend attempting to work out YTMs, however this calculation is the industry standard for the comparison of value in bonds. Luckily, there are many easy routes for establishing a bond's YTM.

> YTMs for sterling bonds are published on the **www.fixedincomeinvestor.co.uk** website. There is also an online yield calculator.

A yield calculator is a must for any serious bond investor. YTMs may be calculated by using the YIELD function in Microsoft Excel or on a dedicated financial calculator such as a Hewlett Packard 12C or 17B (eBay is often a good source of these old-model calculators). Online calculators provide another easy route to determining the value of a bond; an excellent example can be found in the Bonds section of Yahoo Finance:
http://bonds.yahoo.com/calculator.html

Some readers may prefer to download one of the many excellent calculators available as an app on Apple iPhones and other hardware.

Duration

Why do the prices of some bonds move more than others?

Using the example of our theoretical 4% bond with 12 months left to run until maturity, a 1% shift in the yield demanded by investors will produce a change in price roughly equivalent to 1%. In the case of a longer dated bond, with many more years to run until redemption, the price move will be considerably more.

This relationship between a given change in yield and the resulting change in price is known as the *duration* of the bond. Duration is based on the weighted average of the cash flows, broadly speaking how long it will take you to get your money back. This will have a considerable effect on the volatility of the bond over a range of different interest rate scenarios. Let's take three UK gilts as an example (calculated in March 2010).

The following table shows three bonds of different maturities. Note how the longer-dated bonds have longer duration. As mentioned in the paragraph above, duration is a measure of a bond's price volatility over a shift in yield. The table shows how these bond prices move over yield shifts between 2% and 3%.

Table 5.1: Duration example

Bond	Duration	2% YTM	3% YTM	4% YTM	5% YTM
Treasury 5% 2012	1.9	105.8	103.8	101.9	100
Treasury 4.75% 2015	4.89	114.22	108.8	103.7	98.8
Treasury 4.75% 2020	7.9	124.8	115	106	98.05

Note that the higher the duration of the bond the greater the price move shown per change in yield.

Duration, which is expressed in units of years, is determined by the length of time to maturity and the size of the coupon, in effect, the average period of all cash flows. A long bond with a low coupon will have the greatest duration, a short bond with a high coupon will have the lowest duration. Investors looking to benefit from falling yields should look to add duration to their bond portfolios, defensive investors, or those envisioning a rising interest rate scenario will look to reduce duration.

> **Tip**: a zero coupon bond will have a duration equivalent to its maturity.

Convexity

Duration is not set in stone. Obviously, it will shorten with the bond's life, but a drop in price will also reduce the duration.

Why?

Because as the price falls, the fixed coupons are now a greater in proportion to the purchase price, thus shrinking the average life. The relationship between price, yield and the duration of a bond can be plotted on a chart and is known as convexity, due to the shape of the resulting curve (see illustration, below).

Figure 5.1: convexity

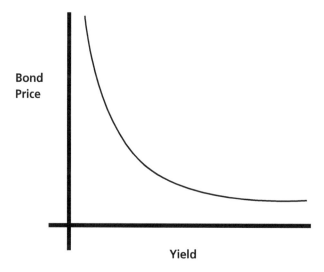

The subject of convexity is also applicable to bond portfolios, and is of some importance to the institutional fund manager who wishes to model how their portfolio might behave in different interest rate scenarios. For the purposes of the private investor, the subject is of rather less importance.

Chapter 6

Credit quality and ratings

Credit quality is a measure of the issuer's ability to service and repay its debt. In the case of gilts, US Treasury bonds and other high-quality government debt, the chance of default is low, even given the West's addiction to deficit funding. However, for issuers lower down the food chain than our sovereign masters, the wise investor must do some homework. Credit ratings will vary greatly from one issuer to another and even between individual bond issuers from the same company, depending on the bond's seniority within the creditor hierarchy.

Buying a bond is a serious business. You will be lending money to an organisation, and you should be comfortable that this organisation has both the ability to service the debt and to repay it in due course. Before we consider the methods of comparing and evaluating credit quality, let us consider what type of loan we will be making.

Types of loan

Secured lending

These types of bonds are comparatively rare but here the bondholders will have a direct charge on an individual pool of assets (often real estate). This, of course, will be of little help if the company is unprofitable and unable to pay the interest due on loans. However, in the event of a bankruptcy, secured lenders will be at the head of the queue and are likely to make a full recovery of their investments.

Senior Unsecured

The most common type of bond. As a senior unsecured bondholder you will rank ahead of the equity holders and subordinated bond holders (see below). However, senior bond holders will stand behind the secured lenders (above) in the event of the company winding up.

Subordinated

Subordinated bonds are securities where the investors claim on the company's assets has been pushed down the credit hierarchy. As such, they are a higher risk than senior or secured bonds from the same organisation.

These types of bonds are generally issued by banks and insurance companies, who have large and complex balance sheets. Such bonds will typically yield more than the two senior bonds above, and show higher volatility. [You can read more about these bonds in chapters 11 and 13.]

And how about government bonds?

Investors should consider that the senior/subordinated structure does not apply to government bonds. Indeed, many aspects of normal commercial law do not apply to governments, and this is something to bear in mind when dealing with the more risky end of the sovereign bond markets.

Note – seniority is not everything. Better a subordinated bond from a high-quality, conservative borrower than a senior bond from a more speculative issuer.

Credit ratings

Credit rating agencies

You may have your own knowledge and views on a company's ability to repay debt – perhaps gained from your experience in the equity market. Alternatively, you can view the credit rating assigned to issuers by several of the credit rating agencies, who deploy considerable resources to assess both the issuer and the individual bond.

It is in the interest of bond issuers to obtain ratings from the credit rating agencies. Without this stamp of approval from an independent body, the bonds will be hard to sell. Indeed, most institutional investors will be unable to purchase a bond that does not have a rating. There are two main international credit ratings agencies, namely Moody's and Standard & Poor's. A simple first stage check on a bond's quality will be to reference such ratings.

Credit ratings are the criteria used by most banks and fund managers when establishing the suitability of a bond as an investment but, remember, situations change quickly, and so can credit ratings. Such ratings, and the change thereof, will be announced via RNS (the Stock Exchange's Regulated News Service) and other publicly accessible news media, but bear in mind that the ratings agencies are notorious for being lagging indicators of credit quality. It is likely that the price of the bond will have moved some time before the change in rating.

You can look up the rating of most bond issuers on **www.moodys.com** and **www.standardandpoors.com**. An honourable mention should also go to Fitch IBCA (**www.fitchratings.com**). Private investors are able to register for free on these websites and view the allocated ratings.

The cost of ratings

The cost of obtaining a credit rating is not insubstantial, particularly for one-off, smaller or infrequent borrowers. Frequent borrowers will generally negotiate a package deal whilst large borrowers will find a rating cost effective on a per-unit basis. Of course, a good rating will drive down the cost of borrowing but the cost/benefit ratio may not be effective for some borrowers. The borrower may also have to devote a significant amount of management time to the ratings process.

The rating agencies are somewhat close-lipped about the cost of providing their testimonial. Moody's documents state that the issuer has agreed,

> "to pay to MIS for appraisal and rating services rendered by it fees ranging from $1,500 to approximately $2,500,000."

Market sources tell me that a typical cost for a UK corporate would be in the region of EUR20,000, for rating. There would also be a running charge for ongoing usage which might be EUR50,000 pa. This fee could rise considerably for more complex organisations such as banks or financial service players.

Credit research is also conducted by broking houses and investment banks, as well as some good independent analysts. However, it is worth bearing in mind that price action in the markets will typically lead any change in the credit rating.

Credit ratings

Here is Standard & Poor's definition of the ratings it awards to organisations issuing bonds.

1. Investment-grade debt

The following credit ratings are known as investment-grade debt. As a rule of thumb, investors managing portfolios where the risk must be minimised, and security of income and capital is paramount, will restrict themselves to bonds rated AAA and AA, with perhaps a few single A investments. Consider also a bond's credit history. Has the rating improved or declined over time? Bonds subject to a potential re-rating will be on "credit watch".

Rating	Description
AAA	Extremely strong capacity to meet its financial commitments. AAA is the highest issuer credit rating by Standard & Poor's.
AA	Very strong capacity to meet its financial commitments. It differs from the highest rated obligors only in small degrees.
A	Strong capacity to meet its financial commitments, but is somewhat more susceptible to the adverse effects of changes in circumstances and economic conditions than obligors in higher-rated categories.
BBB	Adequate capacity to meet its financial commitments. However, adverse economic conditions or changing circumstances are more likely to lead to a weakened capacity of the obligor to meet its financial commitments.

2. Non-investment grade

Bonds rated below BBB are known as non-investment grade. These bonds are of a more speculative nature, and imply a certain degree of risk. In view of this, the yield available on the instrument must be high enough to compensate the investor for this risk. Standard & Poor's gives the following definitions for non-investment grade debt.

Rating	Description
BB	Less vulnerable in the near term than other lower-rated obligors. However, it faces major ongoing uncertainties and exposure to adverse business, financial, or economic conditions that could lead to the obligor's inadequate capacity to meet its financial commitments.
B	More vulnerable than the obligors rated BB, but the obligor currently has the capacity to meet its financial commitments. Adverse business, financial, or economic conditions will likely impair the obligor's capacity or willingness to meet its financial commitments.
CCC	Currently vulnerable, and is dependent upon favourable business, financial, and economic conditions to meet its financial commitments.
CC	Currently highly vulnerable.
C	May be used to cover a situation where a bankruptcy petition has been filed or similar action taken, but payments on this obligation are being continued. C ratings will also be assigned to a preferred stock issue in arrears on dividends or sinking fund payments, but that is currently paying.

Note: The ratings from AA to CCC may be modified by the addition of a plus or minus sign to show relative standing within the major rating categories.

Table 6.1: conversion table for S&P and Moody's credit rating

Standard & Poor's	Moody's
AAA	Aaa
AA+	Aa1
AA	Aa2
AA-	Aa3
A+	A1
A	A2
A-	A3
BBB+	Baa1
BBB	Baa2
BBB-	Baa3
BB+	Ba1
BB	Ba2
B	Ba3

How useful are credit ratings?

The credit ratings agencies do not have a crystal ball – a problem that is faced by anyone attempting to quantify or manage risk, including private investors. One way to measure the accuracy of their work is to study default rates.

The following table shows the results of analysis by Standard & Poor's on bond default rates for their range of ratings for two periods:

1. the year 2005

2. an average of default rates over the period 1981-2008

Table 6.2: bond default analysis

Rating	2005 default rate(%)	1981-2008 default rate(%)
AAA	0	0
AA+	0	0
AA	0	0.02
AA-	0	0.03
A+	0	0.05
A	0	0.06
A-	0	0.08
BBB+	0	0.16
BBB	0.17	0.28
BBB-	0	0.28
BB+	0.36	0.68
BB	0	0.89
BB-	0.25	1.53
B+	0.78	2.44
B	2.59	7.28
B-	2.98	9.97
CCC- C	8.87	22.7

Source: Standard & Poor's

As can be seen, default rates can vary greatly over different time periods.

At risk of making a rather over-optimistic and sweeping statement, I would say that it is rare to experience a default in an investment grade bond. Note, however, that a bond bought with a double-A status may well be downgraded several times before default, so credit ratings are not a "fit and forget" component of risk management.

Finally, consider that default may not be a total loss situation. In portfolios that I have held (or advised on) over the years, I would estimate that recovery rates have been in the range of 20 to 80p in the pound, although recovery of this debt frequently takes some years to achieve.

Non-rated issues

I recently surveyed the readers of my website for their opinion on preferred ratings bands and sectors. 20% of respondents replied that they did not follow the credit ratings agencies, preferring to formulate their own view independently of any rating given. This is not unreasonable. Many private investors have very good judgement and are not slaves to industry orthodoxy. That opens the possibility of buying unrated issues, an area where many fund mangers will be unable to tread.

Consider that an unrated bond is not necessarily a bad credit. There are some issuers who are of the opinion that their name and creditworthiness are sufficient to stand alone without the imprimatur of Moody's or Standard and Poor's. A good example of this would be the mutually-held John Lewis Group, which the market prices as a high-end investment grade corporate, in spite of not having a rating. Tesco Bank, the banking subsidiary of the supermarket group, is also unrated (although its parent carries an investment grade from the major agencies).

However; be advised. There is a danger, particularly with private investors, to confuse the *product with the issuer*. Whilst John Lewis is in good shape, there are numerous producers of well-loved and luxury goods that operate on thin margins, low profitability and a stretched balance sheet. With unrated issuers, take a good long look at the reports and accounts before acting.

Making the credit decision

Credit ratings

Credit ratings and their interpretations are covered earlier in the chapter and it is fair to say that these ratings should be the first port of call. The credit rating agencies are far from perfect but their opinion is generally valid, and, more importantly, their opinion will be closely followed by institutional investors.

Tip: look out for the momentum of upgrades and downgrades. Re-ratings often come in series, and a drop from single-A to triple-B may not be the end of the story.

Do-it-yourself credit analysis

In addition to considering the company's credit rating, you may well wish to perform your own credit analysis, whether the company be rated or otherwise. In some cases, there will not be a credit rating to rely on, the aforementioned John Lewis being a good example.

The first tool to apply is **common sense:** do you trust the management? Are the company's activities, accounts and its balance sheet transparent? The next step is to download a copy of the company report and accounts and start digging. The advent of the internet has made this process much more accessible to the private investor. The company's own website is the first port of call, but there are many resources that can be employed [See the appendix for further information].

On the flip side, be wary of **confusing the product with the company**. As mentioned above, private investors often feel well-disposed towards known high-street brands, and that goodwill may spill over into their analysis of the company's debt. Try to stay objective.

The subject of credit analysis is a complex one, but if I can attempt to boil it down to a few main points, I would focus on the following.

Table 6.3: the main credit questions for investors

Credit questions	Description
Is the company profitable?	A fairly obvious question to ask, but an important one. The excesses of the 2000s proved that there was rather too much focus on the balance sheet, and not enough on the matter of the P&L. Have a good look at the earnings – are they of a good quality and sustainable?
Which part of the company are you lending to?	This can make a big difference. Ideally, you should be lending to the same part of the company that holds the assets. This is usually, but not always, the operating company.
Cover & financial ratios?	Once we have established that the company is profitable, consider what the cover of its debt is. What is the margin on sales? What is the equity/debt ratio? Run some scenarios. If the company suffers a 10% drop in top-line revenue; how will that affect profitability and the ability to service its debt?
Industry risk?	After looking at the individual company's financial situation, give some thought to its peers. Have there been failures in this sector? If so, this is indicative of a general level of risk associated with operating in the sector, however well-run the individual operation may be.
External factors?	Consider what risks and shocks the company might face. These vary from long-term litigation costs (think tobacco), disaster (think BP in the Gulf of Mexico), shifts in government policy (think of the huge bills telecom companies were forced to pay for 3G licences) through to leveraged takeovers. Such events cannot be forecast, but the possibility of an occurrence should be factored into the price paid.
Level indebtedness and maturity profile?	High levels of debt indicate higher levels of risk. Consider also the maturity profile. Does the company have a "hump" of debt to refinance in the near future, or is long term funding locked in place?
The bond's position within the credit hierarchy	Secured, senior or subordinated? With senior bonds (the most common type), watch out for other lenders such as banks pushing themselves above you on the ladder.

Timescale of investment

Very few companies will live forever. Changing social or economic conditions will impact the viability of the company's products and operations. Indeed, one often hears comment that such and such a company is going bust. This may well happen, eventually. Certain industries, such as the manufacturing industry in the west, high-street book/record retailers, or travel agents appear to have a future of long-term decline ahead of them.

However, if we are buying a 5-year bond, the events that may or may not happen in the 22nd century are of relatively little importance to us. Certainly, if I had a pound for every time someone told me Ford is going bust, I would be a wealthy man (I might add that I have frequently held the company's debt, all of which has been serviced and repaid).

A quick glance at the share price

Equity investors and bond investors have different criteria. The former go for growth and may actually encourage risky and highly leveraged business plans. Thus, a soaring share price is not necessarily a good thing for bond investors. Be wary, however, of a persistently sinking share price. This is a sign that all is not well. Also, make use of the copious amount of equity research that is available, generally for free, on the internet.

Summing up

There is market saying that "there are no bad assets, only bad prices". This may be an oversimplification, but the core of the statement is true. After making an assessment of the credit, consider the risk-reward ratio of the trade. Dubious credits may well be worth purchasing if the price is sufficiently advantageous.

Finally, do not forget the three golden rules of running a portfolio full of credits – diversify, diversify and diversify. To be more specific:

1. Diversify by **industry group**. This may include having a mixture of public and non-public borrowers (depending on the credit quality profile of the portfolio) before you move on to the more obvious diversifications across financial services, property, industrial, pharmaceutical and retail issuers.

2. Diversify by **credit quality**. Triple-B credits can show a remarkable degree of commonality across different issuers. Leven the mix with some AAA, some AA and perhaps non-investment grade credits. Consider also that different credit profile groups will behave divergently under various economic scenarios.

3. Diversify by **country**. Try not to have all UK credits in the portfolio.

Types of issuer

Before we go on to look at some examples of individual bonds and their credit ratings, it is worth considering the different classes of issuer that one might be likely to come across in the sterling bonds markets.

Sovereign issuers

As a rule of thumb, the bonds with the least risk of default are the high quality sovereign issuers such as the UK and the larger and wealthier European countries such as France and Germany.

The industry has traditionally considered such assets to be risk free from a default point of view. This type of thinking is perhaps outdated, however the risk of default[2] for bonds issued by these countries can be assumed to be low, and lower than the risk from a bank deposit. Ranking alongside these are the Supranationals, these being agencies such as the World Bank and the European Investment Bank which are guaranteed by their sovereign members.

Second to this are the second-line countries, and those experiencing some economic difficulty. Here I would give Italy and Japan as two examples. While these countries do not have the economic strength of some of their peers, it is fair to say that they have a lower risk of default. This type of debt should not be confused with emerging market bonds, which historically have carried a much higher degree of risk. Recent events have propelled some of the more marginal sovereign credits into the spotlight, with bonds issued by Greece and Ireland trading wildly in the markets as investors consider the likely

---

[2] Note that risk of default should not be confused with market risk, or price volatility. A bond can be 100% guaranteed by all the governments in the world and still experience price swings between issuance and redemption, typically driven by changing interest rates.

outcome of these countries' dire financial situation. It is likely that there will be some instances of at least partial default, and the creditworthiness of second-tier sovereign debt re-evaluated accordingly.

Bank issuers

Next we have high-quality, non-governmental debt. In the past, the highest scorers have often been the banks, some (but not all) of which have credit quality to rival that of a government. However, this situation has been affected by the events post-2008, and bank bonds now often trade on higher yields than corporates. Current moves from Brussels to effectively subordinate bank senior debt to deposits may see this prove to be a permanent development.

The seniority of the issue is of particular importance in bonds issued by banks. Bank debt is usually ranked as follows:

- **Senior Debt**: after secured bonds, this is the best.

- **Lower Tier 2**: the bank does not have the right to defer the coupon. The next best after senior debt.

- **Upper Tier 2**: coupon deferral possible in certain circumstances, but coupons are cumulative (i.e the payments missed will be rolled up and paid when the bank returns to a more favourable situation).

- **Tier 1**: coupon deferral in certain circumstances, non cumulative.

- **Preference Share**: generally coupon payment can be waived, generally non-cumulative.

Corporate issuers

Finally we have corporate bonds. These are bonds issued by corporations, typically large quoted companies. The life of a company is full of ups and downs and it is fair to say that in most cases corporate bonds carry a greater risk than those issued by major governments or banks. Factors affecting a company's credit rating include cash flow, profitability, asset valuations and unforeseen events such as legal action, a takeover or a change of the trading environment. Historically, the yield on these bonds will normally be greater than that available on bank debt and it is unusual for a corporate to achieve triple-A status.

It is notable that during the credit crunch of 2008 onwards this relationship has inverted with bank debt trading wider than corporate debt. Most market participants expect this relationship to revert to the historic norm in due course, but time will tell.

Other types of issuers

There are numerous bonds issued to fund mortgage loans, credit cards loans and other more complex financial transactions. These types of bonds, often known as *mortgage-backed* and *asset-backed*, are not generally available to the investing public in the UK. The credit quality of these varies from excellent to poor, typically depending on their place within the pecking order of claims to the underlying assets. Secondary market liquidity is often poor.

Some sample issuers and their ratings.

In the following table I list some of the better known borrowers and their current credit ratings.

Rating	Borrowers
AAA	Germany, France. Supranational agencies such as the World Bank (also know as the IBRD). UK gilts continue to enjoy a triple A status. Triple-A private sector issuers are comparatively rare, one example being the Dutch agricultural co-op Rabobank.
AA	Sovereigns such as Japan (AA-). A few high quality banks and corporates.
A	Good quality corporates such as Tesco (A-). Lower rated banks.
BBB	More speculative corporates such as Marks & Spencer (BBB-) and British Telecom (BBB-).

Note: These samples are based on the rating in force in early 2011, and are subject to change.

Frequently asked questions

Will a highly rated bond be less volatile than a lowly rated bond?

To a degree, yes. The perception of risk will tend to fluctuate less. However, the influence of interest rates, both in the present and to come will exert a similar influence on both highly and lowly rates bonds alike.

What are junk bonds?

The expression *junk bond* is a colloquialism for a non-investment grade bond (i.e. a bond that is rated below BBB-). In truth the term junk is often a rather harsh description and the majority of these bonds will live a useful and uneventful life, servicing both coupons and redemption payments. Nevertheless, a risk of default is implied in the name and caution should be applied when dealing in these bonds. At the time of writing, examples of bonds with junk status in the sterling markets include GKN, Manchester United and Cable & Wireless. As might be expected, these types of bonds offer a higher yield (7-10%, compared to gilt yields of 2-3%) in order to compensate for the additional risk.

Can credit ratings change?

Yes, indeed they can. Although the ratings that investors follow are described as *long term ratings* by the two main agencies, they can swing around quite quickly as perceptions change. An example of this was the sovereign state of South Korea, downgraded from a comfortable AA- to a worrying BBB- in the late 90s. Another even more dramatic example is Iceland, which was until quite recently rated AAA. This proved to be somewhat optimistic given the small size of the country and the ambitious activity of its bankers. It is now rated BBB-, the lowest possible investment grade rating.

Corporate bonds are even more subject to change as their issuers may be impacted by adverse trading conditions. Leveraged takeovers, in particular, can have sudden and disastrous impact on credit ratings.

PART II:
Bond Markets

This second part of the book explains the different types of bonds available to investors in the market. We will look at the different types of bonds trading in the sterling markets and take a brief glance at some of the overseas currency markets. We start by looking at the UK government bond (or *gilt*) market, this being the most liquid and transparent of all the sub-sets of sterling bonds and the natural reference point or benchmark for assessment of value in other areas.

Chapter 7

Gilts

Bonds issued by the UK government are known as gilts. Why? The issuance of such bonds was originally tied to the bank's gold reserves and, although this is certainly no longer the case, such is the market's faith in the government's ability to repay such debt that the bonds are considered to be "gilt edged".

As with most government bond markets, the size is considerable. In 2001 there were just over 281 billion pounds of gilts outstanding, a sum that has nearly quadrupled in a decade. The market is deep and liquid with the Debt Management Office holding regular auctions of these securities on behalf of the Treasury. Such auctions are for a range of short, medium and long-dated gilts (plus index-linked issues) and typically raise between £1 and £5 billion.

It is vital for any UK investor to understand and follow the gilts market, even if his or her actual interests lie elsewhere, such as equities, corporate bonds or real estate. Why? Because it is the gilt market that will reflect the government's monetary policy, the market's response and a road map of future expectations in the shape of the yield curve.

The liquid and transparent gilt market sets the benchmark for the pricing and corresponding yields of investment-grade corporate bonds, and it is here that we start the practical section of this book.

Before we turn to the nuts and bolts of investing in UK government debt, I thought it might be worth turning back the clock a few years to look at how the gilt market looked in the early stage of my career – a time when Mrs Thatcher was in No. 10 and interest rates were flirting with double-digits.

Back in the day

Dictum meum pactum

My word is my bond. So went the motto of the London Stock Exchange. The mid 1980s saw me as a newly-promoted "yellow button" on the floor of the exchange, an organisation then in a fever of excitement in the run-up to deregulation. I had just taken the role as an "authorised clerk" (or "yellow button"), a position one up the ladder from the lowly "blue button".

I worked for Panmure Gordon, then a respectable firm of mid-cap corporate brokers who fielded a decent gilt broking division operating under the eagle eye of senior partner Ian Cameron, the father of Prime Minister David Cameron.

My job was to check prices and execute gilts trades on the floor of the exchange. At 9.30am (shortly to move to 9am), a giant scrum would form outside the Capel Court door of the exchange, held back by the uniformed stock exchange waiters, who's job was somewhat akin to being a nightclub bouncer. Latecomers at the back of the queue would push forward, causing the keen dealers at the front to be shoved into the waiters and/or the door, an event that would trigger an outburst of strong language, and occasionally violence, from the stalwart waiters.

At 9.30 sharp a motley crew of brokers would burst through the double doors and head for one of the two main gilts jobber's pitches, these being Ackroyd and Smithers and Wedd Durlacher. Here we would stand, pencils poised over our pads to record the gilt "runs", these being a list of gilt prices gabbled off at speed by the jobbers in order or maturity. Next stop was back to the phones situated on the edge of the exchange to relay the prices back to the sales staff in the offices. After this, orders sourced by the sales staff were then relayed to the floor by the two-way VHF radios we carried – mobile phones still being a fairly unknown quantity at that point in time.

Dealing and market practice were an art in themselves and the atmosphere in the virtually all-male exchange was both vigorous and humorous.

Exchange floor nicknames

The best nickname ever? There were two brothers (I believe called Frisby) who worked on the floor of the exchange slightly before my time. Both had been awarded the Military Cross in the Second World War, however the second brother had been awarded the Military Cross and bar, thus, the nickname of the first brother was simply and gloriously "The Coward".

business alternating between frantically busy and nothing (as is so often case in financial markets), there was plenty of opportunity for practical jokes and the like. Further excitement could also be gained by the entry of the government broker into the market. This role was held by Mullens and Co., the staff of whom wore top hats (really). This affectation was extremely useful as it enabled the other dealers to see when the government entered the market, even from the other side of the room.

The market was a clash of cultures at every level. Sharp-eyed lads from Essex jostled with North Londoners and laconic public schoolboys. Meanwhile, the LIFFE futures market had opened up just across the road and advances in communication technology and computerisation were driving head-on against some of the archaic and restrictive practices of the exchange. Prices in those days were expressed in fractions, and this simple expedient was enough to create the role of gilts dealers as a specialized function. Indeed, equity dealers rarely entered the gilt market section of the exchange, perhaps dissuaded by some of the arcane pricing terminology and practices. Barry Lambert, senior dealer at Selftrade has filled in a few gaps (see following box) for me on some of the history of the gilt market over the 70s and 80s and some of the "terms of art" used in face-to-face dealing.

Trading gilts in the 70s and 80s

From 1974 I was a gilt jobber, on the floor of the LSE. There were, for most of the time, two larger jobbers – Akroyd & Smithers and Wedd Durlacher. We used to think that these two accounted for 80% of the volume and 20% of the transactions. The other four smaller jobbers were Charlesworth & Co. (where I was a Partner), Giles & Cresswell, Wedd & Owen and Wilson & Watford; between us we accounted for 20% of the volume and 80% of the transactions.

Just prior to my starting as a jobber, Smith Brothers entered the gilt market in 1972, but pulled out after three months after heavy losses. There were also two country jobbers who had small gilt businesses – they were Aitken Campbell and Moulsdale Rensburg.

In 1978 Pinchin Denny (an established Equity Jobber) started jobbing in gilts (following an injection of cash from County Bank and four other backers) and became the third largest. Sadly, in June 1980 Wedd & Owen ceased trading.

Prices were relatively close, particularly in shorts (in those days only shorts were quoted clean, anything over 5 years was quoted dirty). An average short price would have had a 1/16th spread (quoted, for example, as "a half – nine" = 1/2 to 9/16ths). For mediums and longs a sixteenth was usually the minimum quote denomination, however shorts were quoted to 1/128ths. Under or over related to 1/32nd either side of a fraction and close under or over related to 1/64th either side of a fraction and the slang for that would have been for example "5/16ths clo, clo" (9/32nds to 11/32nds), or it could be a variation such as "under to close over the five" (9/32nds to 21/64ths). Sometimes we would split the 64th, thereby dealing down to 1/128ths.

During those days of rampant inflation we would have to deal with price swings of up to 4 points in a day. I can also remember selling Treasury 15.5% 1998 – under par! And when some of the irredeemable stocks yielded the same as their price.

When I started in the gilt market it opened at 10:00 and the floor closed at 15:30, but we would continue to make prices over the phone until 17:00hrs (while we worked out that day's 'bull and bear' position and our P&L – by hand – we had no computers in those early days!). When I last worked as a GEMM in 1994 I worked from 07:00 to 19:00 – and they call it progress!

Note: for more on bond market nostalgia, I can recommend Philip Augur's excellent book, *The Death of Gentlemanly Capitalism*.

The modern gilt market

Sadly, the archaic splendor and vigor (and let's not forget the terrible thirst) of the old gilt market is no longer with us. Dealing is now online or on the telephone and prices are expressed in simple decimals. The Bank of England issues licenses for Gilt Edged Market Makers (or "GEMMS") and there are 18 firms operating as such at present (a list of these can be found in the appendix at the back of this book).

The GEMMs are the primary dealers in the market – effectively the same role as the market-makers or jobbers of the old system, but with additional responsibility as a conduit for new gilts issues.

The GEMMS have direct access to the Debt Management Office, the agency of the government responsible for gilt issuance, to borrowing facilities (and also the inter-dealer broker network). In return for the licence, the GEMMs agree to make prices in the secondary markets, ensuring a liquid market for the government's debt.

In addition to the above, there are several firms, such the old discount house King & Shaxson, and relative newcomers, such as Evolution, who operate as specialised gilt dealers, albeit not with full market-making capability.

From the standpoint of the private investor buying £10,000 or so of gilts through an online broker, most tickets will be executed with one or two of the GEMMs at most. This execution will typically be transacted via an RSP (retail service provider) – a system where executable prices can be held for 15 seconds or so, enabling the customer and the system enough time to accept the price and seal the deal.

The typical investor accessing the market through an online broker will be able to see a live quote for the majority of gilts.

Rump issues (blocks of bonds left over from very old issues or as a result of conversions or partial redemptions) will not generally have a live price, but workable bids can normally be found in the market by a well-connected broker. Obtaining offers of these illiquid bonds may be more difficult.

Conventional gilts

A good understanding of the UK bond market starts here.

The balance of supply and demand for gilts will dictate the picture for long-term interest rates and the shape of the yield curve accordingly. Most investors will own either a gilt or a gilt fund at some point in their investment career, even if your tastes run to more exotic and high-yielding alternatives.

Let's start with a typical gilt issue.

The Debt Management Office regularly issue new gilts, and here is one that was issued a few years ago – The UK Treasury 4% Sept 2016. The breakdown of the key features of this bond are given in the following table.

Table 7.1: sample gilt terms

Term	Value
Issuer	United Kingdom Treasury
Credit rating	AAA
Coupon	4% (payable semi-annually in two payments of 2%)
Maturity	7 September 2016 at £100
Issue date	March 2006
Issue price	98.36
Issue size	Initially £3 billion (size later increased by fourteen subsequent sales to £34 billion)
ISIN	GB00B0V3WX43

For investors in the gilt market, the first point of reference will be the benchmarks. These are comparatively newly issued bonds with good liquidity, situated on the major popular round number maturity points: 2, 5, 10 and 30 years.

King of the benchmarks is the 10 year gilt; it is on this bond that the futures contracts are based and a large amount of turnover will be seen. At the time of writing, the 10-year benchmark is the UK Treasury 3.75 7 September 2019 (see following chart). It is worth remembering that the status of being a benchmark passes with time. In due course, a ten-year maturity bond will become an eight-year maturity and the crown will pass to a new issue.

Chart 7.1: price chart for sample gilt

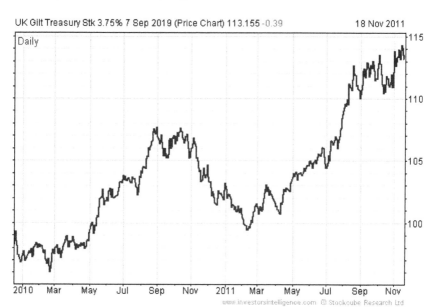

Typical investors in the gilts market will be large institutions, notably the big life insurance companies who love to buy long-dated AAA-rated bonds to meet the long term liabilities created by savings plans, pensions and the dreaded annuities.

A good point about the gilts market is the ease of accessibility for private investors. Gilts have very low minimum denominations and can be dealt with in fractions down to the penny. More importantly, gilts can usually be dealt online through several stockbroker platforms, enabling low-cost, speedy dealing for the man on the street. It should be possible for a private investor to deal in an "on-the run" gilt (i.e. one of the large and liquid issues) on a bid-offer spread of perhaps 5p (0.05%); for instance 110.05 bid to 110.10 offer. However this spread will be wider in less liquid issues.

So will the investor be able to get a good return on gilts?

As a buy and hold investment, I would suggest that gilts offer a low risk investment but will typically offer rather lower YTMs than that provided by corporate bonds or other bonds where the credit risk is higher. This is because of their good credit and high liquidity – and the premium price thus afforded to them by the market. Indeed, most corporate and other bonds are priced on a spread over gilts – the incremental margin provided over gilts. It is comparatively rare to see a GBP bond trade with a yield lower than that available on a gilt of an equivalent maturity. This is known as trading *through* gilts and usually only happens when there is a short-squeeze or some other issue-specific event.

From a trading or even medium-term investment point of view, gilts can be much more rewarding, offering tight bid-offer spreads and fairly rapid price moves. The YTM of the Treasury 3.75% 2019 bond shown is less than 2%, but investors enjoyed a 17 point rally over 2011.

The yield curve

Bonds of different maturities offer different yields. This is understandable. Very short-dated securities will have yields similar to those seen on bank deposits (although credit quality will be a factor). All things being equal, investors will usually demand a greater return for longer-term lending. This means that longer-dated gilts will typically yield more than their shorter-dated cousins. However, expectations for future interest rates changes may alter this natural relationship between short and long-dated bonds.

Plotting the YTMs of bonds against their maturity gives us the *yield curve*, a graphical representation of how investors value the market, and an insight into their expectations for future interest rates.

Positive and negative curves

In an environment where interest rates are expected to rise in the future, longer-term bonds will command higher YTMs than shorter term bonds. This is known as a *positive yield curve*.

In an environment where interest rates are expected to fall, the yield curve will be negative. Longer-term bonds may offer lower YTMs than their shorter-dated cousins.

The gilt yield curves shown (below) from March 2000 and March 2010 are a good illustration of this. The dotted line shows the plot of the gilt yield curve in 2000, showing the yields of bond with maturities ranging from 3 months to 30 years along the X axis. At that point in time interest rates were expected to fall; longer-dated gilts yielded less than short-dated gilts, an example of a negative yield curve.

By 2010, yields had fallen, perhaps rather more than some people expected. The curve had shifted to a more conventional positive relationship.

Chart 7.2: gilt yield curve (2000, 2010)

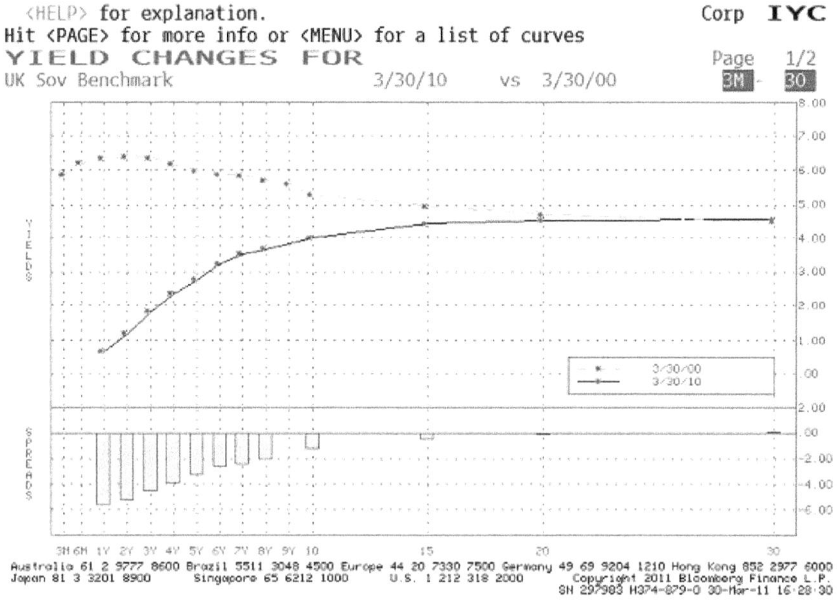

Source: Bloomberg

The gilt yield curve will be the first port of call for most sterling bond investors when assessing value both in gilts and relative value in corporate bonds.

The table below, taken from my website at **www.fixedincomeinvestor.co.uk** and fed by closing prices from the Bondscape platform, shows the majority of gilts outstanding as of March 2011. The positive shape of the gilt yield curve is evident with longer maturities offering higher YTMs than the short-dated bonds.

Table 7.2: UK gilts (March 2011)

Ccy	Issuer	ISIN	Coupon	Maturity	Life	Price	Yield
GBP	UK Gilt Treasury Stk	GB00B0LNX641	4.25	7 Mar 2011	1 days	100.065	0
GBP	UK Gilt Conversion Stk	GB0002215225	9.0	12 Jul 2011	4 mths	102.935	0.61
GBP	UK Gilt Treasury Stk	GB00B3F2K012	3.25	7 Dec 2011	9 mths	101.885	0.73
GBP	UK Gilt Treasury Stk	GB0030468747	5.0	7 Mar 2012	1 yr	104.045	0.93
GBP	UK Gilt Treasury Stk	GB00B1L6WG32	5.25	7 Jun 2012	1 yr 3 mths	105.225	1.04
GBP	UK Gilt Treasury Stk	GB0008938465	9.0	6 Aug 2012	1 yr 5 mths	110.97	1.18
GBP	UK Gilt Treasury Stk	GB00B29WRG55	4.5	7 Mar 2013	2 yrs	106.115	1.39
GBP	UK Gilt Treasury Stk	GB0008921883	8.0	27 Sep 2013	2 yrs 6 mths	116.4	1.44
GBP	UK Gilt Treasury Stk	GB0031829509	5.0	7 Sep 2014	3 yrs 6 mths	109.79	2.09
GBP	UK Gilt Treasury Stk	GB0009026674	7.75	26 Jan 2015	3 yrs 10 mths	105.865	1.1
GBP	UK Gilt Treasury Stk	GB0033280339	4.75	7 Sep 2015	4 yrs 6 mths	109.575	2.49
GBP	UK Gilt Treasury Stk	GB0008881541	8.0	7 Dec 2015	4 yrs 9 mths	124.545	2.49
GBP	UK Gilt Treasury Stk	GB00B0V3WX43	4.0	7 Sep 2016	5 yrs 6 mths	106.195	2.78
GBP	UK Gilt Treasury Stk	GB0008931148	8.75	25 Aug 2017	6 yrs 5 mths	134.3	2.9
GBP	UK Gilt Exchequer Stk	GB0003252318	12.0	12 Dec 2017	6 yrs 9 mths	135.13	1.55
GBP	UK Gilt Treasury Stk	GB00B1VWPC84	5.0	7 Mar 2018	7 yrs	111.255	3.19
GBP	UK Gilt Treasury Stk	GB00B39R3F84	4.5	7 Mar 2019	8 yrs	107.145	3.47

Ccy	Issuer	ISIN	Coupon	Maturity	Life	Price	Yield
GBP	UK Gilt Treasury Stk	GB00B4YRFP41	3.75	7 Sep 2019	8 yrs 6 mths	101.295	3.57
GBP	UK Gilt Treasury Stk	GB00B058DQ55	4.75	7 Mar 2020	9 yrs	108.53	3.63
GBP	UK Gilt Treasury Stk	GB0009997999	8.0	7 Jun 2021	10 yrs 3 mths	136.145	3.73
GBP	UK Gilt Treasury Stk	GB00B3KJDQ49	4.0	7 Mar 2022	11 yrs	101.08	3.88
GBP	UK Gilt Treasury Stk	GB0030880693	5.0	7 Mar 2025	14 yrs	109.895	4.07
GBP	UK Gilt Treasury Stk	GB00B16NNR78	4.25	7 Dec 2027	16 yrs 9 mths	100.13	4.24
GBP	UK Gilt Treasury Stk	GB0002404191	6.0	7 Dec 2028	17 yrs 9 mths	122.005	4.22
GBP	UK Gilt Treasury Stk	GB00B24FF097	4.75	7 Dec 2030	19 yrs 9 mths	105.43	4.34
GBP	UK Gilt Treasury Stk	GB0004893086	4.25	7 Jun 2032	21 yrs 3 mths	98.605	4.35
GBP	UK Gilt Treasury Stk	GB0032452392	4.25	7 Mar 2036	25 yrs	97.915	4.39
GBP	UK Gilt Treasury Stk	GB00B00NY175	4.75	7 Dec 2038	27 yrs 9 mths	106.12	4.37
GBP	UK Gilt Treasury Stk	GB00B1VWPJ53	4.5	7 Dec 2042	31 yrs 9 mths	102.49	4.35
GBP	UK Gilt Treasury Stk	GB00B128DP45	4.25	7 Dec 2046	35 yrs 9 mths	98.44	4.34
GBP	UK Gilt Treasury Stk	GB00B06YGN05	4.25	7 Dec 2055	44 yrs 9 mths	99.065	4.3
GBP	UK Gilt Treasury Stk	GB00B54QLM75	4.0	22 Jan 2060	48 yrs 10 mths	94.085	4.29
GBP	UK Gilt Treasury Stk	GB0009031211	3.0	Undated		61.855	4.85
GBP	UK Gilt Consols	GB0002163805	2.5	Undated		52.36	4.8
GBP	UK Gilt Treasury Stk	GB0009031096	2.5	Undated		52.68	4.75
GBP	UK Gilt Consols	GB0002163466	4.0	Undated		80.615	4.96
GBP	UK Gilt Conversion Stk	GB0002212099	3.5	Undated		72.905	4.8
GBP	UK Gilt War Loan Stk	GB0009386284	3.5	Undated		72.09	4.85

Taking the columns from left to right:

- **Currency** is self explanatory. The UK government does occasionally issue in other currencies but such bonds are not referred to as gilts.

- With regard to **name,** all modern gilts are simply called "UK Treasury Stock". Older issues may have a variety of names, but there is no difference in credit quality etc. They are all HMG obligations.

- **ISIN** is the security code used by most bond traders.

- **Coupon** is the interest payment on the bond per £100 nominal.

- **Life** is the time remaining between the date at which the table was drawn up and the **Maturity** date.

- **Price** is the level at which the bond is trading in the market, and this of course is a factor in the.

- **Yield** – the yield to maturity, factoring in coupon, price and life.

A few observations that can be made from the preceding table:

- Yield typically increases with maturity – this is known as a *positive yield curve* and is, broadly speaking, a natural feature of bond markets.

- Coupons vary greatly – from 3% through to 8% or more. This is generally a feature of the prevailing level of interest rates at the time of issuance. Most gilts are issued at or around par.

- Coupon payment dates vary – this is a useful attribute. Gilts pay coupons twice a year, so with a little juggling a portfolio of six bonds will create a monthly income flow.

- The gilts at the bottom of the table are undated [more on this later in the chapter].

Some peculiarities of gilts

Gilts are straightforward to own and deal in. Although, there are a few wrinkles that the investors may need to be aware of:

Accrued interest

Market convention accrues the interest on gilts on an actual/actual basis between coupon payments. Thus to calculate the accrued, simply count the number of days since the last coupon payment and divide by the number of days within the semi-annual period. [There's more detail on accrued interest later.]

Sub-division to the penny

It is possible to invest odd lot sums in gilts. The minimum price is just 1p. This is quite different to most corporate bonds, which are less frangible and have much larger minimum dealing sizes. Indeed, many institutionally-targeted corporate bonds have minimum denominations of GBP100,000, making them extremely inaccessible for the private investors.

Ex-dividend

Gilts trade in a broadly conventional manner, with the accrued rolling up on the 6 month coupons in the normal way. Gilts are normally deemed to be dealt *ex-div* seven days before the coupon. War Loan is deemed to be ex-div ten days before the coupon.

The convention of allowing gilts to trade *special ex dividend,* a process where investors often sold cum and bought ex, is no longer in practice.

Gilts and taxation

Capital gains on gilts are free of capital gains tax. This is a useful attribute, but investors should be aware that capital losses from this asset class can not be offset against gains elsewhere.

Income, sadly, is taxable (unless the gilt is held in an ISA or SIPP wrapper). Thus, the investor will need to select his gilt by balancing both the YTM and the tax-efficiency of the bond. Low coupon, discounted gilts are the most tax efficient for income-tax payers; doubly so for higher rate payers.

The gilt market has an overhang of older, higher-coupon issues, left over from the 80s and 90s when headline interest rates where somewhat higher. These are unlikely to be tax efficient for the private investor. Looking further out it will be more interesting to play around with the recent low-coupon issuance (for instance the 3.75% 2019) in a higher rate environment.

Many stockbrokers publish tables with the effective yield at various taxation rates, and these are a useful guide. The example below is taken from stockbroker Redmayne Bentley's monthly recommendations list.

Table 7.3: effective yields on gilts (accounting for tax)

Gilts	Mid price	Flat Yield	YTM	Interest paid	Yield to 40% taxpayer
4% Treasury 07/09/16	105.5	3.80%	3.0%	March/Sept	1.45%
4.25% Treasury 07/12/27	98.53	4.31	4.37%	June/Dec	2.65%

> **Tip**: just as low coupon gilts are tax efficient, high coupon gilts may be the opposite! High rate tax payers will have to pay the full Monty on the coupon, but may be unable to offset the capital loss on the bond's natural "roll down" to par.

Gilt strips

All bonds can, and indeed should, be viewed as a series of cash flows; the loan from investor to borrower is followed by a series of payments back to the investor – typically one or two coupons a year followed by a final chunk at maturity.

The simplest type of bond is the *zero coupon* bond (often referred to as a *zero*). Treasury Bills are a good example of these types of securities. Longer dated versions of these kinds of discounted securities are known as *zero coupons*. As with Treasury Bills, an investor purchasing a zero will buy the asset at a discount to its future redemption value. However, in the case of the zero, this event may be some years in the future rather than a few months. No coupons are paid; the investor profits as the security rolls up towards par at maturity. The zero coupon bond is simple to understand and useful.

Sadly the UK government does not issue zeros *per se*, however these instruments are replicated by what is known as a *gilt strip*. Here the investor agrees to buy just one cash flow from the bond – either a coupon or a principal. Effectively, an existing gilt is stripped down to create a family of zero coupon bonds.

As with many financial innovations, strips first emerged in the United States. The instruments first hit the street in 1985 and an active market has been maintained since. The letters stand for Separate Trading of Registered Interest and Principal Securities, and I take my hat off to the chap who must have spent hours wrestling with the description in order to come up with such a punchy sounding acronym. Gilt strips followed in 1997, broadly following the US model.

How do strips work?

Turning to the excellent Debt Management Office's website, our man from the ministry explains:

Gilt strips

"Stripping" a gilt refers to breaking it down into its individual cash flows which can be traded separately as zero-coupon gilts. A three-year gilt will have seven individual cash flows: six (semi-annual) coupon payments and a principal repayment. Gilts can also be reconstituted from all of the individual strips. Not all gilts are strippable. Official strip facilities have been available in the United States since 1985, and France since 1991. Official strip markets also now exist in many countries including Austria, Belgium, Canada, Germany, Italy, Japan, the Netherlands, South Africa and Spain. The strip market began in the UK on 8 December 1997.

All strippable gilts are currently conventional fixed coupon instruments. At end-March 2010 there were 30 strippable gilts in two series with a total amount outstanding of £655.6 billion (£543 billion in market hands). However, only £2.3 billion (nominal) were held in stripped form.

Although anyone can trade or hold strips, only a GEMM, the DMO or the Bank of England can strip (or reconstitute) a strippable gilt.

GEMMs are obliged to make a market in strips, as they are in the underlying gilts. The market in gilt strips has grown slowly since its inception. Factors that have contributed to this slow development may have included the need for pension fund trustees to give the appropriate authority to fund managers to invest in strips and the inversion of the yield curve over much of the early period of the DMO's operations, which made strips *appear* more expensive relative to conventionals. Retail demand for strips has reportedly been affected by the necessary tax treatment, whereby the securities are taxed each year on their unrealised capital gain or loss even though no income payment has been made. However, the ability to hold gilt strips within Individual Savings Accounts (ISAs) may reduce the tax disincentives to personal investment in strips.

Source: DMO

Why buy strips?

The typical buyer of a strip will be looking to invest money to meet a known forward liability – perhaps school fees or other outgoings. There are advantages and disadvantages to this type of assets, some of which I summarise below:

Advantages

- Self re-investing. Strips have no coupon to re-invest. This can be useful for long-term financial planning and also reduces the re-investment risk that may occur in falling rate scenarios.

- High gearing to market moves. The low-priced and typically long duration strips will display gearing in price terms to a shift in gilts' market yields. The table below shows the price moves of a 10 year gilt strip (The PS20 Sept 2020) against a conventional gilts of the same maturity (the UKT3.75% Sept 2020).

Table 7.4: price comparison of strip v gilt

Yield to Maturity	Strip Sept 2020	UKT 3.75% Sept 2020
3%	74	106
4%	67	98
5%	61	90
6%	55	83

Disadvantages

- Not suitable for income investors

- Volatile

- Less liquid than conventional gilts (typically wider bid/offer spreads)

- The roll up effect of these deeply discounted gilts is likely to be taxed as income.

Double-dated gilts

These used to be more common than they are now, but in the past the Treasury has issued double-dated gilts with either a band of maturity dates or an early call option. There are now only two of these bonds remaining in issue, with first and final maturity dates fairly close together (3-4 years apart). These are *rump gilts* – smaller amounts of older gilts that do not have much of a liquid market.

The two are:

- Treasury 7.75% 26th January 2012 – 2015 (issued 1972)

- Treasury 12% 12 Dec 2013 – 2017 (issued 1978)

The Government can choose to redeem these gilts in whole, or in part, on any day between the first date and the final maturity dates. Three months' notice will be provided but the market will generally know if the bonds are likely to be called by comparing the coupon with re-financing rates.

> **Tip**: a rule of thumb for investors will be – if it is standing below par, expectations are that it will not be called.

Undated gilts

There are a number of undated (or "perpetual") gilts that trade in the market. These have no stated maturity but are redeemable at the government's option at any time (and thus should not really be considered perpetual). As such, they share characteristics with equities, or perhaps fixed income preference shares, in as much that no yield to redemption can be calculated, only a basic running yield. The outstanding sums of such issues are small, and liquidity typically poor – although I would comment that these issues traded much more freely in the 1980s and it is not immediately apparent to me why the situation has deteriorated.

No bond of this nature has been issued for many years, but the undated nature of the securities means that they stay around virtually for ever. The government typically only redeems such instruments if:

1. they can refinance more cheaply, and/or

2. the issue has become so small that it is no longer cost-effective to support.

These bonds have been issued over the years, with Consols first issued in 1751. Trading in such instruments is a slightly Dickensean experience. Bonds such as Consols appear regularly in 19th century literature. Indeed, the fortunes of John Galsworthy's Forsyte family (many of whom appeared to be an idle bunch) much rested on the price of these bonds.

The following table shows the majority of the UK's remaining undated gilts. Note the very small issue sizes of these older bonds.

Table 7.5: UK undated gilts

First date of issue	Common Name	ISIN Code	Coupon (%)	Price	Running yield	Outstanding (GBP million)
1946	UK Gilt Treasury Stk	GB0009031211	3.0	61.8	4.85	£38
1752	UK Gilt Consols	GB0002163805	2.5	52.3	4.81	£180
1946	UK Gilt Treasury Stk	GB0009031096	2.5	52.66	4.75	£390
1926	UK Gilt Consols	GB0002163466	4.0	79.905	5.01	£270
1921	UK Gilt Conversion Stk	GB0002212099	3.5	72.915	4.8	£17
1917	UK Gilt War Loan Stk	GB0009386284	3.5	72	4.86	£1900

These instruments have their uses. Undated gilts have the following beneficial features for investors:

- Typically higher yielding than long dated gilts (see below).

- Undated bonds maintain constant maturity – and are thus a very useful benchmark for studying long-dated gilt yields over the decades.

- Low coupon and undated maturity (i.e. very long duration) gives gearing to market.

Range-trading history (see following chart of War Loan).

Chart 7.3: price chart of War Loan

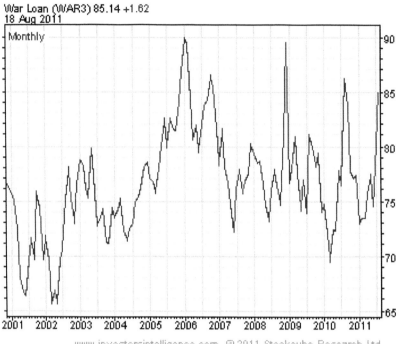

War Loan (WAR3) 85.14 +1.62
18 Aug 2011

www.investorsintelligence.com © 2011 Stockcube Research Ltd

Undated gilts and the yield premium

Undated gilts, sometimes referred to somewhat inaccurately as perpetuals, typically trade at a higher yield than long-dated conventional gilts. In a way, this is strange. The duration of a War Loan at the current price/yield is 21 years. That is almost exactly the same as the super-long Treasury 4% 2060. However, the undated War Loan offers an extra 50bp of yield, quite a large margin.

Note: many people will ask; how can an undated bond have the same duration as a dated bond? Simple – duration is the weighted average of all the cash flows. A high yield, high coupon bond may well have a short duration even if the maturity is well outside of the human lifespan.

Many market participants put this price differential down to the poor liquidity of the War Loan. This is only partially true. The real reason is the adverse *optionality* aspect of the War Loan – should long term interest rates in the UK drop sharply below 3.5% (as indeed they have been in Japan for many years), the government will call the bond. However, holders of the super-long 4% 2060 can continue to enjoy their coupons for many years to come. Thus, a risk premium is priced into the War Loan and other undated gilts.

Treasury Bills

A Treasury Bill is a short-dated government security. They are issued without a coupon, but sold at a discount to par. They are, effectively, the simplest type of fixed income security. It is unlikely that the typical private investor or his advisor will have much to do with the UK Treasury Bill market. However, there are times when it may come in useful. For instance, during the 2008 credit crunch, many investors feared for the security of banks deposits and moved their cash into Treasury Bills as a best option move to protect their capital. Yields were extremely low but the liquidity and short-dated maturity of these government securities made Treasury Bills a natural defensive move. This certainly made sense at the time.

The short-maturity Treasury Bills are a vital component of the money markets. Bills are issued routinely in weekly tenders. Maturities are typically 3-month, 6-month and 9-month. As far as I am aware, no 12-month UK Treasury Bills have been issued to date.

UK Treasury Bills can be delivered into CREST or Euroclear and settlement protocol is T+1 (1 day after the date of trade). There is no theoretical minimum dealing size. Two-way prices are tight in the secondary market at the institutional level (which typically trades in clips of tens of millions of pounds). Unlike bonds, which are generally quoted on a price basis (e.g. 99.875 bid, 99.9375 offered), Treasury Bills are quoted on a yield basis.

Private investor participation is comparatively rare and very small-size orders may prove difficult to execute. In my experience deals around the £100,000 and above are viable.

Members of the public are not able to participate directly in the issuance of new bills, but can participate through a *primary participant*, typically one of the major investment banks. The minimum size at the primary level is £500,000 nominal.

Chapter 8
Index-linked gilts

It is often said that the main risk that bond investors face is that of inflation. This is, broadly speaking, true. A bond investor purchases an asset with a fixed forward stream of cash flows. If the purchasing power of those cash flows is eroded over time, the investor will lose out.

One might argue that this is equally true of equity and property investments, but these types of investments have a degree of natural hedge against inflation – typically dividends and rental incomes rise with inflation over time.

From the point of view of pension fund managers and trustees, hedging against the risk of inflation has always been one of the main priorities. Funds of this nature have long-term liabilities, often linked to inflation or earnings and thus have a strong appetite for inflation-linked assets to balance their liabilities.

Given the demand from the UK's pension fund industry, the creation of index linked bonds was not surprising. Perhaps what was surprising was the first government off the block to issue them was none other than our own HM Treasury. 1981 saw the first issue of UK index-linked gilts (commonly known as "linkers") hit the market. Amazingly, the more sophisticated US Treasury market did not follow suit with its own index-linked securities (Treasury Inflation Protected Securities, or TIPS) until 1997.

Let's take a look at that first index-linked security.

Treasury 2% Index-linked 1996 – the first index-linked bond

£1 billion of the Treasury 2% Index-linked 1996 was issued on 27 March 1981, following the announcement of this new class of security by the then chancellor, Geoffrey Howe, in the previous budget. Purchase of the instrument was restricted to pension funds and the like, although this restriction was sensibly removed the next year in order to improve the marketability of the security.

How did this security work?

The basic principle was very simple. All future cash flows (both the semi-annual coupon and redemption payments) were to be linked to the UK's Retail Price Index (RPI). Thus, if the RPI shows an increase of 5% over year one, an index-linked gilt's coupon will be adjusted by this increment. In other words, a 2% coupon will become 2.1% coupon.

Should the value of the RPI double by the bond's maturity date, by the end of the holding period, the investor will receive coupons at the rate of twice the initial 2% coupon and a redemption payment of twice the par (100) redemption value.

The technicalities were a little more complex than conventional gilts. It was important to ensure that the next payable coupon was a known quantity in order to facilitate secondary market trading (particularly the calculation of accrued interest). In order to ensure this, an eight-month lag was applied to the indexation process. All subsequent payments were then adjusted by the ratio of the 8-month lagged RPI to the base RPI, the latter being determined by the value of the RPI 8 month's prior to the launch. This system worked well enough, although cynics will point out these bonds offer no protection against inflation for the last eight months of its life.

The best way to understand any process is to look at an example. Turning our attention to the slightly newer Treasury 2% 2006 Index Linked bond, also issued in 1981, here are the actual payments received by investors holding the bond from issue to maturity, based on a £100 nominal value initial investment.

Table 8.1: actual payments made for sample index-linked gilt

Date	Payment	Date	Payment	Date	Payment
19-Jan-1982	£0.92	19-Jan-1991	£1.81	19-Jan-2000	£2.38
19-Jul-1982	£1.11	19-Jul-1991	£1.87	19-Jul-2000	£2.39
19-Jan-1983	£1.17	19-Jan-1992	£1.92	19-Jan-2001	£2.45
19-Jul-1983	£1.18	19-Jul-1992	£1.95	19-Jul-2001	£2.47
19-Jan-1984	£1.21	19-Jan-1993	£2.00	19-Jan-2002	£2.50
19-Jul-1984	£1.24	19-Jul-1993	£2.01	19-Jul-2002	£2.49
19-Jan-1985	£1.28	19-Jan-1994	£2.03	19-Jan-2003	£2.53
19-Jul-1985	£1.30	19-Jul-1994	£2.03	19-Jul-2003	£2.56
19-Jan-1986	£1.37	19-Jan-1995	£2.08	19-Jan-2004	£2.61
19-Jul-1986	£1.38	19-Jul-1995	£2.09	19-Jul-2004	£2.62
19-Jan-1987	£1.40	19-Jan-1996	£2.15	19-Jan-2005	£2.68
19-Jul-1987	£1.42	19-Jul-1996	£2.15	19-Jul-2005	£2.72
19-Jan-1988	£1.46	19-Jan-1997	£2.20	19-Jan-2006	£2.76
19-Jul-1988	£1.48	19-Jul-1997	£2.21	19-Jul-2006	£2.78
19-Jan-1989	£1.52	19-Jan-1998	£2.25	19-July-2006	£278.63 redemption
19-Jul-1989	£1.58	19-Jul-1998	£2.29		
19-Jan-1990	£1.65	19-Jan-1999	£2.35		
19-Jul-1990	£1.70	19-Jul-1999	£2.36		

The first point to note is that the first sum received of 92p (in January 1982) was less than the 100p one might expect from a semi-annual payment of the 2% coupon. My first assumption was that this was due to a short-lived spell of deflation. However this was not the case. The first coupon was fixed at the time of issue and took account of the fact that the bond was part-paid in three instalments (March, August and September), reflecting the delayed investment process.

From then on, the process was straightforward.

The base RPI was set at 274.1 – which was the level of the RPI eight months prior to the July issue date.

The amount payable for the second coupon in July 1982 was then calculated by applying the appropriate RPI data point, in this case the RPI eight months before July 1982 and comparing it to the base. Thus, for £100 nominal of the bond:

RPI (Nov 1981)/RPI (base) x semi annual coupon(1%)

306.9/274.1 x 1% = 1.1197

So, the amount paid as coupon was £1.11 (coupon payments are rounded down to the nearest penny).

And so on and so forth.

Each semi-annual payment is adjusted for the RPI. This was almost always upwards; but I note that July 2002 saw a very small downward move. Illustrating the point that indexation on these bonds is not upward only!

Finally, in 2006 this index-linked bond was retired, and the holders received the maturity payment of £278.63.

How good did this protection against inflation prove to be?

Certainly, the holders enjoyed the comfort of a quantifiable hedge against the RPI, but it might be worth considering that conventional gilts offered yields of 9-11% in the early 1980s, a figure that would have considerably outperformed the total return seen on our index-linked bond.

Consider also that the so-called inflation link may not have been perfect. If I remember correctly a pint of beer could be had for about 65p in most areas; perhaps 95p in a more fashionable establishment. By 2006 I'd say that £3 was the norm. On the other hand, the price of clothing has fallen enormously over the last decade or so – it is perhaps a case of what you spend your money on.

Many linkers then followed

Numerous *linkers* followed the first issue, with the new asset class finding strong demand from the pension fund industry. Many examples of these Mark I index-linked gilts are still trading in the markets and their relatively simple calculation basis makes them a popular choice.

As of late 2011, the following index-linked gilts were available on my website and available for trade on most platforms. Note the high prices of many of these bonds, a result of the fairly distant issue date and the subsequent rise in the RPI. In this aspect, index-linked gilts differ from conventional gilts. Linker price will roll upwards towards redemption, tracking the rise of the RPI, whilst conventional gilts have a tendency to gravitate towards their redemption price at par.

Table 8.2: UK index-linked gilts (18 Nov 2011)

ISIN	Coupon	Maturity	Life	Price	Yield
GB0009036715	2.5	16 Aug 2013	1 yr 9 mths	284.04	0.8
GB0009075325	2.5	26 Jul 2016	4 yrs 8 mths	340.39	1.58
GB00B0V3WQ75	1.25	22 Nov 2017	6 yrs	114.485	1.88
GB0009081828	2.5	16 Apr 2020	8 yrs 5 mths	357.435	2.37
GB00B1Z5HQ14	1.875	22 Nov 2022	11 yrs	124.25	2.68
GB0008983024	2.5	17 Jul 2024	12 yrs 8 mths	318.74	2.88
GB00B128DH60	1.25	22 Nov 2027	16 yrs	119.94	2.98
GB0008932666	4.125	22 Jul 2030	18 yrs 8 mths	306.135	2.99
GB00B3D4VD98	1.25	22 Nov 2032	21 yrs	125.13	3.02
GB0031790826	2.0	26 Jan 2035	23 yrs 2 mths	194.94	3.04
GB00B1L6W962	1.125	22 Nov 2037	26 yrs	127.655	3.03
GB00B3LZBF68	0.625	22 Mar 2040	28 yrs 4 mths	116.36	3.02
GB00B3MYD345	0.625	22 Nov 2042	31 yrs	118.705	3
GB00B24FFM16	0.75	22 Nov 2047	36 yrs	125.65	3.01
GB00B421JZ66	0.5	22 Mar 2050	38 yrs 4 mths	117.74	3.01
GB00B0CNHZ09	1.25	22 Nov 2055	44 yrs	152.95	

The columns are broadly speaking self-explanatory, however the yield calculation used for index-linked gilts varies from that used on conventional gilts. Various methods can be employed, which typically have to use some assumption of the future rate of inflation.

The yield calculation basis used here applies a theoretical 3% inflation rate. The actual return to the investor may prove to be higher or lower than this.

Type-two linkers

Since the 1981 launch of the original UK index-linked gilts, various developments occurred in the international markets, notably the emergence of the US Treasury Inflation Protected Securities (TIPS). The US had followed a model established by the Canadian government in the structure of its index-linked bonds and this gradually become the norm in the international capital markets and in 2005 the UK government followed suit (as indeed did many other governments) with the establishment of Canadian style index-linked gilts.

These new type of linkers were not, as many gilts dealers expected at the time, issued with a side of maple syrup. The Canadian style structure referred to a three-month lag structure for the calculation of coupons and redemption amounts. Arguably, this is a fairer method of calculation, given that the shorter lag means a tighter relationship between the index and the security. However, it does make the calculation of the accrued interest from the six-monthly coupons fairly tricky. An estimate has to be made, using the *index ratio* – a factor published daily by the DMO.

The next complexity for investors to get their heads round is the pricing convention. Old-style linkers trade on a conventional price basis. As we can see from the table above, this means that the cumulative effect of inflation has increased the secondary market price of these bonds to two or even three times their original issue price. However, the type two (or Canadian style) linkers trade on what is known as a *real price basis*. This means that the inflation has been stripped out and as a result prices tend to gravitate around par. However, when the bonds are settled, the consideration will reflect the accrued inflation effect on the price. The "inflation-adjusted dirty price" is calculated as follows:

$$\text{Inflation -}\ \substack{\text{adjusted} \\ \text{dirty price}} = \left(\substack{\text{Index} \\ \text{Ratio}} \times \substack{\text{Real} \\ \text{Clean Price}} \right) + \left(\substack{\text{Index} \\ \text{Ratio}} \times \substack{\text{Real} \\ \text{Accrued Interest}} \right)$$

The table below shows the "type two" linkers trading in the market as of September 2010 with the respective clean and dirty prices.

Table 8.3: type two index-linked gilts

Gilt	Price without inflation	Price with inflation	Interest (with inflation)	Yield with inflation assumption at 5.18%	DMO Real Yield
Treasury 1.25% 2017	107.25	123.50	0.199	5.438%	0.257%
Treasury1.875% 2022	112.15	121.65	0.282	6.030%	0.832%
Treasury 1.25% 2027	105.2	120.93	0.199	6.121%	0.920%
Treasury 1.25% 2032	108.47	111.44	0.178	6.037%	0.837%
Treasury 1.125% 2037	109.44	120.72	0.172	5.935%	0.738%
Treasury 0.625% 2040	97.30	100.25	0.289	5.924%	0.727%
Treasury 0.625% 2042	98.56	100.25	0.091	5.872%	0.676%
Treasury 0.75% 2047%	104.54	103.48	0.112	5.804%	0.609%
Treasury 0.5% 2050%	96.72	101.19	0.159	5.793%	0.599%
Treasury 1.25% 2055	128.22	148.82	0.201	5.742%	0.548%

Source: Winterflood Securities

On the subject of new linkers vs old linkers, there is one observation to be made. It is notable that the fixed element of the coupons of the more recent issues are in the range 0.5 – 1.25%, considerably lower than the 2.5% seen on the original 1980s issues. This perhaps reflects the generally lower expectations of investment returns of the modern world.

Estimating value in index-linked gilts

With conventional bonds, an accurate assessment can be made of the return on the asset. Future cash flows are known and investors can lock in a yield to maturity based on the current market level.

Not so index-linked bonds. Both the future coupons and the future redemption price are unknown, so how can value be established? The best one can do is to make an educated guess. An assumption (that most dangerous of concepts!) must be made as to the future rate of inflation.

However, it is fair to say that with conventional gilts or bonds it is not possible to calculate the real (inflation-adjusted) returns. With linkers, this is possible.

Real yield

The most popular calculation method for valuing index linked bonds is the "real yield". This calculates the margin above (or below) the rate of inflation for the bond. For a conventional index-linked bond issued at par, the real yield will be the same as the coupon at the point of issue.

Money yield

One technique to apply is the calculation of the "money yield" of the bond. To perform this calculation, the core (or average rate of) inflation is applied to the future cash flows of the bond, and this in turn can be discounted back to calculate a conventional YTM.

Breakeven inflation rate

Another popular tool for valuation, or at least comparative judgement, is the "breakeven inflation rate". This data is published in the FT and other financial publications and shows the inflation rate at which index-linked bonds will break even with conventional gilts of an equivalent maturity. This is handy tool. Typically a buyer of index-linked bonds will have a good idea of what level of inflation he expects or needs to beat and this concept will tell him or her whether he'd be better off with conventional or index-linked gilts over the given scenario.

Real return at X% inflation

Another technique for valuation is the "real return at X% inflation". With this technique a preset assumption for inflation is applied to the bonds, and the results calculated in real, or inflation-adjusted, terms. Of course, the end result for the investor may differ very greatly from this projection. Should inflation come back with a vengeance, the bonds will show considerable growth in both coupon and redemption value over the holding period.

Calculating the current par

Another useful tip for identifying the degree of premium attached to MKI index-linked gilts is to look at what might be considered the *net asset value* of the bond. To do this, check the RPI reference rate of the bond (the starting level from which future indexation is based). This is available from the DMO website or can be found in the RPI/CPI tables at the back of this book. Compare the reference rate with the current RPI to determine what the neutral price (sometimes known as the *current par*) of the bond would be. This gives a good mental picture of where the bond is trading relative to its theoretical flight-path to maturity. You will find that the bond's market price will rise above, or fall below, this theoretical current par level according to supply and demand – this in turn will be influenced by future inflation expectations and the credit quality of the issuer.

This technique does not apply to the MKII index-linked gilts.

The future

At the time of writing, in 2011, the coalition government is attempting to reduce the enormous pension fund liabilities of the public sector. One technique to tackle this is to move the indexation benchmark for such pensions from the RPI to the CPI, the latter having been a historical underperformer. What is good for the goose is good for the gander and should the public sector shift to CPI indexation, it is likely that many private sector defined benefit schemes will also move to this slightly less arduous benchmark. This will create a curious situation of fund managers attempting to balance future CPI-linked liabilities with RPI-based assets. No doubt, ingenious investment bankers will come up with some solutions, but from a longer-term point of view, the obvious solution is for the government to commence issuance of CPI-linked gilts.

Conclusion

Index-linked gilts: yes or no?

The natural buyer of index-linked gilts is a large pension fund, the trustees of whom need to match long-term index-linked liabilities. Such investors are prepared to give up a degree of performance in the security in return for a government-guaranteed hedge against inflation. Thus, all things being equal, one might expect index-linked gilts to underperform other more risk-positive assets over time.

This is a fair assumption, however, with index-linked gilts, as with most other asset classes, every dog will have its day. An investor or trader purchasing inflation-linked securities during a period of low inflation expectations may be pleasantly surprised by the performance of such bonds when those expectations shift. They can also offer a surprisingly tax-efficient solution during periods of high inflation.

Linkers are not one of my favourite types of bonds, but they are undoubtedly worth monitoring as the performance of the UKTI 2.5% 2020 over the 2009-2010 period demonstrates in the chart below.

Chart 8.1: price performance of index-linked gilt (2007-2010)

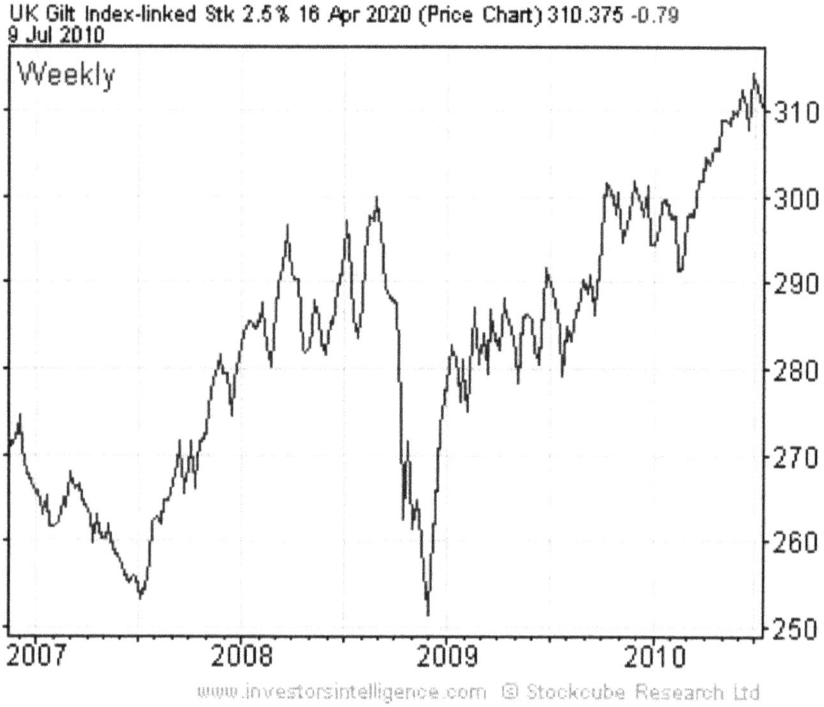
UK Gilt Index-linked Stk 2.5% 16 Apr 2020 (Price Chart) 310.375 -0.79
9 Jul 2010
Weekly
310
300
290
280
270
260
250
2007
2008
2009
2010
www.investorsintelligence.com © Stockcube Research Ltd

Consider also that capital gains for the private investor will be tax free. In times of high inflation, this may put this asset class firmly on the buying list for higher-rate taxpayers.

Note: Unlike the index-linked saving certificates issued by the government's NS&I (until recently, available through the Post Office), index-linked gilts do not have a floor. If inflation proves to be negative over the holding period, the investor may receive less than he put in. However, this event has yet to occur over the 30-year history of these instruments.

Chapter 9

Domestic and Eurosterling corporate bonds

The majority of corporate bonds that the investor will encounter in the sterling bond markets are technically defined as *Eurosterling bonds* (i.e. sterling-denominated Eurobonds). British investors should not be put off by this, the term simply refers to the basic structure of the bond. Sterling Eurobonds will usually be referred to simply as corporate bonds in the market but it is worth taking some time to consider the nature of Eurobonds. These are curious beasts, which are broadly speaking defined more by what they are not, rather than what they are.

Development of the Eurobond market

The instrument arose out of a curious vacuum in the 1960s, when JF Kennedy imposed the IET tax (or Interest Equalization Tax), a domestic tax measure, intended to make it less profitable for U.S. investors to invest abroad by taxing the purchase of foreign securities. The design of the tax was to reduce the balance-of-payment deficit, but the effect was to drive bond issuance and trading offshore. The City of London has good reason to be thankful to JFK.

According to historians, the first Eurobond seems to have been the 1963 issue for the Italian government agency Autostrade, led by the then-leading investment bank SG Warburg & Co for the dizzying amount of $15 million. The early issues were predominately USD-denominated, reputedly soaking up the large amounts of US dollars then in European hands from the Marshall plan. These Eurodollar bonds were followed by Euro-DM bonds, Euro-Franc bonds, Euro-Lira and Euro-Sterling and non-European currencies such as the JPY and the CAD. With the advent of the single European currency in the 1990s, the various European currency sectors where unified, confusingly creating Euro-Eurobonds (a term that is never used).

The main features of a Eurobond can be classified as follows:

1. Issued into the international capital markets

2. Underwritten and sold by a syndicate of banks. Settles via Euroclear

3. Pays coupons and redemption sum free from withholding tax.

What about listing?

Eurobonds generally trade off-exchange; a listing is less important than it would be for an equity. However, most bonds have what I would describe as "courtesy" listing – typically on the Luxembourg stock exchange. This amounts to little more than filing the paperwork and is no guarantee (or even indication) that the bond will trade on that exchange.

However, a listing is a useful characteristic for a bond to have and is a ticked box for some fund managers, investment schemes or wrappers. In the UK, a listing is a requirement for SIPP account holdings (in most cases).

Domestic and Bulldog bonds

A couple of decades back, sterling denominated bonds would have been segregated between the following:

1. Domestic bonds – sterling bonds issued by UK institutions

2. Bulldog bonds – bonds issued by foreign entities (often overseas governments) into the UK bond market

3. Eurosterling – (see above)

Prior to the 1997 budget, both gilts[3] and domestic bonds were subject to a withholding tax of 25%. This was abolished to bring the UK in line with other jurisdictions. Before this date there was a considerable gap between the domestic and Eurosterling issues, however the difference is now somewhat arcane and broadly down to settlement procedures.

In truth, the growth of the Eurosterling format for debt issuance has eclipsed the domestic market, and it's in this category of bonds that the private investor will spend most of his time hunting for bargains. Older Bulldog issues with long maturities may still be found trading from time to time, but as bearer bonds with gross-paying coupons, these instruments will behave broadly in the same manner as a Eurosterling bond.

Investors may encounter a number of older domestic issues including debentures [discussed in more detail in a later chapter]. Such instruments

---

[3] In a splendidly Fabian piece of logic, private investors who bought gilts through the Post Office were able to receive coupons gross.

often have unusual features and should be analysed on a case by case basis (make sure you read the prospectus). Whilst liquidity will often be limited in such instruments, bargains can certainly be found.

Meat in the sandwich

At this point I would like to point out that we have reached the "meat in the sandwich" for the bond markets. Part II of this book deals with the bond market and the types of bonds that can be found in this wide-ranging asset class. Chapter 7 deals with gilts, and it is this large and liquid market that acts as the benchmark or reference point for comparative value in the sterling bond market.

Chapter 10 and beyond deal with some of the more esoteric bonds, often with unusual features and higher yields. However, the type of bond I describe in this chapter, "Domestic and Eurosterling bonds" are what the investor will typically buy when investing in corporate bonds.

How big is the sterling bond market?

I have already touched upon the vast size of the international bond market, but is it possible to get a measure of the sterling sub-set? I have previously mentioned that the sterling bond market is a relatively small sub-set of the international bond market. It is also true that the vast growth of the gilt market (over £1 trillion at the end of 2011) has to a degree overshadowed corporate bonds.

Figures from the Bank for International Settlements (BIS) show the total size of the sterling market to be just over £1.3 trillion at the end of 2011. For comparison, the BIS record the amount of Euro-denominated bonds outstanding at around £7.8 trillion equivalent.

Another interesting metric is supplied by debt capital markets specialist Dealogic, who keep a track of new issue activity in the bond markets. Their figures show that issuance in the sterling market for 2011 consisted of 395 new bonds, raising a total of £86 billion.

The Dealogic data ties in with my own experience; although the BIS figures appear to be overly large to me. Market sources suggest that a more realistic estimate of the outstanding amount of sterling bonds in issue would place it in the hundreds of billions. Nevertheless, the market is substantial, with several thousand issues outstanding at any one time. The size of these issues will vary greatly from just a few tens of millions to blockbusters with £1 billion or more outstanding. One interesting facet of the sterling bond market is its bias towards domestic issuers – around 70% of the companies issuing on the sterling market are from the home team. Banks are the largest constituent amongst these issuers and this is perhaps a reflection of the size of the financial services industry in the UK relative to other industries.

Of course, these estimates of size and constituents are a movable feast. Bonds are issues and redeemed all the time. Consider also that many of these thousands of issues will be effectively private placements – issued on institutional investor demand and often held to maturity. Thus, a large proportion of the securities issued will be irrelevant from our point of view.

The private investor will be more interested in those issues with a reasonable degree of transparency and liquidity. The excellent BondMarketPrices.com website shows 3,000 sterling issues with prices reported; but an individual market maker will typically make prices in only a fraction of this number, perhaps 200 or so. Individual investment banks will cover different sectors and issuers, making the market somewhat fragmented.

Institutional or retail?

This book, and many brokers, will often describe a bond as being either an *institutional* or a *retail* bond.

What does this mean?

If we rewind the clock back a couple of decades to the good old days of the Eurobond market, there was no attempt to segregate institutional and private investors. The latter were extremely active buyers of Eurobond issues across a range of currencies. The archetypical investor was the "Belgian dentist", a reasonably well-to-do professional who would tuck his savings away in bonds, often issued by well-known multi-national corporations. In those days the issuers might well have been Nestlé, Coca-Cola or the World Bank. The currency of issue might have been US dollars or perhaps the DM. It is said that the attractions of such investments were given a boost by the gross coupons paid and it would be naive to deny this. Witholding tax was in force in many countries, and bonds were squirreled away in private banks and secretive countries such as Switzerland and Luxembourg.

Whatever the rights and wrongs of this, private investor participation was strong. However, with the growth of the financial markets over the 1980s through to the 21st century, institutional investors became more prominent. Bond issues became larger, and in some cases more complex. What is more, the issuance process became a very fast moving B2B environment, with little opportunity for the private investor to get a toe-hold at the primary stage.

By the middle of the last decade, the cold gaze of the regulators had begun to settle on this historically unregulated market. At one point, the subject of withholding tax was discussed. This would probably have driven the entire bond market to a new location in Dubai, Singapore or Switzerland within 48hrs. Luckily, a reprieve was granted.

European Prospectus Directive (EPD)

Another problem came from a different direction. The EU wished to adopt a standard set of rules for issuing new securities. This was the European Prospectus Directive (EPD). HM Treasury States:

> The Prospectus Directive is the EU framework for the preparation of prospectuses in public offers of securities and where securities are admitted to trading on a regulated market. The purpose of the Directive is to harmonise requirements for the drawing up, approval and distribution of the prospectuses that are published when securities are offered to the public or admitted to trading on a regulated market.

The Prospectus Directive seeks to enhance investor protection and improve the efficiency of the single market. Its key innovation is that a prospectus approved in one Member State is valid across the EU, giving issuers a "passport" across the EU capital markets. The Directive came into force on 1 July 2005.

So far, so good.

But, as ever, there was an unintended consequence of this plan. The directive allowed for institutionally target issues to be fast tracked to market with a short-form prospectus. In the case of bonds, such issues had to have a EUR50,000 or local-currency equivalent minimum denomination (later increased to EUR100,000). This was intended to help prevent such issues falling into the hands of private investors, a plan that was broadly effective.

Thus issuers and investment banks naturally took the line of least resistance and most bond issues, including those in the sterling market, came to market with large minimum denominations. The EU had once again saved the private investor from himself!

LSE - Order Book for Retail Bonds

But, just as nature abhors a vacuum, financial markets fill the gap. In the sterling market, the London Stock Exchange launched the *Order Book for Retail Bonds* in February 2010, a market modelled on the successful Italian MOT market. This market taps into the unrequited demand from private investors abandoned by the conventional issuers' retreat from these grass-roots buyers.

The new market is producing a template for this type of bond. Such issues are slightly more laborious to issue, but are fully EPD compliant. Typically, the bonds are straightforward issues from relatively well-known companies (often FTSE350 members). Issuers to date have included consumer finance operator Provident Financial, utility National Grid, housing association Places for People, Tesco Bank, and Lloyds TSB. Bonds to date have been simple in their structure with typical attributes as follows:

- 5-10 years maturity,

- senior,

- fixed or floating coupons,

- size £25 to £200 million, and

- importantly, with minimum denominations of £100 or £1,000.

Such bonds have a relatively slow issuance process over 1-2 weeks, allowing time for brokers to offer the instruments to their client base. By 2011, around half a dozen new bond issues have been launched on this platform, with more on the way.

A typical example of the new type of sterling retail bond issue is the **Tesco Bank 5.2% 24 August 2018** bond (XS0591029409). Launched in Feb 2011 with a maturity of 7.5 years, the bond paid two semi annual coupons of 2.6% per annum and was well-received by investors, raising £125 million for the supermarket's banking subsidiary. The bond went to a small premium above its launch price at 100 and has traded up as high as 108 subsequently.

There are now approximately 100 bonds listed on the LSE ORB, this being a combination of the growing new issue market and older bonds in retail-friendly denominations that have been adopted by the new platform. Strong demand suggests that this universe of bonds is set to grow.

Chapter 10
Zeros, FRNs, convertibles and others

Overview

This book has so far largely concerned itself with conventional fixed rate bonds where the instrument carries a fixed coupon and matures at a given date. These instruments are comparatively easy to understand and utilise as investments.

The bond market has always been a place of innovation and new types of bond are constantly being issued in order to fulfil investors' demand or provide an efficient source of funds for borrowers. Frequently, a special situation will arise, sometimes driven by a change in the taxation or regulatory environment that will lead to the issuance of bonds with unusual structures. Investment bankers will look to exploit these situations and over the years, many weird and wonderful structures have been issued. In both the primary and particularly in the secondary markets, these bonds can provide excellent opportunities, but investors must be sure that they fully understand the terms and conditions of the issue before purchasing.

> **Tip**: A word to the wise: if you don't understand it, don't buy it!

Investors who wish to delve deeper into the amazing range of structures available in the international bond markets will need to familiarise themselves with some of the more common variants and how they may be utilised as a trading or investment vehicle.

In this chapter we'll be looking at,

1. zero coupon bonds

2. floating rate notes

3. equity convertibles

4. mortgage & asset-backed bonds

5. corporate index-linked bonds

1. Zero Coupon Bonds

Zeros are the very simplest form of bond, consisting of only two cash flow events: investment and redemption. We have already covered this concept in the section on gilt market strips and Treasury Bills.

The asset class is a common structure traditionally popular amongst European private investors. Zero Coupon bonds are in effect one discounted cashflow, purchased in advance by the investor and maturing at par. The yield on the bond is obtained for the holder by the increase in price (or roll up) to maturity. The yield to maturity can be calculated by the conventional formula or by simple discounted cash flow calculations.

An example of a typical zero is the EIB 0% 5 November 2026. This was issued by the AAA-rated Supranational, the European Investment Bank in 1996 at a price of 13.75%.

I looked at this bond a few years ago. At that time the bond stood at 31.25%, the large price move since issue being a factor of both the roll up to maturity and the very long duration (and hence high sensitivity) of the instrument during a falling interest rate environment. Here is a table of the calculations I performed at the time.

Table 10.1: volatility analysis of EIB 0% 5th November 2026

Yield to Maturity	Price
7%	20.10
6%	25.12
5%	31.45
4%	39.46

As an example of the level of gearing inherent in long dated zeros, if the above bond experienced a 1% shift from its then current yield of 4.98% to 5.98%, the corresponding price fall would be from 31.54% to 25.19%, a fall of 6.35 points, an impressive 20% (6.35/31.54) of the current price.

I have previously covered the subject of duration, and how this measures a bond's price sensitivity (or gearing) to interest rate shifts. Zero coupon bonds have longer-dated duration than coupon-bearing bonds of the same maturity. The table illustrates the potential volatility of this long-dated zero. Note that a 3% drop in yield nearly doubles the price of the asset.

Figure 10.1: effect of interest changes on bonds

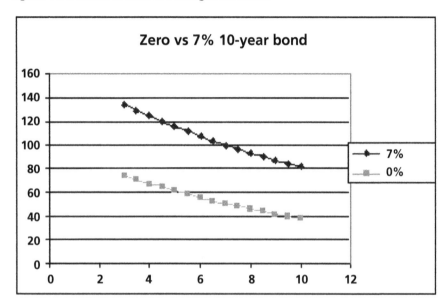

On this subject, the chart above shows the price performance of two 10-year bonds, one with a zero coupon, the other with a 7% coupon over a range of interest rate scenarios. Note how the low-priced zero shows greater price volatility over the given yield range of 2% to 10% YTM. The zero's price moves from below 40 to over 70p, nearly doubling in price. The higher-priced coupon-bearing bond shows a more modest capital gain of around 60%. As we saw on the long-dated EIB bond, this gearing is magnified in longer-dated bonds.

Government bonds are also available in zero coupon form [explained in the chapter on gilts]. These are known as *strips*, and are effectively a single coupon or principle payment taken from an outstanding government bond issue. These instruments have long been popular in the United States but have only become available in the UK comparatively recently.

Advantages of zero coupon bonds

Zeros have some advantages for the private investor. They are ideal for meeting fixed forward liabilities and are effectively self-reinvesting, without the requirement for growth investors to receive and re-invest coupons.

Note: in times of falling interest rates, coupon re-investment can be a major problem for long-term portfolios. For instance, an investor who bought with YTM of 8% ten years ago may be forced to re-invest the coupons at 4% if rates have fallen significantly in the meantime. Zero-coupon bonds help alleviate this risk.

A simple investment of a given amount will produce a known lump sum at a forward. Long-dated zeros also have exceptionally high duration (see chapter 5 on duration), making then a good vehicle for investors or traders who wish to have gearing to falling interest rates.

Disadvantages of zero coupon bonds

Zero coupon bonds pay out no income. Credit risk is thus effectively extended with no repayments from the issuer ahead of redemption. Long-dated zero's display high duration, making for mark-to-market losses when interest rates move adversely. Rising rates may cause sharp falls in the price.

UK-based investors may also be disadvantaged by the tax treatment of zeros, which requires that income tax be paid each year on the theoretical interest gained by the holder. This effectively means the investor will pay the tax many years before receiving any income! This situation will not affect investors utilising offshore structures or other forms of tax shelter.

Dealing in zero Coupon bonds

Although fairly rare in the sterling markets, zeros are theoretically easy to deal in and trade on a simple price basis. There's no accrued interest to worry about! Secondary and primary market issues may be purchased through brokers when available. However, secondary market liquidity in zeros is often poor.

2. Floating Rate Notes

Floating Rate Notes (FRNs) are popular with bank and corporate treasurers. These bonds do not have a fixed coupon, but pay a rate linked to a market benchmark. Typically, the coupon will be linked to 3-month LIBOR (the London Interbank Offered Rate). The issuer will agree to pay the holder a coupon related to the current rate; for instance a FRN might pay 3-month LIBOR + 1/8% (the quoted margin). The market is dominated by issuance from the banks and effectively FRNs are a type of tradeable interbank loan.

So how does one calculate the yield?

Alas, it is not possible to calculate a Yield to Maturity for a FRN, due to the unknown future coupon flows. Market practitioners instead use the discounted margin calculation to assess the yearly income from the bond compared to that available in the money markets. This calculation compares the sum of the income received from the bond's coupon with capital gain (or loss) created by holding the bond to maturity, discounted at current money-market rates.

Private investors, who have no need of single basis point accuracy, can use the rather more straightforward simple margin calculation, as follows:

simple margin = (100/price * quoted margin) + ((100–price)/years to maturity)

For instance, an FRN trading at 99.50, and paying a coupon of LIBOR + 1/8% which matures in 4.5 years time will have the following simple margin,

(100/99.5 * 1/8) + (0.5/4.5) = 0.237

The simple margin is thus LIBOR plus 23.7 basis points (0.237%). This means that the holder will receive approximately a quarter of a point over LIBOR if he holds the bond to maturity.

Note that as the FRN's discount or premium to par increases, so the fixed income element of the calculation increases. However, under normal circumstances, investment grade FRNs trade fairly close to par, making this aspect of the calculation fairly marginal. When dealing in deeply discounted (or premium priced) FRNs, discounted cash flows should be taken into account.

Here's some examples of typical FRNs trading in the secondary market recently. The prices of the bonds will move up and down with perceived credit quality, and margins will move in an out accordingly.

Table 10.2: list of example FRNs

Issuer	Credit Rating	Currency	Coupon	Maturity	Price	Discounted Margin
HSBC	AA	GBP	Lib + 70[4]	Sep 2012	100.68	23bp
BAC	A	GBP	Lib + 10	Jun 2012	99.14	83bp
Credit Agricolé	AA-	GBP	Lib + 25	Sep 2014	98.75	62bp

Advantages of FRNs

A good defensive investment when in a rising interest rate environment. High quality FRNs display low volatility. Useful for matching future income streams against floating rate liabilities (for instance mortgage payments). Some defensive quality against inflation (interest rates generally rise in line with inflation). Rates achieved may be higher than that available on deposit.

Disadvantages of FRN

Effectively low duration means that holders will not benefit from rising bond prices if interest rates fall. Quality of issuers variable. Some issues subordinated.

Dealing in FRNs

FRNs generally trade in wholesale sizes of £5 million and above, although dealing sizes and turnover have reduced following the credit crunch. However, the market is liquid with a large number of issues outstanding at

---

[4] Note the high margin on the coupon – this is a result of the bond being issued during the credit crunch.

any given time, although USD and Euro-denominated issues are more common than sterling. Banks and financial institutions are by far the most common issuer of these types of bonds and these types of institutions also make up the majority of the investor base. Because of this, the number of FRNs available to the private investor in suitable small size blocks is often quite restricted, but offers are available from time to time from good brokers.

The discounted floater gearing effect

The majority of FRNs are senior-debt issues, generally issued by creditworthy banks. This, combined with their low price sensitivity to interest rate shifts has meant that historically the bonds have generally traded around par.

Sometimes this is not the case. Some FRNs are subordinated and bonds issued by distressed borrowers can trade at a significant discount to par. At this point, the instrument effectively becomes a hybrid – floating coupons and a fixed-interest component from the discount between the market price and the future redemption price.

The calculation of the internal rate of return from the discount to par is fairly straightforward. However, it is worth taking time to consider the effect of the discount on the coupon. The gearing obtained by a sub-par purchase price for the bond effectively boosts the coupon and thus has a significant impact on the income flows of the instrument, particularly in a rising interest rate environment.

Example

Consider an FRN with a coupon set at LIBOR plus 25bp. Let us assume that it is an unloved subordinated floater and that the bond is trading at 70p in the pound.

Our next assumption is that LIBOR is 3%.

What running yield will we receive?

running yield = (LIBOR + margin) x 100/price

(3% + 0.25%) x 100/70 = 4.64%

Thus, we have a bond that is returning a running yield of LIBOR + 1.64%.

What happens to that margin when rates go up?

Let us say that LIBOR hits 7% a few years down the road. Now:

(7% + 0.25%) x 100/70 = 10.35%

The effective margin is now 3.35% over LIBOR. The investor has significantly increased his margin over LIBOR.

Perpetual Floating Rate Notes

The UK investor may well encounter this strange beast. During the late 1980s, many UK banks issued subordinated perpetual FRNs. These bonds were issued in order to boost the capital reserves of the banks and are subordinated to the debt of depositors and senior bondholders. This means that in the event of the bank going into liquidation, subordinated note holders would stand behind other creditors, although they still rank above the equity holders. The credit rating for a subordinated FRN will thus be lower than that for a senior bond from the same issuer

The market for subordinated perpetual FRNs was initially very strong, with the extra margin over LIBOR proving very attractive to institutional investors. However, during the late 1980s, the asset class suffered when investors re-evaluated the bonds and realised that they held what was, in effect, a glorified preference share. Prices fell sharply.

The value of the asset class gradually recovered to the low 90s, but took another severe setback during the Russian debt crisis (1998), when fears were raised for the health of the entire western banking system. Prices fell to the low 60s. Prices subsequently recovered with the higher quality names trading back up in the 70-80 area, but have fallen back over the latest banking crisis. See the table below for some examples of recent levels for perpetual FRNs.

Table 10.3: some sample perpetual FRN issues

Issuer	Credit Rating	Currency	Coupon	Maturity	Price
HSBC	A3	USD	LIBOR +25bp	Perpetual	65
Standard Chartered	Baa1	GBP	LIBOR +18.75bp	Perpetual	61.5
Barclays	Baa1	GBP	LIBOR +100	Perpetual	70
Lloyds[5]	Ba2	USD	LIBOR +25	Perpetual	55

How does one calculate the yield on a perpetual FRN?

With no fixed redemption date, the running yield (or *running margin*) is the only measure that we can use. Any running yield calculation assumes that the bond can be sold at the same price at which it was purchased, an event for which there is clearly no guarantee!

running margin = quoted margin * 100/price

Advantages of Perpetual FRNs

Typically, high margin over LIBOR. Volatility of instrument in bad times creates opportunities to acquire asset cheaply. Although asset is subordinated, the underlying credit of the issuer is often sound (for instance, a UK clearing bank), making the actual likelihood of total default low. No need to re-invest on maturity.

Disadvantages of Perpetual FRNs

Subordination weakens credit quality. No redemption date, thus any liquidation of asset subject to availability and level of market bid. Price may be volatile. Some issues carry minimum or maximum coupon clauses, which may affect the asset's future performance. Rates may be linked to unusual benchmarks. Check the small print!

---

[5] Coupon suspended to Jan 2012.

3. Equity Convertibles

An equity convertible bond carries an option enabling the holder to switch his bonds into the issuer's equity at a prearranged price. Convertible bonds offer the investor a combination of income combined with an equity kicker, enabling the bondholder to profit from a rise in price in the company's shares. Investors should be aware that there are two types of convertible bond,

1. **mandatory convertible**, which converts to equity on the redemption date (arguably an *equity forward*), and

2. **optional convertible**, which has a fixed redemption date and price and the option to convert the proceeds into equity at a pre-set rate.

The latter is a more suitable instrument for fixed income investors.

Convertibles have typically been purchased by investors who wish to obtain income, while keeping some exposure to the equity market for potential capital growth. The UK market in these bonds has somewhat diminished over the last decade.

Valuing convertibles

There are two components to the valuation of a convertible,

1. the value of any potential conversion to the underlying equity, and

2. the value of the known cash flows of the bond, this being a combination of coupon and redemption payments.

The value of the equity component of the bond can be calculated by applying the conversion rate and comparing this to the price of the underlying equity. Convertible bonds may well show a premium to the value that might theoretically be achieved by immediate conversion, reflecting a combination of investor optimism and the differential between the equity's dividend and the convertible's coupon.

So how does one work out the premium?

The first concept to grasp is that of the parity price. This is the neutral price at which the convertible would trade in the event of a trader buying the instruments, converting the bond into equity and selling at the current market price. The parity price is calculated as follows:

parity = conversion ratio x current market price

The incremental value of the current market price above parity is known as the *premium*.

Buying "busted" convertibles

As the shares of a company rise in value, the price of the convertible will follow, reducing the yield available from the instrument. In the case of very strong stocks the convertible will effectively trade as an equity, often with a price at a multiple of its redemption value. Instruments of this nature will be of little interest to the fixed income investor and are somewhat outside the scope of this book.

Perhaps of more interest will be the low priced, or "busted", convertible. If the company's fortunes are weak, the share price may fall well below the convertible bond's strike price. At this point they will trade on the basis of fixed-income valuations (i.e. yield, credit risk etc).

What is interesting is that such issues frequently fall off the radar of the equity traders, but fail to make it on to the radar of fixed income investors. As such, they are a fertile hunting ground for value investors.

Advantages of convertibles

Provides income combined with the potential for capital growth. Old or "busted" convertibles that no longer have a realistic chance of conversion to equity may sometimes be neglected by the market, enabling fixed income investors to purchase them purely for the fixed income component of the bond, often at advantageous levels.

Disadvantages of convertibles

The yield may be lower than a straight bond of the same maturity if the market perceives value in the equity option. Convertible bonds may be subordinated to senior debt, thus increasing the potential risk. Investors should carefully examine the terms and conditions.

4. Mortgage & asset-backed bonds

Conventional fixed income bonds have a claim on the issuing company's assets. In some cases the security may be improved by having a direct claim on a specified asset or pool of assets of the company. [You can read more on this subject in the section on Debentures.]

In addition to such bonds, there is a huge international market in mortgage-backed bonds, the most well-known of which is in the US. Mortgage-backed securities (MBS) are one of the backbones of the US fixed income markets and there are many investors, traders and firms that do nothing but deal in such securities.

The complex and important MBS market is beyond the scope of this book, and sterling-based investors are unlikely to have much contact with such securities. However, it is important to understand the concept as the impact of the multi-trillion pound MBS market on other securities should not be understated.

In a nutshell, when the typical American takes out a mortgage, he or she will enter into a 25 year contract at a fixed interest rate with the right to repay the debt at an earlier date if he or she wishes. In many ways, this is better than the typical British mortgage which is typically a variable rate or fixed with redemption penalties. However, consider that our US householder will be locking in a rate that is priced off 25-year interest rates (rather than the typically lower short-term rates) and will be paying an additional premium for the optionality of the early repayment rights.

A large pool of such mortgages will then be bundled up and resold as an MBS. The simplest form of this is the pass-through security. Here, the householders pay the interest and repayment elements of the loan whilst the investors (i.e. the purchasers of the bond) receive fixed coupons.

A slightly more complex version of the above is the Collateralised Mortgage Obligation (CMO). Here, the security of such bonds is often enhanced by a senior/subordinated structure. This works by passing the risk of default (inevitably there will be some mortgagees that fail to meet payments) down the line to unsecured investors. The following diagram explains the process. Note how the senior secured investors have a lower coupon.

Figure 10.2: Collateralised Mortgage Obligation structure

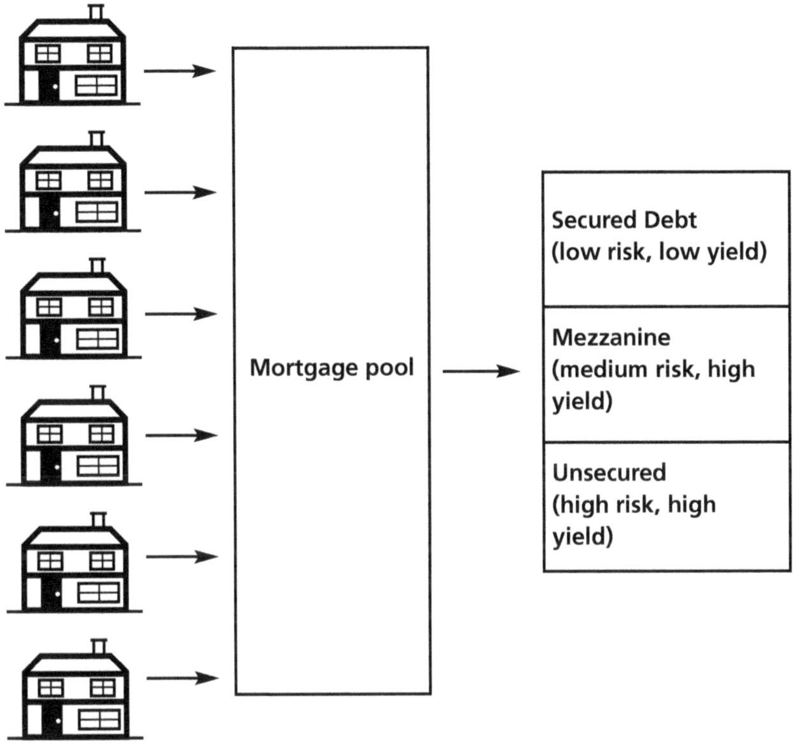

Somewhat different from the risk of default is the risk of pre-payment. This optionality aspect is an important aspect of MBS. If interest rates fall, or indeed if the mortgagees move house at a faster-than-expected rate, it is likely that the pool of mortgages will be diminished. The investors have no risk to capital, but will have a proportion of their investment redeemed. That is not great news for an investor in a falling interest rate environment, as you can imagine.

Pfandbriefs and European mortgage bonds

Rather nearer to home exists the not-inconsiderable European mortgage backed market, including the German Pfandbriefs – a well established, regulated and liquid market that provides financing for commercial and residential loans. Such bonds are typically of a medium-dated maturity and are a popular investment in the Eurozone (although they may have a limited appeal to the GBP-based investor).

UK mortgage-backed bonds do exist, but are very much restricted to a specialist professional market. Looking forward, it is not inconceivable that a Pfandbrief-like market will develop in the UK, and the government has sponsored academic studies to investigate this possibility. However, such development will take many years and for the moment the UK market looks set to continue with its model of floating rate, customer-to-bank mortgages for many years to come.

Covered bond

A recent development to emerge from the banking industry is the *covered bond*. Such bonds are both guaranteed by the banks and have a claim on specific assets. This is a belt-and-braces approach, driven out of the necessity to raise funding post credit-crunch.

5. Corporate index-linked bonds

These creatures are comparatively rare, but may become more common as time goes on. The majority of such bonds are issued by companies with experience in matching RPI or CPI- linked liabilities. Utility companies are a case in point, but I would suggest that some of the retailers (particularly the supermarkets) have a top line closely matched to the rate of inflation and might well be able to make a case for increased funding in this manner going forward.

One sticking point is the tax situation. If the holder has to pay tax on the index-linked element of the capital appreciation, any advantage gained will be lost. This is a particular problem for index-linked corporate bonds. Unlike index-linked gilts, the capital gains from the indexation increase of the redemption value are chargeable to income under HMRC's current tax rules.

I reproduce below my "Bond of the week" from January 2011, which addressed the salient points of this type of security.

National Grid 2.983% 2018

Investors are familiar with index-linked gilts. These instruments have been around since the 1980s and enable the government to raise cheap funds, thanks to the insatiable demand from pension funds and insurance companies for inflation-protected assets. Given the current above-target level of inflation (November's RPI figures came in at +4.7%), this month's increase in VAT and rising energy prices, many bond investors are beginning to think that the pension funds may have a point.

The problem is index-linked gilts offer only a very narrow margin over inflation – many new issues now carry a miserly coupon of less than 1%. Can corporate bonds offer investors a better deal?

Certainly, inflation-linked bonds from corporate issuers do exist, although they are comparatively rare. Such bonds are usually issued by organisations that have both experience and commercial exposure to inflation. Supermarkets and utilities are two such industries that fit this description. Both Tesco and National Grid have issued RPI-linked bonds over the past few years. We will look here at the National Grid 2.983% July 2018 (ISIN XS0150037405).

£300 million of the bond was issued in June 2002, with a fairly conventional structure. The bond has both the coupon and redemption payments linked to the RPI and was issued at par. At that time, the bond offered 68bp more than the UK Treasury index-linked 2.5% 2016.

Some eight years have passed since the issue date. The RPI has increased by 29% over the period, and the bond has gained 44% to its current market price of around 144 – an outperformance indicating the continuing demand for such assets. It is also worth noting that the coupon is ticking up fairly steadily. Searching through the RNS (regulated news service) for the security, I note that the last three coupon fixes have been as follows:

July 2008 – 3.70%

July 2009 – 3.66% (a rare example of negative RPI growth)

July 2010 – 3.84%

Given that RPI growth is surging ahead, we can expect a coupon of just over 4% to be announced in June 2011. The redemption price is not yet known, but if we were to project the last RPI data forward to the July 2018 redemption date at the current 4.7% rate of growth, and then apply it to the bond's reference-level in 2002, a level of 190 can be inferred.

> **My view**: The bond is a useful hedge against inflation, which looks set to continue to run, at least over the shorter term. Credit-wise, the asset is a comfortable hold with A-rating from S&P and the cushion of a defensive income stream from the company's virtual monopoly.

Unusually, for a corporate linker, the bond has a sensible minimum price of £1,000, and this makes the instrument accessible for private investors. The bond is also deliverable into the Crest system, and this means that investors utilising execution-only stockbroker accounts should be able to purchase the bond.

Retail-targeted index-linked bonds and structured products

With the demise of the excellent National Savings and Investments Index-linked certificates in 2010 (which curiously disappeared from the Post Office shelves at roughly the time that inflation took off), investors looking for inflation-linked savings products have had little to choose from.

Some of the building societies responded by issuing index-linked fixed-term deposits (3 and 5 year), and these products quickly proved successful. The investment banks soon followed with index-linked products of their own, aimed squarely at the retail and wealth-management market. Barclays and RBS were first to market, with both banks bringing issues around the ten-year area with a "RPI plus floor" structure. This meant that the bond would pay the higher of either the minimum coupon or the change in RPI for the period. The bonds had at par redemption price and the RPI-linkage was paid entirely through the coupon payment. For practical reasons, the bonds are traded dirty (with any accrued interest rolled into the price).

Details of RBS "RPBI" issue:

Name	Royal Bank of Scotland "RPBI" (ISIN GB00B4P95L57)
Issuer	RBS senior obligation
Issued	Oct 2010
Maturity	Nov 2022
Coupon	3.9% p/a, or the increase in RPI (whichever greater). Paid quarterly

The problem with such products is that they are effectively a securitised structured product. This means that the secondary market price is largely controlled by the issuer and priced off swaps and/or the banks' internal price models for the appropriate period. As such, I have some reservations about such issues, as follows:

1. Should the issuer cease to make a market in the bonds, the conventional market makers may not step in.

2. The bonds are issued off the investment bank's book, and supply will increase with demand. Because of this, they are unlikely to trade at any significant premium over their peers.

3. All index-linkage is via the coupon, and for some investors, this may not be tax efficient.

Index-linked retail bonds

More recently, the growing UK retail bond market has seen issuance from some good-quality names including the aforementioned National Grid. These bonds have small-size minimum denominations and trade on the LSE ORB market.

To date, the structure has been conventional, following the template of the old index-linked gilts. One interesting point to note about these issues is that a precedent has been set in having a minimum redemption price at par (rather like the NS&I index-linked certificates). If we experience long-term deflation, this could prove to be a valuable option for the investor.

Chapter 11
Other types of bonds

Arguably, the most attractive feature of bonds as a class of investment is their simplicity; a high-quality financial asset with a fixed coupon and a set redemption date. Many investors choose bonds for this type of straightforward predictability. But, the financial markets are rich in variety and many other types of fixed income asset are available other than the plain vanilla straight bond. These include a wide variety of subordinated issues, including the popular building society (and ex building society) PIBS.

It is also worth noting that it is in these backwaters, which are often underesearched, that value is to be found by the investor who is prepared to do some spadework. This chapter takes a look at some of these instruments.

In this chapter we will look at:

1. debentures

2. fixed income preference shares

3. PIBS

4. contingent capital instruments

1. Debentures

The expression *debenture* is somewhat of a term of art. In the UK market, *debenture* generally refers to an older security, often a relatively high quality in terms of the collateral, and often a charge on property. There are still a few of these older debt instruments, issued in the 1980s and before knocking around and offers will surface from time to time, often through specialist brokers such as Collins Stewart or Evolution. Sizes will generally be odd lots of a few tens of thousands or hundreds of thousands and dealing will be by negotiation.

An example is the **British Empire Securities & General Trust 8.125% Debenture Stock 2023**. £15 million of this security was issued in 1993 by the eponymous investment trust for "the furtherance of the Company's investment policy". The issue presumably also added gearing to the ordinary shareholder's equity.

In terms of the security, the prospectus states that:

> The New Stock will be secured by a first floating charge over the whole of the undertaking, property, assets and rights, both present and future, wherever situate, (including any uncalled capital) of the Company and will rank pari passu in point of security with the Existing Stock.

I last saw these bonds trading in late 2010; £21,000 were offered at a price of 105 giving a YTM of 9.8%. Such securities are unlikely to have a credit rating and should be treated on a case-by-case basis with a long hard look at the company's report and accounts.

One fascinating backwater of this market are sporting club debentures. These are issued by sports clubs such as Wimbledon LTA in order to raise money for new grounds, etc. and are generally for a fixed term of five years or so. Holders have the right to subscribe for tickets on a priority basis. Such assets are normally closely held by the investor, but do change hands from time to time.

Note: in the US, the term debenture refers to an unsecured asset – holders will be considered general creditors in the event of bankruptcy. (A good example of two countries separated by a common language!)

2. Fixed income preference shares

As the name suggests, fixed income preference shares (FIPS) are not bonds – they are a class of equity which pay a fixed coupon. In terms of the ranking on the balance sheet, FIPS rank above equities – hence the "preference share" terminology. If there is not enough money at the end of the year, the dividend on the FIPS will be paid ahead of any dividend on the ordinary share. However, from a bond investor's point of view, these instruments are deeply subordinated. The dividend can be suspended during hard times and in the event of a liquidation, virtually everyone bar the ordinary shareholders are ahead of you in the queue.

Not only are FIPS subordinated, they are also comparatively rare. Changes in the accounting rules in 2005 made issuing this type of instrument less attractive for companies. Nowadays, the only new issues seen are from companies who have limited choice in terms of equity-type fund raising; an example being the 2010 issue for Ecclesiastical Insurance.

Nevertheless, FIPS are popular holdings for private investors. The highly subordinated nature of the asset means that the yield will be high. Also, the UK preference share market is a thin one; under-researched and with comparatively little institutional demand. This is ideal territory for the informed value investor to poke around for bargains.

Cumulative & non-cumulative

A key difference to note is the division between "cumulative" and "non-cumulative" preference shares. In the event of the company suspending payment of the dividend, the liability will "roll up" on cumulative preference shares. Of course, while the going is good the holders may not notice the difference, but in thin times the cumulative share will be the better performer. Market valuations for the two classes vary accordingly.

Redeemable, perpetual or convertible?

Many preference shares are perpetual or irredeemable – similar in concept to ordinary shares. Others may be redeemable at the issuer's option. The issuer's call feature should be seen as a negative factor for investors and valued accordingly.

Finally there are convertible preference shares that convert into ordinary equity. These used to be much more common than they are now.

Zero dividend prefs

These types of instrument were issued by split capital trusts, a scheme that was embroiled in scandal in the middle part of 1990s. There are relatively few of these instruments that continue to trade.

Dealing in FIPS

There are no theoretical problems with dealing in FIPS. Liquidity, and particularly depth of market, is not great, but for the private investor looking to buy or sell a few thousand pounds, the market works.

Checking the price of the Royal Sun Alliance 7.875% Cumulative Preference share (RSAB) on Selftrade's online platform, I note a one-point bid/offer spread (this will vary from day to day). Buyers should also factor in the ½% stamp duty payable on purchases on this class of security.

The less liquid preference shares will turn over fairly infrequently and investors should position themselves to take advantage of offers as and when they appear.

> **Tip**: buy preference shares as a new issue – no stamp duty is payable.

The table opposite shows Collins Stewart's useful weekly price and information update of popular preference shares. Note the relatively small issue sizes of these instruments.

▶ Collins Stewart

9th Floor 88 Wood Street London EC2V 7QR
Preference Shares: call 020 7523 88878 or STX 67925/6

LEADING PREFERENCE SHARES

CSCS 288

September 12, 2011

STOCK	TICKER	OFFER PRICE	YIELDS		MARGIN OVER TREASURY 4.25% 2055 NET BASIS			ISSUE SIZE	DIVIDEND DATES	FUTURE XD DATE IF KNOWN
			NET	BOND COMPARISON	CURRENT	SINCE 1/1/01 HIGH	LOW			
Aviva 8 3/8% Cum	AV.B	109 xd	7.62	9.52	403	609 (18/3/09)	122 (21/3/02)	£100m	31/3 , 30/9	
Aviva 8 3/4% Cum	AV.A	113	7.83	9.83	425	671 (18/3/09)	127 (21/3/02)	£100m	30/6 , 31/12	9/11
Bristol & West 8 1/8% Non-Cum	BWSA	77	10.88	13.73	730	1596 (18/3/09)	139 (30/7/03)	£32m	15/5 , 15/11	5/10
Co-operative Bank 9 1/4% Non-Cum	CPBB	122.5	7.68	9.66	410	431 (9/9/09)	158 (23/3/05)	£60m	31/5 , 30/11	
Ecclesiastical Ins. 8 5/8% Non-Cum	ELLA	111.5	7.82	9.82	424	515 (4/12/08)	200 (17/4/07)	£106m	30/6 , 31/12	
General Accident 7 7/8% Cum	GACB	98 xd	7.97	9.95	438	559 (2/4/09)	133 (21/3/02)	£110m	1/4 , 1/10	
General Accident 8 7/8% Cum	GACA	108.5	8.28	10.39	469	653 (2/4/09)	135 (21/3/02)	£140m	1/1 , 1/7	
Investec Non-Cum Floating Rate (£10) †	INVR	415	3.62	4.53	312	312 (9/9/11)	260 (8/3/11)	£151m	7/7 , 14/12	
Lloyds Banking 6.475% Non-Cum (call 15/9/2024)	LLPE	62.5	*	*	-	1749 (21/1/09)	86 (30/1/07)	£56m	15/3 , 15/9	
Lloyds Banking 9 1/4% Non-Cum	LLPC	79.75	*	*	-	1857 (22/1/09)	121 (21/3/02)	£300m	31/5 , 30/11	
Lloyds Banking 9 3/4% Non-Cum	LLPD	81.5	*	*	-	1648 (24/2/09)	132 (9/3/05)	£56m	31/5 , 30/11	
National Westminster 9% Non-Cum	NWBD	98.5 xd	9.02	11.26	543	2596 (22/1/09)	109 (9/3/05)	£140m	16/4 , 16/10	
Northern Electric 8.061p Cum	NTEA	118 xd	6.78	8.47	319	322 (1/9/10)	134 (18/2/10)	£111m	31/3 , 30/9	
R.E.A Holdings 9% Cum	REB	106.5	8.56	10.75	497	497 (12/9/11)	401 (7/7/11)	£42m	30/6 , 31/12	
RSA Insurance Group 7 3/8% Cum	RSAB	98.75 xd	7.41	9.25	382	879 (4/3/03)	155 (11/9/01)	£125m	1/4 , 1/10	
Santander UK 8 5/8% Gross Non-Cum	SANB	89 xd	8.64	10.78	505	603 (13/3/09)	124 (21/3/02)	£24m	6/4 , 6/10	
Santander UK 10 3/8% Gross Non-Cum	SAN	98.5 xd	9.38	11.71	579	712 (2/4/09)	136 (21/3/02)	£136m	6/4 , 6/10	
Standard Chartered 7 3/8% Non-Cum	STAB	106.5	7.11	8.97	353	513 (9/3/09)	115 (9/3/05)	£96m	1/4 , 1/10	14/9
Standard Chartered 8 1/4% Non-Cum	STAC	116.5	7.28	9.18	369	585 (13/3/09)	115 (9/3/05)	£99m	1/4 , 1/10	14/9

Source: Collins Stewart

3. PIBS

PIBS (Permanent Interest Bearing Securities) are a type of instrument issued by UK building societies. Technically they are not bonds, but a type of risk capital, being subordinated to deposits and other senior obligations of the society. The reason for the issuance of these instruments was simple. Building societies are mutual organizations and are thus unable to issue equity to bolster their capital. Thus, the PIBS structure was created in order to raise capital and ensure that the societies were able to grow their balance sheets without having to wait for the slow process of building core capital through retained profits.

Typically, the structure of PIBS was fairly straightforward: an undated security with a fixed coupon. The issuer usually reserves the right to call the bond at some point in the future. The coupons on individual issues vary from around 6% to over 13% (generally reflecting the level of market rates at the time of issue).

Because of their fixed coupons, PIBS behave in a manner similar to bonds and offer investors a long-term income stream. Many of these instruments were issued in the 1990s and the following decade. They found ready demand and, apart from gilts, are perhaps the most widely-held of all types of fixed income instruments amongst UK private investors.

The public generally have great faith in the building society movement and in spite of the evident subordination and undated nature of these types of issues, income-hungry investors drove up the price of PIBS in the secondary markets to considerable premiums. In 2006, the Manchester Building Society 8% PIBS (which was issued at par) traded as high as 150. At that price, the running yield was just 5.3%.

Effect of the credit crunch

However, times change, and so does investor sentiment. The events of 2008/9 demonstrated that this subordination is a real risk for investors and holders of PIBS in many building societies and ex-building societies have been adversely affected.

For the more stable societies, such as Nationwide, the credit crunch has resulted in much lower secondary market prices for its PIBS, but little in the way of disruption to the income flows for the holder.

In the case of some of the more troubled members of the building society movement, holders of these instruments have been forced to accept a refinancing package, typically resulting in a substitution of the PIBS for the less desirable PPDS (see below).

Ex-building societies

To muddy the waters still further, it is worth remembering that many of the building societies shed their mutual status in the 1990s, propelled by a frenzy of carpet bagging and great hopes for the future. As with many things, it may have seemed like a good idea at the time, but none of the ex-builders still exist as a stand-alone entity and most of the PIBS of these issuers now exist as subordinated liabilities of the acquiring banks.

In some cases, it is worse with B&B and Northern Rock now nationalised. This has resulted in the PIBS coupons of these banks being frozen, and the holders joining a long queue in the hope of either resumption of interest payment or some type of settlement.

Dealing in PIBS

Dealing in PIBS is fairly straightforward, with most of the instruments available on the execution-only platforms. Liquidity, however, may be variable and bid-offer spreads are wide. Investors will have to pick their moment to achieve good bargains in this area. As ever with less liquid securities, it may be worth negotiating or leaving a limit order rather than simply paying the full offered price.

Call dates on PIBS

The majority of PIBS have call dates, the details of which will be found in the prospectus. This is an important factor to consider. An investor buying a PIBS over par could reasonably expect the issue to be called, whilst even an under-par purchase may be affected, with the future upside potentially capped by the call.

Call dates on PIBS are often accompanied by the additional option for the issuer to re-set the coupon, usually to a margin over LIBOR or benchmark gilt. Historically, such events were a "step up", meaning that the issuer was more likely to call the issue than reset the coupon, but in the post-credit crunch world, the optionality of this situation has swung against the investor.

Be wary of confusing a call with a fixed redemption date. I have met investors whose portfolio planning was based on assumed redemption of their PIBS holdings on the call dates. This, of course, may happen (depending on the issuer's cost of funding at the call date), but it should certainly not be relied on.

> **Tip**: holders of PIBS are full members of the issuing society. Whilst profitable opportunities for demutualisation are limited in the current environment, one never knows what will happen in five or ten years time.

Case study – The Portman 7.25% PIBS

The Portman Building Society was a fairly typical example of a mid-sized player amongst the then numerous mutually-owned building societies (my 1994 copy of the Butlers Building Society Guide shows 84 such organisations). The society can trace its roots back to 1846, but the smaller Bournemouth-based Portman threw in its lot with the larger Nationwide Building Society in 2007, part of the general trend towards consolidation in the industry.

The instrument in question is the Portman 7.25% PIBS, £60 million of which was issued in 2001 at a price of 100p. In due course, this instrument became a liability of the Nationwide Building Society, an event that was viewed as positive for investors, given the greater size and strength of the latter. The security is now generally known as the "Nationwide" 7.25% PIBS, but may also be referred to by its old title. The security, ticker and ISIN will be, of course, the same. The chart shows the instrument's price history over the past five years.

Chart 11.1: price history of Portman 7.25% PIBS

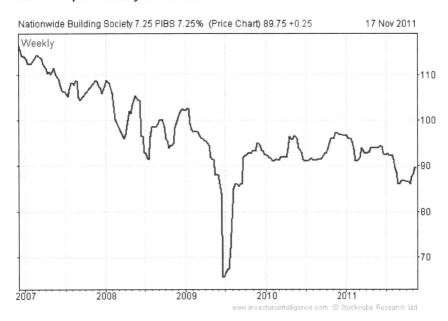

Nationwide Building Society 7.25 PIBS 7.25% (Price Chart) 89.75 +0.25   17 Nov 2011

www.investorsintelligence.com © Stockcube Research Ltd

PIBS are, broadly speaking, subordinated undated fixed income securities, but the details vary from issue to issue and it is worth reading through the prospectus to identify all the features of the instrument. For example, the following box gives an extract from page 8 of the Portman 7.25% PIBS prospectus, on risk factors.

Extract from Portman 7.25% PIBS prospectus

Investors should be aware that the PIBS are undated and subordinated and that the terms of the PIBS vary considerably from the terms of ordinary building society share accounts and deposit products. They should particularly note the following characteristics of the PIBS:

(a) Permanence – The PIBS will be repayable only at the option of the Society on 5 December 2021 and every fifth successive 5 December thereafter, or in certain limited circumstances as described in "Special Conditions of the Issue of the PIBS – 4 Repayment" on page 10 of this document in each case subject to the permission of the statutory

---

authority responsible for regulating building societies, which is currently the Building Societies Commission (the "Commission", which expression shall include any successor body performing for the time being the same or similar functions in relation to building societies, including the Financial Services Authority to whom the responsibilities of the Building Societies Commission are expected to be transferred with effect from 1 December 2001). The Society is under no obligation to the investor to seek any such permission to repay the PIBS.

(b) Liquidity – In order to realise his capital investment in the PIBS, an investor must either go to an established secondary market or look to make a private sale. There is no guarantee that the investor will be able to liquidate his investment in the PIBS for cash either because the future liquidity of the secondary market is not guaranteed or alternatively the investor may be unable to find any potential private purchasers. Therefore, there is a risk that an investor cannot realise his investment in the PIBS when he wishes to do so.

(c) Capital value of investment – As the capital value of the PIBS will vary with market interest rates, the market perception of the value of the Society and the availability of purchasers, there is a real chance that the investor will make a capital loss when he comes to sell his PIBS.

(d) Subordination – The PIBS are subordinated to all other liabilities of the Society. In a winding up or dissolution of the Society, the claims of the PIBS holders will rank behind all other creditors of the Society and the claims of Members holding shares (other than deferred shares) as to principal and interest. Investors should be aware that this subordination is a primary factor behind the higher interest rate that is paid on the PIBS when compared to other investment products of the Society i.e. that there is a direct trade-off between higher interest and higher risk.

(e) Investor protection – Unlike normal building society investment products, the PIBS are not protected investments for the purposes of the Building Societies Investor Protection Scheme and are not expected to be protected investments under the Financial Services

Compensation Scheme following the introduction of that scheme, the date for which is proposed to be 1 December 2001.

(f) Payments of interest may be missed – Interest in respect of the PIBS will not be payable where the Directors of the Society resolve that to make payment would result in the Society's capital falling below prescribed minimum levels and that accordingly such interest should not be paid or where the Society has not paid interest in respect of deposits or shares (other than deferred shares).

(g) Interest – If the Society does not make an interest payment in respect of the PIBS in accordance with paragraph (f) above, such interest will be cancelled. Interest is paid without withholding or deduction for tax under current law. Nevertheless, tax may be withheld or deducted if there is a change of law.

(h) Rights – The rights of the PIBS holders are markedly different from those of shareholders in a company, e.g. as to voting rights and protection of minorities. For example, as indicated in paragraph 6 on page 6 of this document, each PIBS holder only has one vote at general meetings of the Society, irrespective of the number of PIBS he holds, whereas shareholders at a general meeting of a company would normally have one vote on a poll for each share held.

(i) Amalgamation, conversion or takeover of the Society – If the Society amalgamates with, or transfers all or part of its engagements to, another building society, the PIBS will not become repayable as a consequence thereof, but will become deferred shares in that society. If the Society transfers the whole of its business to any other body, the transfer will incorporate arrangements to secure that the PIBS are effectively converted into perpetual subordinated debt of that body, and do not become repayable other than at the option of that body on 5 December 2021 and every fifth successive 5 December thereafter or in the limited circumstances as described in "Special Conditions of the issue of the PIBS - 4 Repayment", in each case subject to the permission of the Commission.

Perhaps the main points to note here are (a) (d) and (f). The security is callable at the issuer's option, and that means that upside is limited. Point (d) reinforces our knowledge of the subordinated nature of these securities whilst (f) highlights the fact that during bad times the coupon payment may be skipped.

Summary

To summarise on PIBS, times have changed. In the early 2000s some investors believed these instruments to be "as good as gilts", to quote one over-optimistic bulletin board poster at the time. Post-credit crunch, the risk is more evident, and this can be seen in the price action on the chart. In many ways, investors' sentiment towards the sector is now more balanced, with both risk and reward considered.

4 Contingent capital instruments

Contingent Convertibles (CoCos), sometimes known as Enhanced Capital Notes (ECNs), or Hybrids, are a relatively new breed of security, forged out of the fires of the 2008 credit crunch. Such instruments are effectively subordinated bonds, but with a feature that allows the issuer to force a mandatory conversion on the holders into equity[6].

The prime issuers of such structures are banks and building societies who may have urgent need in the future to boost their capital ratios. Conversion triggers are set at certain ratios, varying between 5% and 8%. That means that if the capital held by the bank falls below these levels (perhaps triggered by write-downs on bad loans), such securities will be forcibly converted to equity. The equity conversion would occur at a point in time of maximum stress and it is fair to say that this would be a very disadvantageous move for the holders.

As banks and building societies endeavour to rebuild their capital after the credit crunch, such instruments are becoming more common. Lloyds were

---

[6] Building societies can not issue equity, so in order to improve their capital ratios, hybrid bonds issued by building societies convert into "PPDS" – profit participating deferred shares. Should this event happen, it would not be a happy one for the bond holders. Dividend payments for PPDS are related to the profits of the company and are discretionary. What is more, the PPDS are unlikely to have the long-term recovery capability of ordinary shares.

one of the leaders with the complex series of ECNs issued in late 2009[7], but other issues of this nature have been seen from Yorkshire Building Society and UBS over 2010/11.

For instance, if a building society's tier one capital falls below a set ratio, perhaps 5 per cent of the assets, the hybrid bond holders will suffer a forced conversion to profit-participating deferred shares (PPDS). Dividend payments on PPDS are related to the profits of the company and are discretionary.

Specialist bond brokers RIA Securities offers the following informed view on hybrid bonds.

> When the financial crisis struck in 2008/09, banks ran up massive losses which undermined their capacity to pay dividends and, in the more extreme cases, eroded their capital base to an extent that injections of funds from taxpayers were required. In either case, shareholders suffered severe losses but bondholders generally got to hold onto their claims. Senior bondholders were intentionally protected to limit the systemic damage. Many subordinated bonds had 'burden sharing' language embedded such as maturity extension and coupon deferral option imbedded. However, these features turned out to be difficult to use. Bond investors insisted on coupons and repayment schedules as deviating from them would upset the pricing of the securities.

> Maturity extensions and coupon deferrals were seen as a break with convention, signalling 'distress'. Hence banks were extremely reluctant to use them. At the peak of the credit crisis in 2008 regulators then used the special state-aid powers endorsed by the European Commission to enforce coupon deferrals and extensions on a broader scale (ING, KBC, Commerzbank, RBS, Lloyds, Irish banks, some Spanish and German regional banks). Tier-1 and Upper-tier 2 bonds, which were meant to shelter bank equity and thus counted as 'regulatory capital', simply did not do a good 'burden sharing' job.

---

[7] Thank you to Collins Stewart (Canaccord Genuity since 2012) for providing their informative weekly publication on the Lloyds CoCo's.

Two different kinds of 'new' hybrid bonds are being introduced, which both meet the need for a more flexible 'capital buffer' but still have essential bond features. The two approaches are either Contingent convertible bonds or debt securities with write-down features. Contingent convertibles, or CoCos, are debt instruments that automatically convert to equity when a pre-determined floor of capital adequacy is breached. The issuer will determine the trigger level in the prospectus, leaving it to the investor to judge the probability for this trigger to be hit. The trigger is defined as a certain level of core capital relative to total assets, a formula first used in the case of the Enhanced Capital Notes issued by Lloyds Banking Group in November 2009. Bond investors would become equity providers should losses erode the bank's capital to below this threshold. Investors face the difficulty of having to monitor bank capital on the basis of figures published by the issuer itself. Poor visibility and some moral hazard risk would mean that the market price of CoCos would become very sensitive to short-term risk factors as soon as the capital ratio moves closer to the trigger level, even if a considerable margin is left. This 'equity' risk element may keep conservative investors away from CoCos, but it also means that issuers have to offer an attractive risk premium relative to other types of bank bonds. The agencies appear uncertain about how to rate these new securities, but no more than a low investment grade rating is achievable.

Analyst Harald Eggerstedt at RIA goes on to offer the opinion that new structures may be developed as time goes on:

The second approach uses bonds which contain write-down language rather than equity-conversion features. The write down would be triggered by the regulator if this is needed to ensure a minimum capital level relative to risk weighted assets. The principal would be written back to 100% out of profits generated in subsequent years. For such bonds to be acceptable to investors on a broader basis, regulators have to lay out the rules under which they have a mandate to trigger haircuts. This is now underway with the implementation of the new Basel capital adequacy guidelines. To offset the effect of a potential capital loss, issuers need to be committed to reverse write-downs as early as possible. Redemptions must be made at par at a target date. If redemption is delayed for capital adequacy reasons, every reasonable effort should be made to redeem the bonds at par in subsequent years.

The clear advantage of this model is that swift action is possible, minimizing market disruption. Bond prices would have reflected the write-down already after negative net-income is reported, so that the haircut itself would not exert any further pressure on prices. The write-down could be defined in fixed proportion to the loss-impact on the balance sheet. NordLB, Rabobank and Unicredit have issued such bonds. For mutuals and state-owned banks such bonds are particularly attractive as an alternative to issuing new shares or contingent convertibles (which may not be an option for them).

My thoughts

I am not a huge fan of the CoCo structure. My fundamental objection is that the instrument operates on a "one strike and you are out" principle. Thus, should investors suffer forced conversion to equity, they are stuck with a new lower-quality security. My preference is for conventional subordinated debt, where the bond holder can hang on for long-term recovery. Nevertheless, there is a saying that there is no such thing as a bad asset, only a bad price. At the right level, CoCo's can offer an attractive risk-reward ratio.

Looking forward, the CoCo structure may already be redundant. The rules concerning bank capital ratios are in a state of flux and the future is likely to see a variety of new types of subordinated and loss-absorbing instruments emerge.

The following table lists the enhanced capital notes issued by Lloyds Banking Group.

Collins Stewart

9th Floor 88 Wood Street London EC2V 7QR
Lloyds ECNs: call 020 7523 8887/8 or STX 67925/6

CSCS 288

September 12, 2011

LLOYDS BANKING GROUP - ENHANCED CAPITAL NOTES

STOCK	TICKER	DEALING UNIT (£'000)	OFFER PRICE	GROSS YIELD	YIELD TO MATURITY	MARGIN OVER TREASURY 4.25% 2055 GROSS BASIS CURRENT	HIGH (SINCE 1/12/09)	LOW (SINCE 1/12/09)	PREMIUM (DISCOUNT) IF CONVERTED BASED ON LLOYDS ORDINARY AT 30**	ISSUE SIZE £m	PAY DATES
LBG Capital 1 7.5884% (12/5/2020)	LB1G	1	75	10.12	12.36	653	653 (12/9/11)	317 (14/4/11)	47.9%	732	12/5 , 12/11
LBG Capital 1 7.8673% (17/12/2019)	LB1I	1	76.5	10.28	12.59	670	670 (12/9/11)	349 (14/4/11)	50.9%	331	17/6
LBG Capital 1 7.869% (25/8/2020)	LB1H	50+1	93	8.46	9.01	487	522 (5/7/10)	356 (19/11/10)	83.4%	596	25/2 , 25/8
LBG Capital 1 7.975% (15/9/2024)	LB1J	1 Share	76	10.49	11.59	691	691 (12/9/11)	405 (26/4/10)	49.9%	102	15/3 , 15/9
LBG Capital 1 8.125% (15/12/2019)	LB1D	1	90	9.03	9.94	544	552 (5/7/10)	381 (16/11/10)	77.5%	4	15/11
LBG Capital 1 11.04% (19/3/2020)	LB1F	50+1	103	10.72	10.48	713	713 (12/9/11)	529 (16/11/10)	103.1%	736	19/3 , 19/9
LBG Capital 2 7.625% (9/12/2019)	LB2C	1	89	8.57	9.60	498	517 (16/7/10)	368 (15/11/10)	75.5%	151	9/12
LBG Capital 2 8.5% (7/6/2032)	LB2G	1	85	10.00	10.25	641	641 (12/9/11)	427 (16/11/10)	67.6%	104	7/6
LBG Capital 2 9% (15/12/2019)	LB2D	1	94	9.57	10.14	599	599 (12/9/11)	458 (12/4/11)	85.4%	96	15/7
LBG Capital 2 9% (15/7/2029)	LB2F	1	101	8.91	8.88	532	548 (5/3/10)	460 (19/11/10)	99.2%	107	15/7
LBG Capital 2 9.125% (15/7/2020)	LB2A	1	92	9.92	10.55	633	633 (12/9/11)	438 (19/11/10)	81.4%	147	15/7
LBG Capital 2 9.334% (7/2/2020)	LB2Q	1	84.5	11.05	12.38	746	746 (12/9/11)	418 (14/4/11)	66.6%	207	7/2
LBG Capital 2 9.875% (10/2/2023)	LB2L	1	97.5	10.13	10.24	654	654 (12/9/11)	501 (22/11/10)	92.3%	57	10/2
LBG Capital 2 10.5% (29/9/2023)	LB2E	1	109	9.63	9.24	605	690 (25/10/10)	490 (19/11/10)	114.9%	68	29/9
LBG Capital 2 11.125% (4/11/2020)	LB2H	1	112	9.93	9.13	635	661 (1/9/10)	561 (1/7/11)	120.9%	38	4/11
LBG Capital 2 11.25% (14/9/2023)	LB2M	50	108	10.42	10.08	683	710 (5/7/10)	547 (19/11/10)	113.0%	95	1/3 , 1/9
LBG Capital 2 11.875% (1/9/2024)	LB2N	1	106	11.20	10.99	762	762 (12/9/11)	558 (16/11/10)	109.0%	35	1/3 , 1/9
LBG Capital 2 12.75% (1/08/2020)	LB2I	10	113	11.28	10.42	770	770 (12/9/11)	605 (16/11/10)	122.8%	57	1/8
LBG Capital 2 14.5% (30/1/2022)	LB2K	50	123	11.79	10.76	820	859 (1/12/09)	662 (12/4/10)	142.6%	79	1/3 , 1/9
LBG Capital 2 15% ECNs (21/12/2019)	LB2S	100+1	135	11.11	8.91	752	834 (26/5/10)	638 (11/4/11)	166.2%	775	21/1 , 21/7
LBG Capital 2 15% (22/1/2029)	LB2U	100+1	139.5	10.75	10.18	717	784 (26/5/10)	583 (1/7/11)	175.1%	67	21/1 , 21/7
LBG Capital 2 16.125% (10/12/2024)	LB2O	50	135	11.94	11.02	836	888 (1/12/09)	689 (1/7/11)	166.2%	61	10/6 , 10/12

**LBG ECNs will convert into ordinary shares if the Group's published consolidated core tier 1 capital ratio falls below 5%: the most recent published ratio is 10.1% (5/8/2011)

The conversion price is 59.2093 or 1.68892 ordinary shares per £1 of ECNs

Stamp Duty is payable on LBG Capital stocks settled in Crest. Yields are quoted for three day settlement in Euroclear.

While every effort has been made to ensure that the above details are correct, Collins Stewart Europe Ltd accepts no responsibility for any errors or omissions.

Prices are indicative only, and should not be taken as offers or recommendations.

To deal call Rik Edwards or Chris Burgoyne on STX 67925/6 or 020 7523 8887/8 (redwards@collinsstewart.com / cburgoyne@collinsstewart.com)

Source: Collins Stewart

Chapter 12
Overseas and foreign currency bonds

This book is intended for the sterling-based investor. Typically such an investor will have sterling-based liabilities such as school fees or retirement and as such will look to secure future cash flows (be they income or roll up capital gains) in sterling. But, we live in a global economy. Developments in Europe, America or China will impact the UK and its bond markets within minutes or hours. As such, even the most died-in-the-wool enthusiast will need to keep a weather eye open for moves in US Treasuries and Bunds, if only to contextualise and better understand what is happening in gilts and other sterling bonds. Above and beyond this, there will be times when the sterling bond buyer may wish to venture overseas. Such a broad subject would easily fill another book (or three), but this section offers a brief overview.

Think currency first, bonds next

The world of foreign bonds is full of opportunities, but investors should heed this word of warning – when buying foreign currency bonds, the greatest source of volatility will be the FX rate, not the bond. The following chart shows the 5 year German Government bond (the BOBL) and the GBPEUR exchange rate.

Over the period (just 6 months), the BOBL dropped 5 point from its EUR120 starting point – that's around 4%; meanwhile the GBPEUR pair moved around twice that over just the Oct-Nov period.

Over longer periods the moves can be even more extreme. The GBPUSD pair can move 30% over a couple of years, whilst the GBPEUR has seen huge shifts over the decade. Of course, such moves may well be in your favour, but consider that when buying foreign currency bonds – you are really making a long-term FX trade.

Chart 12.1: BOBL v GBPEUR

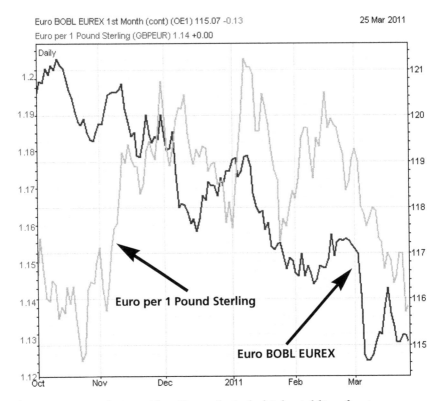

Euro BOBL EUREX 1st Month (cont) (OE1) 115.07 -0.13   25 Mar 2011
Euro per 1 Pound Sterling (GBPEUR) 1.14 +0.00

The win-win trade is to identify a relatively high-yielding foreign-currency bond with a fair chance of currency appreciation over the holding period. Such trades certainly do occur, but they should not be considered low risk.

Covering the full extent of the international bond markets is beyond the scope of this book, but I have attempted a short overview below.

US dollar bonds

US Treasury Bonds will be the first port of call for any investor studying the US market. The yield curve (see following chart) in this large and liquid market will determine the base level of yield offered by corporate bonds of various maturities. Benchmarks are the 3 month bill, the 2, 5 and 10 year notes and the 30 year bond (also known as the *long bond*). The US also offers a range of TIPS (Treasury Inflation Protected Securities).

Chart 12.2: US treasury yield curve

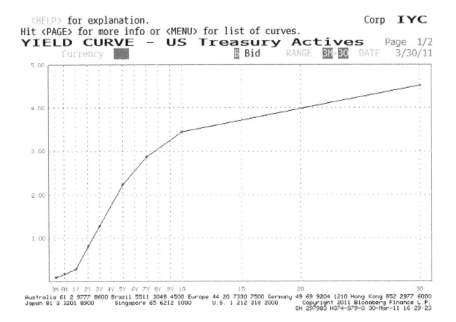

Investors seeking liquidity would be advised to steer their brokers towards the US Treasury market. It is easy to deal in and a low-cost option from a bid-offer spread point of view. From the point of view of income generation, the private investor will be better off looking at the EuroDollar market (i.e. USD-denominated Eurobonds). There is a wide selection of credits available in this sector of the market; indeed, considerably wider than that which is seen in the EuroSterling markets, with more representation in the sub-investment grade class.

One of the best sources of data for USD bonds available to the private investor is the **www.BondMarketPrices.com** website. This website streams post-trade prices from the TRAXX system (a trade matching system used by market professionals in the Eurobond market). The system is free to view due to recent EU legislation/guidance on openness and market access. Post-trade reports are available on bonds with the following criteria:

- Bonds must have 1 year or more to maturity.
- Bonds must have a current rating of A- or above.

- Bonds must have an issue amount of €1,000m or above (or currency equivalent).
- Trades must be in bonds (i.e. straights, floating rate notes or convertibles).
- Trade quantities must be between €15,000 and €1,000,000 (or currency equivalent).

The following table shows an extract from this website of USD-denominated corporate bonds.

Security Name	Currency	High	Low	Median	No. Trades	Volume
ABU DHABI NATL ENERGY 5.875 27/10/2016 S	USD	105.25	104.86	105.00	2	950000
ABU DHABI NATL ENERGY 6.6 01/08/2013 S	USD	107.25	107.25	107.25	1	341904
AMERICAN HONDA FINANCE 2.5 21/09/2015 S	USD	99.05	98.94	98.99	< 1	57142
AT&T CORP 5.6 15/05/2018 S	USD	110.71	110.71	110.71	< 1	952
AT&T INC 2.5 15/08/2015 S	USD	99.79	99.69	99.74	< 1	113857
BP CAPITAL MARKETS 3.625 08/05/2014 S	USD	104.28	104.18	104.23	1	447666
BP CAPITAL MARKETS 3.875 10/03/2015 S	USD	104.66	104.61	104.64	1	455571
BP CAPITAL MARKETS 4.742 11/03/2021 S	USD	100.98	100.98	100.98		
BRITISH GAS INTL FINANCE ZERO 04/11/2021	USD	56.85	56.85	56.85	1	124285
CNOOC FINANCE (2011) 4.25 26/01/2021 S	USD	97.70	97.48	97.59	1	1338095
DOLPHIN ENERGY 5.888 15/06/2019 S	USD	106.88	106.72	106.72	1	595571
EDP FINANCE 4.9 01/10/2019 S	USD	89.94	89.05	89.50	1	326333
EDP FINANCE 5.375 02/11/2012 S	USD	103.02	102.95	102.98	< 1	164190
EDP FINANCE 6.0 02/02/2018 S	USD	96.91	96.45	96.68	3	744619
ELECTRICITE DE FRANCE 4.6 27/01/2020 S	USD	102.17	101.80	101.98	1	247238
ELECTRICITE DE FRANCE 5.5 26/01/2014 S	USD	109.95	109.89	109.92	2	289952
ENEL FINANCE INTL S.A. 5.125 07/10/2019 S	USD	101.59	101.51	101.51	2	433666
ENEL FINANCE INTL S.A. 5.7 15/01/2013 S	USD	106.12	106.12	106.12	1	353857
FRANCE TELECOM 4.375 08/07/2014 S	USD	107.77	107.77	107.77	< 1	72904
GENERAL ELECTRIC CO 5.0 01/02/2013 S	USD	106.72	106.72	106.72	2	372904

Sample taken from **www.bondmarketprices.com** 25 March 2011

The US market also offers an interesting range of preference shares and quasi-bond instruments. It is fair to say that due to the difference in the scale of the two economies and their respective stock markets, the preference share market is deeper and more liquid than the rather thin market that exists in the UK. An interesting source of information for investors looking for opportunities in this sector of the US market is the *Forbes Lehman Income Securities* newsletter, a monthly email subscription publication ($199 per annum) with a good track record.

Investors should also consider the very wide variety of USD bond ETFs available – everything from specific sectors of the Treasury curve, through to high yield, Municipal Bonds and preference shares.

Euro-denominated bonds

European government bonds

When looking at European government bonds, the first point of call will be the German Bund market. This is considered to be the most liquid and most creditworthy of all European government bond markets. Consequently, the German Bunds trade at the lowest yields of all the European bond markets.

The Benchmarks in the German market are as follows:

- Bundesschatzanweisungen (Schätze) – 2 year notes

- Bundesobligationen (Bobls) – 5 year notes

- Bundesanleihen (Bunds and Buxl) – 10 and 30 year bonds

All of which trade in a free and transparent manner across a liquid yield curve. Any good broker should be able to deal in Bunds, which are normally settled in Euroclear, although CREST settlement is possible.

Other major European government bonds include:

- The French OAT (Obligations Assimilables du Trésor) market – is often considered a close second to the Bund in terms of quality

- Spanish Bonos (2-5 years) and Obligaciones del Estado (5 years plus)

- Italian BTP (Buoni del Tesoro Polianualis)

Again most brokers will, at least in theory, be able to trade in these instruments, although Euroclear settlement facilities will usually be required. The path here is slightly less well trodden for the UK private investor than in Bunds.

As one moves away from the Teutonic high ground of the European bonds markets, credit quality typically diminishes, and thus yields rise. This relationship varies over time, and by some considerable extent.

Prior to monetary unification the individual bonds markets traded in local currencies and at local rates. As the member countries of the Eurozone pulled together ahead of the launch of the Euro, traders across the globe were running the convergence trade – shorting the Bund and buying the higher yielding debt in countries such as Italy. This trade came good. As the chart shows, by late 1999, there was virtually no yield spread or premium attached to the Italian BTPS.

Chart 12.3: yield spread on the 10 year Italian BTPS

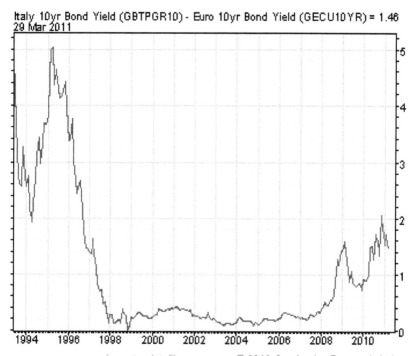

Italy 10yr Bond Yield (GBTPGR10) - Euro 10yr Bond Yield (GECU10YR) = 1.46
29 Mar 2011

www.investorsintelligence.com © 2013 Stockcube Research Ltd

This proved to be a triumph of hope over reality. Spreads started moving out again by the end of the decade.

The European government bond market is once again populated by bonds with wildly differing yields, dictated by the market's opinion of the creditworthiness or otherwise of the issuer. The following table gives a snapshot of the 10 year benchmarks with their respective yields.

Table 12.1: 10 year Euro government bond yields (March 2011)

Country	10 govt bond yld(%)
Germany	3.34
France	3.69
Belgium	4.28
Italy	4.77
Spain	5.18
Portugal	7.89
Ireland	9.73
Greece	12.50

There will no doubt be further movements in this pecking order over the years to come.

Non-government Euro-denominated bonds

Moving away from the world of government bonds, there are numerous non-government Euro-denominated bonds, which one might describe as *Euro Eurobonds*.

It is worth pointing out that the market for fixed income for private investors in Europe is much more highly developed than in the UK. Borsa Italiana run the successful MOT platform which turns over around 300,000 tickets a month in a variety of issues. This is a more established version of our own LSE ORB platform and is a good point of reference for investors looking for potential investments in the huge Euro-denominated bond market. A wealth of information can be found at the Borsa Italiana website at **www.borsaitaliana.it**. The following table shows a snapshot of some of the 700-odd issue available on the platform.

Table 12.2: sample of bonds traded on Italian MOT

ISIN Code	Issuer	Name	Coupon	Expiry Date	Currency	Bid Price	Ask Price
IT0001264792	Dexia Crediop	Opere-98/18 Cap Rf	5.50	10/15/18	EUR	99.50	100.20
IT0001267381	Centrobanca	Centrob-98/18 Cap Rf	5.50	10/20/18	EUR	100.15	100.61
IT0001271003	Banca Imi	Bim-Imi-98/18 Sd	5.00	11/4/18	ITL	107.71	109.90
IT0001271649	Intesa Sanpaolo	Medio Lomb-18 75 R F	5.50	11/6/18	EUR	100.90	101.44
IT0001277406	Dexia Crediop	Opere-98/18 11 F/Rf	5.50	11/27/18	EUR	98.81	99.53
IT0001278404	Unicredit Mediocredito Centrale	Medio Cen-98/18 Fts	0.39	12/3/18	EUR	86.90	87.00
IT0001278941	Centrobanca	Centrob-13Equity Lkd		10/10/13	EUR	94.82	95.49
IT0001282299	Dexia Crediop	Opere-13 12 Tf/Frf	6.49	12/18/13	EUR	102.62	103.15
IT0001282414	Intesa Sanpaolo	Sp Imi-98/13 7 Sd	5.00	12/2/13	EUR	134.79	135.73
IT0001287249	Unicredit Mediocredito Centrale	Medio Cen-98/18 S-D		12/24/18	EUR	99.55	100.05
IT0001292850	Intesa Sanpaolo	Mcr Lomb-19Eu Sd Ind	2.22	1/15/19	EUR	88.35	88.75
IT0001296133	Banca Monte Dei Paschi Di Siena	Mpaschi-99/14Eu 3 Sd	3.00	1/4/14	EUR	99.42	99.80
IT0001300992	Centrobanca	Centrob-19 Eu Sd/Ind	2.36	1/22/19	EUR	87.42	87.78
IT0001302659	Intesa Sanpaolo	Sp Imi-99/19 7 Ind	3.25	1/25/19	EUR	95.60	95.79
IT0001302733	Banca Monte Dei Paschi Di Siena	Mpaschi-99/29 4 Tm	5.00	2/1/29	EUR	87.50	87.68

Comment

The snapshot shows a variety of bonds, but I would observe that there is a strong bias towards banks and other financial institutions. This is a factor to be wary of in many bond markets. Otherwise, I observe fairly reasonable bid-offer spreads, which range from a tight 0.18 cents to around 150 cents.

Other foreign currency bonds

There are numerous markets for investors to get involved in – from the huge but somewhat inaccessible JGB (Japanese government bond) market to more marginal foreign currency markets such as Iceland or Turkey, or the Latin American countries.

Canada and Australia also make strong candidates for overseas investment. At the time of writing, these currencies are strong, boosted by the respective regions' mineral exports. Also the government bond markets are of a good quality in terms of liquidity and the credit outlook. However, the usual caveats about currency moves continue to apply. In addition to this, watch out for withholding tax and currency controls which are from time-to-time applied in some of these markets.

Investors wishing to trade or invest in these markets will need a good broker with full international settlement capability. Such markets will largely be beyond the capabilities of the low-cost execution only brokers.

Chapter 13

A walk on the wild side – distressed and illiquid debt

Some key concepts

While most equities are bought in the hope of great things to come, namely growth, profit, rising dividends and takeovers, the psychology behind the average purchase of a bond is somewhat different. Typically a bond is purchased on the premise of an absolute certainty of the return of capital and income. Should the capability of the issuer of a bond to service and repay debt come into doubt, fixed income investors head for the exit with astonishing rapidity.

Fallen angels

Selling pressure is generally exacerbated by a decline in the issuer's credit rating. Most fund managers are restricted to holding bonds considered to be investment grade. This is generally defined by a credit rating above Standard & Poor's BBB- and Moody's Baa3. Bonds with a rating below this level are considered to be non investment grade, colloquially known as junk bonds. Should a bond drop to this status, the majority of funds will be forced to sell.

This investor behaviour creates considerable selling pressure, with few people on the other side of the trade to pick up the pieces. Understandably, valuation undershoot can arise as sheer weight of money drives the price below what the fundamentals, or indeed common sense, would suggest to be reasonable. This type of bond is known as a *fallen angel*.

Examples of this type of behaviour occur time and time again in the bond markets – sometimes restricted to individual sectors or countries and sometimes, as was seen in the 2008 credit crunch, across the board. The table below shows some of the prices and approximate yields available to investors in sterling bonds during the darkest hour of the credit crunch – October 2008, a couple of months after Lehman Brothers folded on 15 September. Bear in mind that the bonds selected are comparatively liquid on-the-run sterling bonds (i.e. those with reasonable transparency that can be found quoted on broker and investment bank systems). These issues were to a degree underpinned by private investors and held their value somewhat better than less frequently traded bonds. Prices traded in other issues during those dark days could vary by ten percent or more on a day-by-day basis.

Table 13.1: sample bond prices and yields – October 2008 to Sept 2010

Bond	Price (Oct 08)	Yield (Oct 08)	Price (Sep 10)	Yield (Sep 10)
Goldman Sachs 5.25% 2015 (senior debt)	70	11%	107.15	4.7%
GE Capital 4.625% 2016 (then rated AAA)	75	10%	106.07	3.3%
Segro 5.5% 2018	62	12.5%	105.4	4.6%
Citigroup 5.125% 2018 (subordinated)	45	16%	95.03	5.8%

We should put these moves in context. All of the above are (or at least were!) well-regarded investment-grade bonds of medium-dated maturities. In normal market conditions one might expect such bonds to move by no more than a ten or twenty point range over their life, and such a range might take many years to achieve. Over the 2008-10 period, moves of 30-50 points were seen across a wide range of securities.

Perhaps the best example I can find of this dramatic sell-off and recovery is in the subordinated financial sector during this period. This area understandably took the worst of the punishment over the credit crunch and the deeply subordinated Euro-denominated **RBS 7.0916% perpetual issue** provides a case in point.

The following chart shows the price history bottoming out at 8.5c (yes, that's 8.5c, not 85c!) – although I am reliably informed that in 2009 bonds changed hands at 7cents and possibly lower. At the time of writing the bond's coupon was suspended under the blanket EU ruling on discretionary coupon payments. However, coupon payments look set to resume in due course and the bond now trades in the mid-seventies, making the security a seven bagger over a two-year period for those investors courageous enough to step in at the lows.

Chart 13.1: price chart of RBS 7.0916% perpetual issue

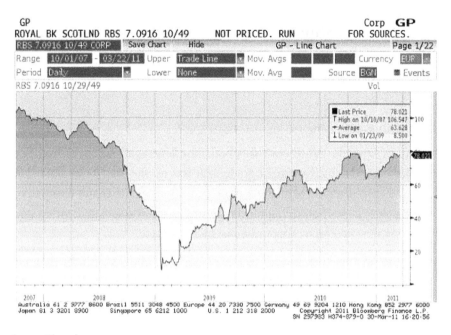

Source: Bloomberg

New issue vs fallen angel

Sub-investment grade bonds are often referred to as junk bonds. This is an emotive expression and suggests that the asset is of little worth.

I would beg to differ, but before putting forward my case it is worth differentiating between those bonds issued with sub-investment grade ratings and previously creditworthy bonds that have fallen from grace.

Michael Milken and Drexel Burnham Lambert

A name forever synonymous with junk bonds is that of Michael Milken. Milken, a native of California, had identified that the non-investment grade bonds had historically produced superior risk-adjusted returns. With this kernel of an idea, Milken was to develop strategies at the LA-based Drexel Burnham Lambert that were to turn the fairly complacent US corporate world upside down. The surge in availability of capital from the creation of the junk bond market fuelled the huge boom in leveraged takeovers that was responsible for driving much of the 1980s equity bull market.

Like many so many over-leveraged financial empires, it ended badly. In 1989 Milken was indicted by a federal grand jury on securities fraud charges and subsequently banned from operating in the securities market.

Junk bonds established as an asset class

Not all of Drexel's handiwork was bad. The leveraged takeover had been established and sub-investment grade debt was on the map as an asset class. However, the problem with new issue junk bonds is that the company is starting from a position of high leverage, and is often associated with a story regarding new products, corporate restructuring, etc.

It is fair to say that such issues are sold rather than bought with the sales and marketing arms of investment banks running at full speed ahead to place the debt. From time to time, good value is to be found, but the area is not a favourite of mine.

But not all junk bonds are new issues. My preference in the asset class is for fallen angels. Such degraded secondary market instruments have a lower profile and may well be under-researched and hence under-valued. It is here that the informed investor can identify and actively seek value.

The following chart of the Brixton Estates 6% Dec 2010 is an illustration of how a bond can be valued at a very low level, and then make a full recovery. We will look at a few strategies for these later in this chapter.

Chart 13.2: a Brixton angel falls

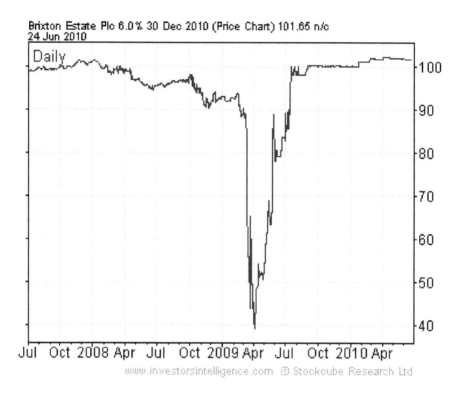

The chart of Brixton Estates 6% December 2010 bond demonstrates the high level of volatility that can be exhibited by distressed bonds. Note the equally rapid recovery.

High yield bonds and the credit cycle

The natural direction of the corporate bond market is that of tightening. Corporate bonds are issued with yields offering a margin over treasuries or funding benchmarks such as swaps or LIBOR rates and it is fair to say that these margins are generally eroded, slowly and steadily, over time.

Why might this be?

The effect can viewed as a natural part of the credit cycle. In times of economic growth investors' confidence grows, and this in turn leads to an increased willingness to pay a higher price for assets. Risk aversion falls away, and the premiums demanded by investors likewise.

The other factor that fuels the natural tightening cycle of bonds is a feature of the market itself. Financial institutions are both the biggest issuers and the biggest investors in the bond markets. Positions held by banks create demand for bonds. This demand in turn lowers the funding cost of the issuing institutions, who are in many cases, the banks themselves. With these cheaper funds, the banks are able to buy yet more bonds, expanding their balance sheets at ever lower margins. Add to this, the pressure from management and shareholders to make more profit each and every year and what happens? You've guessed it – expand the size of the balance sheet by buying more bonds.

This merry dance can go on for some years in benign credit conditions – gradually tightening the incremental yields offered by corporate bonds until over-valuation sets in. The resulting sell-offs bring the conditions that the distressed debt investor thrives in.

Investing in high-yield bonds

Know your asset

So how should an investor go about identifying and purchasing high-yield bonds?

When buying investment grade bonds, a degree of largesse is acceptable. It is not necessary to read the prospectus every time you buy a gilt or a AAA-rated vanilla bond. However, high yield bonds are different. There is real risk, and one issue may differ greatly from the next, both in terms of its structure and the return achieved.

The first step is to obtain a copy of the prospectus. Here you will find the full details of the bond, the seniority (or otherwise) of the credits, plus information on puts, calls or other event-triggered actions.

Next, read the company accounts, nowadays easily available on the internet. It's a boring job, but someone has to do it. Interpret the account from a bondholder's point of view. Remember that it is not rapid growth, hopes for the future or exciting new product launches that will affect the short-term credit picture.

Finally, keep an eye on the company's share price and monitor the bulletin boards. For example, in the UK, the Motley Fool's "banks" board has a good body of well-informed punters that spend their days reading prospectuses and swapping information.

The equity markets have a higher degree of visibility and participation than the bond markets and whilst equity investors have no particular edge when it comes to obtaining information, the impact of any such information or changes in sentiment can (and I stress can) be visible in the equity market before the bond market. Share prices can be a leading indicator; and note that distressed debt prices will show a much higher level of correlation with equities than would usually be the case for a bond.

Get a good broker

The discount brokers provide a good service. Buying £10,000 of bonds for £12.50 commission is good value in anybody's book. In liquid bonds, the price differential achieved on execution between an online discount broker and specialist will be minimal

But the game changes in the world of illiquid and distressed debt. The same bond may trade at three dramatically different prices between six counterparties on the same day. Remember, this is not a stock exchange. There is no centralized mechanism for routing quotes and trades – there are multiple peer-to-peer transactions taking place. During major market pullbacks and crises, the widely-held concept of an efficient market goes out the window – at times there is neither the capital or the risk appetite to make such a huge and disparate market efficient. This makes dealing much harder, but opens up an enormous opportunity for investors willing to back their own convictions with hard cash.

A wholesale block of GBP million plus may trade at a dramatically different price to a £10,000 lot. Online brokers will typically attempt to execute the trade through their usual RSP (retail service provider) whilst a more old-school broker will be able to use his market contacts to your advantage. This can make a big difference. A switched-on broker that spends his time searching through offers and inventory can identify odd-lots that are up for sale, and in a market with very limited transparency and erratic liquidity, the difference in price can be several percent (rather than basis points), or even tens of percent.

Broker criteria

If you are serious about dealing in distressed and illiquid debt, you will need a broker who can provide the following:

1. **Multi-currency dealing and custody facilities**

   As mentioned earlier, distressed and illiquid bond investors will need to cast their net beyond the shores of the UK. The USD and Euro are the main currencies for bond issuance but opportunities this decade have been seen in local currency denominated debt such as the Russian Rouble and the Icelandic Krona.

2. **Euroclear settlement (an absolute must) plus UK and US domestic custody (DTC)**

   Many conventional UK stockbrokers only offer certificated or Crest settlement and custody and will be left scratching their heads with astonishment if you suggest buying anything slightly outside these facilities. Investors will either need a broker that can offer flexible custody services as part of the account or an independent custodian service. The latter is only likely to be commercially viable for larger accounts.

3. **Knowledge**

   As a private investor, there is only so much information, analysis and flow that you will be able to see. A good broker will be plugged in to the dealing desks at the major investment banks. He or she will also be able to see what other investors in the market are focusing on and reflect this "colour" back to you. A good advisory broker will also have ideas of his own to run past you.

4. **Access to prospectuses**

   You will need to be intimately acquainted with the bonds that you are considering buying. The best way to do this is by reading the prospectus of the original issue. These are sometimes available from the IR section of company websites. Users of the Bloomberg Terminal are also able to read and download numerous issue documents.

For a list of brokers offering execution and advisory services in bonds to UK investors, see the appendix.

Investment considerations

Before embarking on an adventure in the world of high-yield debt, it is worth pausing to consider a few of the more quirky aspects of this asset class:

Transparency and liquidity

When the solids hit the fan, the first thing to go is transparency. Bonds in the affected sector will virtually cease to trade and market makers will be reluctant to quote prices. This situation has been improved somewhat over the last few years by the advent of the credit derivatives market and credit default swaps (CDS) which can provide a good snapshot of where the market is pricing the risk of a particular credit. CDS levels can be hard to access for the private investor, although a limited amount of data is now starting to flow through to free-access websites and the financial press.

The constraints of the market are such that a trading approach is not viable. By all means take profits on positions that show healthy gains, but attempting to hop in and out of the market on small price variations will not benefit a high yield portfolio.

CDS specialist, CMA Quotevision, provides an excellent free email update on movers in this market which you can sign up to on their website at **www.cmavision.com**.

The inverse yield curve – getting more bang for your buck

Longer-dated bonds yield more than short-dated bonds; right? Not in the wacky world of high yield. In normal market conditions, with a positive or even flat curve, it is reasonable to expect investors to charge a premium for the incremental risk of lending longer – hence a positive credit curve. Curiously, the opposite is true in distressed debt. Longer dated bonds have lower prices and thus offer superior gearing to the recovery – hence giving more bang for your buck. As a result, demand is slightly greater for these long-dated bonds and an inverse yield curve will set up.

Here is an illustration of this effect from the General Electric sterling credit curve in October 2008. At the time, the issue had a triple-A rating but was widely considered to be at risk from the contagion of the global financial industry. Given the nature of these bonds, one might expect GE's debt to trade perhaps a 50 to100bp wider than US treasuries. However, as a glance at the low price and high yields show, our once triple-A giant was trading as junk, with YTMs of 10% and up. Even more alarmingly, the GE yield curve had inverted. The short-dated 2011 bond was yielding more than the long-dated 2028.

Table 13.2: General Electric sterling yield curve

Bond	Life	Price	YTM
GE 4.75% March 2011	3 yr	87	11%
GE 5.625% March 2014	6 yr	79	10%
GE 6.75% Aug 2018	10yr	80	9.8%
GE 5.25% Dec 2028	20yr	62	9.2%

Sell or hold – consider your exit

Generally, when one buys an asset, shares, real estate or bonds, it is good to know that it can be resold. Investors will, quite rightly, pay a premium for liquidity. Such things cannot be assumed in illiquid bonds, but I venture the opinion that it matters less in this environment. If an asset is throwing off 10, 11 or 15% per annum, your original capital will be returned via income in just a few years and the bonds can simply be held until maturity. In this important aspect, the bond market is greatly superior to the equity market where investors are reliant on the future market price of the instrument (a factor Donald Rumsfeld would categorise as a "known unknown") in order to realise their investment.

Undated issues are also a strong possibility if the yield is high enough to view the asset as a keeper, but consider both the likelihood of securing an eventual sale/realisation, the transaction costs of doing so and your own future needs for realising the investment.

Some types of trades

Some investors will simply take the approach of buying the highest yielding bond on the list. However, there are several distinctive types of trade that might be entered into – each with its own merits. In this section we will at a few them:

1. overreaction to bad news

2. yield – and plenty of it

3. calls and corporate events

4. takeovers

5. it's going bust – but not just yet

6. high-yielding currency plays

7. odd-lots and oddities

8. busted bonds

9. no-premium convertibles

10. selling short

1. Overreaction to bad news

The classic opportunity. As discussed earlier, valuation undershoot quickly sets in. Take a look at BP bonds (chart below) after the Gulf of Mexico oil rig disaster. The event was an expensive ecological nightmare with possibly an over-strong response from a showboating US president. But was the US government really planning to drive the company into liquidation? Even if it did, BP has an awful lot of assets! Keep an eye open for such knee-jerk sell-offs.

Chart 13.3: reaction of BP 4% 2014 bond to Gulf of Mexico disaster

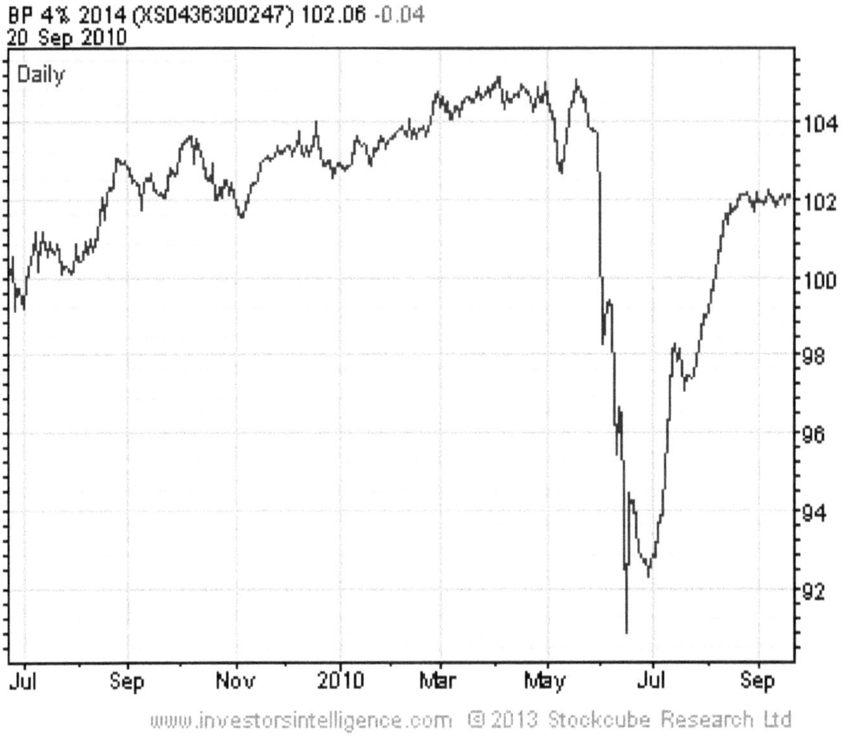
BP 4% 2014 (XS0436300247) 102.06 -0.04
20 Sep 2010
Daily
104
102
100
98
96
94
92
Jul
Sep
Nov
2010
Mar
May
Jul
Sep
www.investorsintelligence.com © 2013 Stockcube Research Ltd

2. Yield – and plenty of it

When a bond is trading at a very distressed level, but continuing to service its coupon. Perhaps a prime example of this is Equitable Life bonds in the first few years of the millennium. The mutually-owned life insurer was in bad shape, being unable to meet the unhedged liabilities of the guaranteed annuity policies (GAR) it had unwisely issued in the previous three decades. In hindsight, this was a fairly basic error, which makes one wonder what actuaries actually do for a living. However, there was no easy solution and the members were effectively reduced to a game of beggar-they-neighbour, with holders of the GAR attempting to sue the society and the bulk of the other policy holders suffering a haircut on their savings.

Equitable life had a bond issue outstanding at the time – the Equitable Life 8% subordinated perpetual. By 2002 the issue was trading at around 25p in the pound. Anyone you asked at the time would tell you that Equitable Life was bust – and this was technically true, but the important point was that the zombie-like mutual was continuing to service its debt. To have ceased to do so would have made matters even worse. At 25p, the gearing effect on this fairly high coupon issue was phenomenal. A £10,000 investment would purchase £40,000 nominal of bonds – paying £3,200 in coupons each year.

By 2005, the bond was trading at 98p in the pound. How did it all end? Equitable Life was wound-up, sold off and generally torn to pieces. The bond was redeemed at par in 2007.

3. Calls and corporate events

Bonds will be called by their issuer on a commercial basis. If the company can arrange cheaper funding elsewhere, it will do so. Thus, investors value bonds on a worst case basis. Bonds trading above par are assumed to be likely to be called, bonds trading below par are assumed to run to maturity. However, in certain cases, bonds may be called as part of the company's program of investor relation programs – if there is an expectation on the part of the investor that the issue will be called, the company may feel that it is in its best interests to do so, even if it does not make immediate commercial sense. Japanese issuers have a reputation for upholding their commercial honour in this manner, as do frequent issuers such as banks (this generally happens within the subordinated sector). This behaviour can create an opportunity for switched-on investors who can purchase below-par bonds trading on the market on a yield-to-maturity basis that have a strong likelihood of a premature redemption. The buyer will then be able to benefit from a rapid price appreciation as and when the call is exercised.

4. Takeovers

The prospect of a leveraged takeover can put the fear of God into most bond holders.

Why?

Such bids, particularly those from private equity load up the target company's balance sheet and are extremely detrimental for the credit. Investors head for the hills and, as usual, spreads explode. However, private investors can afford the luxury of objectivity. A good example of this was Phillip Green's proposed bid for Marks & Spencer in the middle of the 2000s (see following chart). The deal would have dropped about £10 billion of new debt onto the balance sheet of the then-struggling retailer, so the market's reaction was understandable. But if the takeover had gone through, would a highly-experienced and competent retailer such as Phillip Green have driven M&S into bankruptcy over the ten-year life of the bond? I would suggest that that is an extremely unlikely scenario. The bond, then offering a yield of around 8.5% in 2004, was excellent value.

Chart 13.4: M&S 5.625% 2014

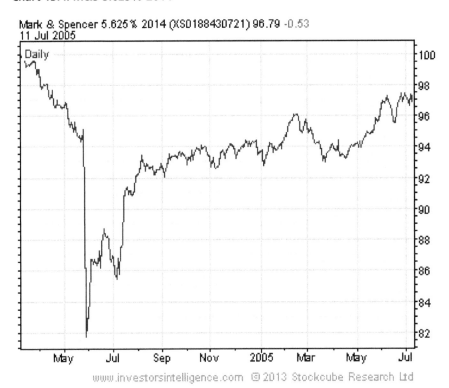

Mark & Spencer 5.625% 2014 (XS0188430721) 96.79 -0.53
11 Jul 2005

www.investorsintelligence.com © 2013 Stockcube Research Ltd

5. It's going bust – but not just yet

In the 1990s the telecom industry embarked on an unprecedented wave of fund raising. Spurred on by the white-heat of the technology, media and telecommunication revolution and the phenomenal growth of networked computers and mobile phones, the telco companies issued bond after bond. Much of this was to fund the required infrastructure, but rather less welcome was the requirement to pay unbelievable sums for the new 3G licences to the

UK and European governments. This was probably the greatest single tax cheque ever written in history; the auction of the UK licence alone raised the sum of £22 billion. Much of the tax revenue was then raised by bond issues, many of which are still with us today.

Somewhere towards the lower quartile of this sector was the mid-sized, fixed-line player Colt Telecom. As with many companies in the sector, its business revenue was reliant on fast-growing, top-line revenues. But, in the early years of the new century, this growth was not coming through, or at least not fast enough. The share price plunged from a heady £12 on the eve of the millennium to below a pound in 2002.

The company also had outstanding debt, and general opinion at the time was that the company would struggle to refinance. Indeed, forward projections showed that hiatus would occur later in the decade. In other words, popular opinion was that the company would go bust. Such opinions are music to the ears of distressed debt traders, creating the negative investor sentiment that produces rich opportunities. What was interesting about Colt was that the maturity profile of its debt was staggered towards the end of the decade. A fund I advised was able to pick up DM-denominated Colt convertibles with a 2005 maturity for around 55 cents in the Euro. The moral is – who cares about the disaster if it's after the redemption date! I am glad to say Colt Telecom went on to make a full recovery.

6. High-yielding currency plays

High yielding bonds denominated in foreign currencies often hit the headlines in the general financial media. Double-digit yields sound great, particularly on sovereign credits.

There are two things going on at once here: the bond's price action and the currency moves. The latter is often more important than the former. Get it right and you get a double benefit – for instance, a trader buying the Icelandic T-note (chart below) in November 2008 would have seen a 25 point gain in the bond and an appreciation in the Icelandic Krona against the Euro from ISK180 to around ISK98.

Opportunities can also be found in countries with strong export-driven economic growth – these areas can have the winning combo of firm rates and appreciating currencies.

Chart 13.5: Iceland T-note 7.25%

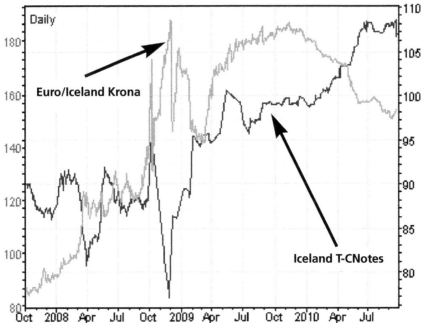

7. Odd-lots and oddities

Small scraps of bonds often end up on trader's books. These positions become aged and the dealer will be under pressure from his managers to dispose of them, particularly at the end of the financial year, and it is possible to pick up bargains from time to time. It is also possible to buy rump positions in bonds, debentures and other income bearing securities that have been partially redeemed, leaving perhaps just a few hundreds of thousands still in issue. The liquidity (and transparency) of such instruments will be such that most fund managers will not get involved, and thus buyers will be scarce. The key point to remember here is that you may be able to negotiate to buy such odd-lot assets cheaply, but you will be forced to take a correspondingly low price if you need to sell them. Positions such as these need to be bought and held for the yield alone.

8. Busted bonds

It is possible to make money buying the debt of bankrupt companies. Here the bet is that the unwinding process will unlock the value of the assets and that the bondholders, as senior creditors, will benefit. This can work, an example being the bankruptcy of British Energy in 2002-04. As senior creditors, debt and bondholders received the lion's share (97%) of the new equity during the re-financing process and emerged as the new owners of the company, a situation that proved advantageous as the new company quickly moved back into profit, boosted by rising energy prices.

But, such bets are not my favourite play on the market: the asset throws off no cash in the short term and the unwinding process can be lengthy – sometimes years.

9. No-premium convertibles

Convertible bonds are typically bought by equity-focused investors. When the underlying share price drops away, so does the natural market for these instruments. The sector is worth keeping an eye on for bargains on conventional yield/value basis.

10. Selling short

All the techniques covered in this chapter involve long-only plays on the market. It would seem reasonable to assume that short-sales might also be profitably traded in distressed debt at certain points of the cycle. I would caution against this. Private investors or smaller institutions will find it difficult to borrow stock or effectively short a bond other than by a simple sale without delivery – a trade that most brokers will not permit. Also, shorting a high-yield bond means that you will effectively be responsible for paying the coupon – a high cost of funding. Finally, the poor liquidity of such instruments means that it may prove difficult to cover back the short. I would therefore recommend that the distressed debt game is one to be played from the long side only.

Putting a high yield portfolio together

Clearly, diversification is a must for any type of higher-risk portfolio. When running equity portfolios, many high-performance fund managers prefer tight portfolios, the rationale being that the greater the number of stocks, the more your performance will tend to track the general market.

This is less of an issue with bond portfolios – our portfolios are driven largely by locking in yield and less by market beta. A high yield portfolio can hold numerous positions without drag on performance, provided each position is sufficiently high yielding. Indeed, subsequent price performance of the assets may be less of an issue providing the income is sufficient. I would suggest that ten positions should be a minimum for a portfolio of this type.

A ladder structure (see chapter 16) is a good start for the portfolio. On top of this, attempt to diversify both by sector and trade type (see above). The high yield investor will naturally be drawn to USD and EUR denominated assets, as these currencies see the greatest level of issuance, and therefore currency exposure should be monitored. However, the higher the yield the less important this factor becomes.

Size and scalability

In portfolios of this nature, which generally rely on the identification and purchase of unloved, non-transparent and illiquid issues, the size of the portfolio will be a key issue. Very large portfolios will not work. Trying to manoeuvre a billion or so in and out of scrappy will-o-the wisp bids and offers would be impractical. Conversely, very small portfolios will also struggle. The majority of bonds are now issued with £50,000 or £100,000 minimum dealing sizes. Even allowing for the probability of discounted prices (the average high yielder or distressed bond will trade below par), a wide-ranging portfolio constructed from bonds sourced from the institutional market will require a sum of half a million pounds or so, assuming a sensible level of 10x diversification is to be maintained.

Perhaps the ideal size for a truly diverse and international high yield bond portfolios lies somewhere between £100,000 and a few million. Not all investors will have funds of this scale, although it may be worth considering banding together to form an investment club, a well-known and sometimes socially rewarding form of collective investment. The ProShare website offers some useful advice on setting up such a scheme.

Can a high yield portfolio be run on a smaller scale?

Yes, but with some reservations. There is an active market in sterling-denominated securities, such as PIBs, preference shares and some of the newly created CoCo's and ECNs (such as the complex family of Lloyds bank issues). In addition to this, conventional retail-targeted bonds with low minimum dealing size (typically, £1,000) do experience sharp sell-offs from time to time. The example of Marks & Spencer 5.625% 2014 shown earlier in this chapter is a case in point. On this basis, a £50,000 to £100,000 portfolio will be perfectly viable, a sum that is well within the reach of many investors with a couple of decades of ISA and SIPP saving under their belt.

Of course, the selection, availability and prices of distressed and high-yield bonds will vary from year to year, But at the time of writing, looking through the markets for bonds available in retail size and offering high yields, throws out the following candidates:

- Enterprise Inns 6.5% 2018, trading at 73 to give a yield of 10.5% YTM. A struggling pub operator, but bond holders benefit from a charge on the company's real estate.

- Bank of Ireland 13.375% PIBS. Circa 40p with a running yield of around 30%. Originally a Bristol and West BS issue, but now part of the Bank of Ireland and subject to ongoing legal battles. However, the security continues to pay its chunky coupon.

- Societe Generalle 5.4% 2018. At 70p in the pound offers a YTM of 12%. An unloved subordinated bank debt.

The distressed debt of the fringe European government bond markets may also be a possibility.

However, such a portfolio will be limited in terms of the selection and availability of assets and may become unduly concentrated in the debt of subordinated UK financials.

Chapter 14
Bond funds

As I discuss later in this book successful fixed income investors build portfolios, rather than simply buying one or more bonds as part of a random selection of assets. I have also covered the barriers presented to private investors by such matters as large minimum dealing size. Given these factors, one might expect bond funds to provide the obvious solution. However, I have some concerns with investing through vehicles of this nature.

Charges

The first reservation that I have regards charges. Headline interest rates and bond yields have been declining since the beginning of the 1980s and the yield offered on most bonds, government and corporate alike, is in the low single-digits. However, many bond funds charge fees that are perhaps more suited to the inflationary 1970s than the current market environment. On top of this may be an upfront charge of between 1% and 5% (although many discount brokers will enable investors to circumvent this obstacle, which is primarily intended as a payment mechanism for the advisor or broker).

Using the handy **www.morningstar.co.uk** website to sort and rank UK bond funds produces some interesting results. Eight funds receive a five-star rating. I have selected three from well-known providers along with some key facts.

Table 14.1: three sample bond funds

Fund	Assets under man (£m)	TER	5yr performance (annualised)	12-month yield
M&G Gilt & Fixed income	673	0.91%	4.3%	2.8%
Legal & General Gilt Index	842	0.23%	3.8%	3.9%
Allianz Pimco Gilt	656	0.53%	4.9%	2.9%

Note, the Total Expense Ratio (TER) which ranges from 0.23% to 0.91%. Consider that the yield on the FTSE Gilt All Stock Index is 3.7% and that the yield on gilts is perhaps 2% on average. That means that in many cases the TER will be taking a good chunk of the long-term return; in the case of the M&G fund, nearly half.

I have no reason to doubt that the managers of these funds are extremely skilled – but in some cases they, and their customers, have quite a headwind to deal with in terms of charges!

Moving on from the fairly straightforward world of gilts. It is fair to say that a good fund manager should be able to add value in the arenas of high-yield, illiquid and emerging market debt and with hopefully higher totals returns available from these more riskier assets, the charges may make a less disproportionate hit on the total return. Again, charges will need to be watched and as with all fixed-income investments, a tax-efficient structure for holding the investments will be vital if compounding is to be achieved over the years.

The last few years have seen the type of hedge fund known as *market-neutral funds* move from purely the professional sphere to attract private investors as well. Such funds operate a mixture of long and short positions and are intended to provide a steady (low volatility) capital growth irrespective of the general market direction. Effectively, you are employing a skilled manager to trade a book for you – and the investor's return will be a reflection of that skill.

Market neutral funds (sometimes known as *absolute return*, and bundled under the general banner of *hedge funds*) are a useful diversification for a portfolio, but I would observe that they are not always successful in their aims, and that charges are generally high. Pick your manager carefully and try to identify those funds with consistent success over three years or more.

The market neutral approach is now also applied to bond funds and mixed or cross-asset funds. Certainly this is logical given the many complex arbitrage and trading strategies available within the bond markets. The £600 million Threadneedle Absolute Return Bond Fund, run by Quentin Fitzsimmons is one of the better known examples. I note that the annual charge on this fund is 1.25%. Similar funds are available from GLG and Barings. As with my observation with the equity-focused equivalent, be aware that you will be investing in the manager, not the market.

My second reservation about bond funds is more conceptual than practical. If you buy a bond fund, the future behaviour of this fund in terms of coupons paid, market valuation and particularly the realisation of assets are unknown. A bond fund has no redemption date. Thus, one is largely dependent on the skills of the fund manager on maintaining what will be, broadly speaking, a constant duration set of assets. One could argue, that on this basis a bond fund is conceptually more akin to an equity – an unknown series of future cash flows. This is quite different to an individual bond, which has fixed coupons and repayments dates, or even a basket of bonds which will gradually redeem down to cash.

ETFs

Exchange Traded Funds (ETFs) are the fastest growing sector of the fund management industry. These instruments are of a straightforward nature and generally track a known index. In the case of equities, such indices are generally household names: the FTSE100 or the Dow Jones. In the case of bond indices, the theory is the same, although bond indices are a slightly more obscure area.

The basic theory of ETFs remains the same for equities and bonds alike – a low cost tracking vehicle that can be accessed via a stockbroking account; opening the door to self-directed investors. These types of funds usually track a capitalisation-weighted index. And fees are cheap, perhaps 0.2% on average.

Now, cap-weighted indices are a tried and true method of investing in the equity market – the better a stock performs, the higher the market cap and thus the more you buy for the portfolios.

But does this work for bonds?

I'm not so sure. Quoting M&G's Jim Leaviss in January 2009 from the company's excellent **www.bondvigilantes.com** website:

> Let me start by restating our opposition to index investing when it comes to corporate bonds (we would say that, wouldn't we). An equity index is an index of success – as the company prospers and its market capitalisation rises, its weighting in the index increases. Bond indices are buckets of failure. The more a company borrows, the greater its weighting in the bond index. If you follow a bond index, and a company within it doubles its leverage, making its failure more likely, you will have to increase your exposure to that company. Companies like Ford and General Motors were at one stage 23% of the European high yield market – today GM bonds trade at between 15 and 30 cents in the dollar. There is no more depressing sight in the world than a

bond fund manager rejoicing in the default of a company because he or she was "underweight" the benchmark. If you don't like a company, or even a whole sector, don't invest in it. The index issue might soon become very important for high yield investors, as bank bonds continue to tumble.

This problem can be very real for investors. One of the first sterling bond ETFs to be launched was the **iShares £ Corporate Bond ETF**. This ETF tracked the capitalisation-weighted Markit iBoxx £ Liquid Corporates Long-Dated Bond Index (SLXX). The problem with this index is that banks (after governments) are traditionally the biggest issuer in the bond markets. As a result, when the credit crunch hit the market, the fund took a major hit (as can be seen in the following chart). To make things worse, the index also had more than its fair share of subordinated paper.

Chart 14.1: iShares £ Corporate Bond ETF (2006-2010)

iShares Sterling Corporate Bond (SLXX) 119.67 -0.67   11 Nov 2010

www.investorsintelligence.com © 2013 Stockcube Research Ltd

It is interesting to compare the 5-year price history of this fund of average corporate bonds with the price history of what many people would describe as an average corporate bond within the sterling market – the **Marks & Spencer 5.625% March 2014**.

What happened next is the real difference. Looking at the M&S bond, we see that the price fully recovered after the 2008 crash. This was largely due to the instrument's fixed redemption date and price, drawing the bond's price ever towards par. Not so the bond ETF.

This is an extremely good example of my point that *a bond fund is quite a different animal from a bond*.

Chart 14.2: Marks & Spencer 5.625% March 2014 (2006-2010)

iShares subsequently launched the **iShares GBP Corporate Bond (ex Financials) ETF (ISXF)** which goes a good way to addressing the problems of imbalance from financials within the bond markets.

In conclusion, the growth of the ETF market (which still has some way to go) provides a useful selection of vehicles in the fixed income market, particularly for investors with a relatively small portfolio who require ready-made diversification.

The following list, which is by no means exhaustive, shows a selection, taken from the **www.investorsintelligence.com** website of popular ETFs. The list also includes money market funds and some trading-orientated swap and short ETFs.

The one week and year-to date performance (showing Jan –Nov 2011) gives an indication of the levels of volatility and price moments that might be experienced by an investor in such assets. These are typically somewhat lower than those seen on equity index ETFs.

Investors should be aware that some ETFS have European listing and some have US, whilst many are dual. This is largely a technical point but I have experienced inconvenience in the past due to some stockbrokers being unable to deal in US ETFs for regulatory reasons.

Table 14.2: selection of bond ETFs

Bloomberg Ticker	Name	Close	1 Week	YTD
XCRG	db x-trackers CURRENCY RETURNS ETF 3C	2834	-0.20%	-3.50%
XEO2	db x-trackers II - EONIA Total Return Index ET	11992	0.00%	0.00%
XGLE	db x-trackers II - iBoxx = Sovereigns Eurozone Total Return Index ETF	165.62	-0.80%	-0.40%
XBUT	db x-trackers II - IBOXX GILTS TOTAL RETURN INDEX ETF	23505	0.60%	9.30%
XBUI	db x-trackers II - IBOXX UK GILT INFLATION-LINKED TOTAL RETURN INDEX ETF	20346	0.80%	13.70%
XUGS	db x-trackers II UK GILTS SHORT DAILY ETF	11308	-0.50%	-12.60%
XGBP	db x-trackers Sterling Money Market ETF	18639.5	0.00%	0.30%
XUSD	db x-trackers US Dollar Money Market ETF	170.89	0.00%	0.00%
XTXC	dbx iTraxx Crossover TRI ETF	113.79	-1.00%	-5.30%
LQDE	iShares - iShares $ Corporate Bond	104.82	-1.80%	1.20%
ITPS	iShares $ TIPS	121.24	1.00%	11.80%
SEML	iShares Barclays Cap Emerging Market Local Govt Bond	58.885	-0.60%	%
IEAG	iShares Barclays Capital Euro Aggregate Bond	102.25	-1.00%	-0.80%
IEAC	iShares Barclays Capital Euro Corporate Bond	111.89	-1.10%	-1.50%
EEXF	iShares Barclays Capital Euro Corporate Bond ex-Financials	89.61	-0.60%	0.70%
EEX5	iShares Barclays Capital Euro Corporate Bond ex-Financials 1-5	89.055	-0.50%	0.40%
IEGZ	iShares Barclays Capital Euro Government Bond 10-15	119.355	-1.40%	-5.60%
IEGY	iShares Barclays Capital Euro Government Bond 5-7	132.095	-0.70%	2.10%
IEGA	iShares Barclays Capital Euro Treasury Bond	98.755	-0.90%	-1.20%
IBTS	iShares Dollar T Bond 1-3 Years	83.705	1.80%	-0.90%
IBCX	iShares Euro Corporate Bond	119.499	-1.10%	-0.70%
IBGL	iShares Euro Government Bond 15-30	127.62	-1.50%	-5.30%
IBGX	iShares Euro Government Bond 3-5	124.615	-0.70%	-2.10%
IBGM	iShares Euro Government Bond 7-10	141.29	-0.60%	3.70%
IBGS	iShares Euro Govt Bond 1-3 Years	114.58	-0.50%	-2.40%
IBCI	iShares Euro Inflation Linked Bond	143.29	-1.70%	-7.50%
IGLT	iShares FTSE UK Gilt All Stocks	11.63	0.60%	9.90%
INXG	iShares GBP Index Linked Gilt	13.075	0.70%	11.10%
IGLO	iShares III PLC – iShares Citigroup Global Government Bond	118.58	-0.60%	6.20%
SEMB	iShares JPMorgan $ Emerging Markets Bond	0084	-0.70%	-2.30%
SHYU	iShares Markit iBoxx $ High Yield Bond	65.445	0.70%	%
SCOV	iShares Markit iBoxx Euro Covered Bond	115.38	-1.50%	-0.40%
SLXX	iShares Sterling Corporate Bond	119.445	-0.40%	2.90%
IBTM	iShares USD Treasury Bond 7-10	122.77	2.50%	9.30%
EMDL	SPDR Barclays Capital Emerging Markets Local Bond	60.305	0.10%	%
UKAG	SPDR Barclays Capital Sterling Aggregate Bond ETF	53.86	0.20%	%

Comment

A variety of different types of assets can be accessed through the above ETFs. Funds such as the iShares Sterling Corporate Bond or the iSharesIndex Linked Gilt give a useful "one click" solution to adding a basket of such securities to one's portfolio. ETFs also give a useful conduit into overseas bond markets, but investors should be aware that where the underlying assets (such as US Treasuries) are denominated in a non-sterling currency, FX volatility may be a major factor, and indeed be greater than any price movements in the underlying bond.

Finally, some ETFs such as the dbx iTraxx Crossover TRI ETF track specialist credit indices and may perform in a manner that is quite different from a conventional bond fund. With ETFs, as with all things, my view is simpler is better. More on that point below.

ETF structure

Another point to consider is the structure of the ETF. Many ETFs operate by simply buying the constituents of the index that they track. A slightly less zealous version of this technique is to buy a representative sample of the underlying index, and this is the approach taken by the popular iShares SLXX mentioned above. These types of ETFs are generally known as *physical* ETFs.

Other ETF providers use a swap-based approach. These are sometimes known as *synthetic* ETFs. Here the ETF provider parks the cash from investors in liquid assets (which may or may not be related to the securities in the target index). The provider then enters into a swap agreement in which the returns achieved from the assets held are exchanged for the theoretical returns that would have been achieved on an index-tracking basket. The Lyxor iBOXX Liquid Corporate Long Dated GBP ETF operates on such a principle.

So, synthetic or physicals?

The synthetic structure frequently has lower charges and tracks the underlying index with more accuracy, and thus there are arguments for the former. However, I aim for simplicity in all things and generally feel comfortable with the more straightforward physical structure.

Finally, I should point out that ETFs open the door for investors to the wonderful world of overseas bonds. That's fine, but be aware that currency movements may throw the sterling value around more than the price of the underlying assets. Get the currency right and you will not have much else to worry about – the opposite is also true!

PART III:
Practical Matters

Chapter 15
Dealing, custody and other mechanics

This chapter will look at the following four topics

1. How to deal

2. Platforms and markets

3. Custody and delivery

4. Choosing a broker

1. How to deal

Bond identification

First, identify your bond. The typical investor will determine which bond or bonds to buy according to appropriate criteria of maturity, credit quality and yield, it is important to correctly identify the security to prevent errors in dealing or other misunderstandings. When dealing in equities this process is usually fairly easy, and most equities will only have one class of share, and one symbol. Not so bonds – and each issuer may have several bonds trading in the market at any given time. It is therefore important to identify the right one, and to pass on accurate instructions to the broker.

Market convention describes bonds in the following way: **issuer, coupon, maturity**.

Thus, the Tesco bond illustrated below would be described as the "Tesco five point five percent 13th December 2019".

Ccy	Issuer	Coupon	Date	Price	Yield
GBP	Tesco Plc	5.5%	13 Dec 2019	105.5	4.72%

For the avoidance of doubt, use the bond's ISIN code (International Security Identification Number). The ISIN identifier is a 12-character alpha-numerical code unique to the security (this is in contrast to tickers, or symbols, which are related to the exchange and are not unique). ISIN codes are used by all market professionals when the avoidance of doubt is paramount.

Many domestic instruments use three, four or more digit LSE alphanumerics, and these are useful for exchange-traded instruments such as preference shares. For instance the Ecclesiastical Insurance 8.625% preference share trades on the LSE under the ticker ELLA. Prices for this instrument can easily be retrieved from popular websites such as ADVFN or interactive investor using these codes. These are often referred to as TDIM codes (previously known as EPIC codes). They are not greatly utilised by bond market professionals although many execution-only platforms rely on then.

Conventional bonds trading on the LSE ORB market will also have an alphanumeric TDIM identifier, generally four digits. The Provident Financial 7% 2020 bond can be found under the PFG7 ticker.

> **Tip**: bond maturities are often described in the US date format (i.e. MM/DD/YYYY). Watch out for this potential source of confusion. If in doubt, write the date as "Dec" not "12".

What will the final cost be?

The price that you see on the screen will typically be around 100, perhaps ranging in the 80 to 120 area. In this aspect bonds are very different from stocks, where prices range from a fraction of a penny for some AIM stocks up to $172,000 for just one share of Warren Buffet's Berkshire Hathaway.

The price is expressed as a percentage of the nominal value (i.e. the redemption value) of the bond. This is known as the *clean* price of the bonds and on this basis an investor buying bonds with a face value of £10,000 at a price of 99.30 will pay £9,930. However, we must also consider the factor of any accrued interest.

What is accrued interest?

If an investor buys a bond on its first day of issue, or just after the last coupon payment, the price seen on the screen will be the total price paid. However, when buying a bond half way through its coupon period (for instance 6 months after the last coupon payment for an annual bond), there will be an adjustment for the income that has accrued to the bond. This is standard practice in the bond market and strikes a fair balance between buyers and sellers, as well as neatly differentiating between cash flows from income and those from capital gains.

With the majority of non-gilt bonds, the basis of this accrued interest is calculated on a "30/360" basis. This assumes that each month has 30 days, and each year has 360 days.

Example

Let us assume that an investor buys £10,000 nominal of the Tesco 5.5% 13 Dec 2019 on the 13th January 2010.

The market price is 99.80 and the trade is for settlement in three days time.

£10,000 nominal of Tesco 5.5% 13 Dec 2019 at 99.80 = £9,980

The settlement date is the 16 January (trade date plus 3 business days, usually referred to as "T+3"). We need to calculate how much accrued interest that we should reimburse the seller for. The bond pays a coupon annually and the last payment was the 13 Dec 2009.

Period 13 Dec 09 through to 16 January 2010 = 33 days (on a 30/360 basis)

So, the accrued interest will equal 33/360 days times the annual coupon, times £10,000 nominal, or:

33/360 x 5.5/100 x £10,000 = £50.42

Thus, our contract note will show roughly the following:

£10,000 nominal of Tesco 5.5% Dec 2019 bonds at 99.80 = 9,980
Accrued interest = £50.42
Commission = £25
Total = £10,055.42

Note: The price shown on the screen will not include accrued interest and will be known as the *clean price*. The effective price that you pay, including any accrued is known as the *dirty price*.

Tip: there are a few bonds and bond-like instruments that trade dirty. Preference shares are quoted in this manner, and a few oddball bonds. It's always good to check.

Accrued interest for gilts

The Debt Management Office produces a detailed document on calculating the accrued interest on gilts which can be downloaded from the DMO website. This covers the subject in some detail, including the more complex calculations performed on both the old-style and new-style index-linked gilts.

At the risk of oversimplifying the subject, the main variations from the calculation process shown above are as follows:

1. Most gilts pay coupons twice a year (the majority of non gilts pay annual coupons). The exceptions to this rule are some of the undated bonds such as 2.5% Consuls.

2. The accrued interest is calculated on "actual/actual" basis, where the true number of calendar days is used to determine the apportionment of the coupon.

Selling your bonds

The best strategy for investing in bonds is typically that of buy and hold. Remember, unlike equities there is no need to sell in order to realise your investment; capital will be returned to you on maturity. In addition to several other advantages, this simple fact saves you one set of commission.

However, from time to time all investors will need to sell a bond in order to raise capital, or perhaps in order to switch into some more tempting investment opportunities elsewhere. In the event of this, bonds can be sold back into the market. The market price may be higher or lower than your purchase price and may impact the return that you receive on the investment.

When selling a bond, the accrued interest must also be factored into the calculation. In this case, any unpaid interest will be paid over from the new buyer to the seller, effectively the reverse of the scenario illustrated above.

Commissions

Brokers need to be paid for their services. Luckily for the share investors, execution prices in equities saw considerable deflationary pressure with the advent of the internet and online dealing. Fixed price commissions of £5, £8 or £12 a deal are now commonplace, making a purchase of a line of stock cheaper than a coffee and a sandwich for many investors.

This deflationary pressure has largely been brought about by the development of STP (straight-through processing). A customer can see an offer on the broker's website, click to buy the stock and have his order instantly routed through to the market maker, who guarantees good execution whilst the price is live (generally a rolling 15 second window).

To date, bond execution in the UK has lagged this model. The Bondscape platform provides live executable quotes sourced from competing market makers, primarily Barclays & Winterflood, as does the new LSE ORB platform. There are also many peer-to-peer quote systems streamed through Bloomberg etc with some newcomers including Evolution and Shore Capital specifically targeting the private investor flows from the brokers. However, with the market fragmented, most brokers use a dealer to source the best bid and offer, often using the tried and tested method of telephone dealing. This means that the cost is likely to be higher, and many brokers charge accordingly, with bond commissions often set at a minimum of £40 or thereabouts.

Commission costs need to be factored in, and the size of the deal is a variable. For a £2,000 deal, £40 commission is 2% – not far off what a unit trust might charge upfront. This may be acceptable on a bond that is held for many years, but a disaster on short-dated instruments.

On a £10,000 deal, £40 amounts to 0.4% as a one-off cost. Not great, but manageable. The moral of the story is to keep a close eye on costs.

Tip: buy bonds as new issues. The broker will often be paid a distribution fee by the selling group (typically 0.25 to 0.5%) and will not charge commission on the other side. If the bonds are held to redemption – no commission will be payable over the whole holding period. No wonder stockbrokers don't like bonds!

Wide bid-offer spreads

One of the most frequent complaints is that bid-offer spreads for private investors dealing in bonds are too wide.

This is broadly speaking true, although it is not universally the case. Gilts will generally be fine with bid-offer spreads as low as 0.05 points (e.g.111.15-111.20) for the main benchmarks. Undated issues are more tricky, and here the bid-offer spread can be 2-3 points (for example War Loans 85-88).

The situation in corporate bonds is very varied. A liquid bond may trade on a quarter-point spread (for instance 99.25 to 99.50 in retail size, or as wide as two or three points). Market makers on the recently issued retail bonds on the LSE ORB aim to quote 1% bid-offer spread (98-99), and competition between multiple market makers may bring the touch in to perhaps 0.5%. However, the situation will vary from day to day.

Some of the less liquid PIBS and subordinated bonds may trade on a ten-point spread – a situation that is likely to nullify any advantage of owning the security if taken at face value.

The bond market is quite unlike the equity market. In equities, small-sized tickets can generally be dealt in on tight spreads, but this spread may move out considerably when the buyer has several million to invest.

In the bond market there is generally an efficient market operating in investment grade credits in commercial size (£10 million and up), but this tight picture may actually deteriorate for the man who wishes to trade a £10,000 ticket.

Tips for keeping down dealing costs

Clearly, input price is everything for a bond portfolio, although I would suggest that secondary market bids are less important, given that much of the portfolio will be held until redemption. Here are some tips for keeping down dealing costs:

1. Buy bonds as new issues – you will also save commission costs.

2. Hold to redemption when possible (no sale costs).

3. Negotiate – prices are not set in stone.

4. Use a good broker – whilst individual bid/offer spreads may be wide, there will be considerable pricing differentials between market makers, making the "touch" or composite price either tight, flat (or better).

5. Work limit orders. I have mentioned the ten-point spread seen in some PIBS, however I have been able to purchase such instruments close to the bid side of the price by using a little patience.

Settlement

The back end of any commercial process is vital. Without the mechanisms of buying, selling, transferring ownership and custody, and discussion of the value of securities and investment planning are nothing more than academic theory.

Good bond practitioners should be familiar with these systems.

Reconcile your statements

A very basic practice, but important for all investments. People make mistakes, and the application of Murphy's Law generally means that these mistakes will not be in your favour. When dealing and investing in bonds, check the following:

1. Basic check – confirm that you have the right instruments in your account.

2. Coupon payments – check that your coupon has been paid, and that no withholding tax has been applied.

3. Purchase – check that the accrued has been calculated properly and that you have not been charged any unnecessary stamp tax.

4. Sales – check that you have received the accrued interest.

2. Platforms and markets

The dematerialized bond market

We have already touched upon the decentralised nature of the fixed income markets. Sadly there is no longer a splendid building in which top-hatted brokers conduct their business.

From the perspective of the UK investor, it is likely that he or she will be dealing through a stockbroker, who in turn will have access to a number of relationships with investment banks.

It is these peer-to-peer relationships that truly form the bond markets. Investment banks and brokers will send out emails before the market opens with indicated levels for bonds. Over the course of the day these levels will be updated with the information available on various systems (generally with restricted access). Probably the most well-known of these systems is Bloomberg and in some, but not all, cases prices are live and executable. Good brokers will need to maintain a number of relationships in order to get good price discovery and executions.

Typically, the levels quoted are simply estimates of where the market makers believe they will be able to bid or offer the bond. The prices will often be expressed as a spread over treasuries or the swap rate. One can not always deal on the indicated price, and execution in the bond market remains somewhat of an art form with deals conducted both on the telephone and via electronic systems.

The table shows a typical sample of indications from a market maker:

Table 15.1: sample bond prices from a market maker

Security	Bid/ask Spr	Bench	ZSP		Px	Mdy
AALLN 6 18	157/147	UKT 5 18	136/126		111.84-112.48	Baa1
ABIBB 6½ 17	143/133	UKT 4 16	98/87		111.70-112.29	Baa1
ABIBB 9¾ 24	135/125	UKT 5 25	152/142		138.69-139.88	Baa1
AKZANA 8 16	134/124	UKT 4 16	116/106		117.08-117.57	Baa1
AZN 5¾ 31	79/69	UKT 4¼ 32	98/88		106.41-107.76	A1
BALN 10¾ 14	188/168	UKT 5 14	144/125		122.08-122.84	Baa2
BASGR 5 17	117/107	UKT 4 16	75/65		109.56-110.10	A1
BAYNGR 5 18	120/110	UKT 5 18	95/86		106.88-107.48	A3
BGGRP 5 17	145/135	UKT 4 16	88/79		104.52-105.09	A2
BGGRP 5 25	111/101	UKT 5 25	112/102		98.15-99.13	A2
BIRMIN 6¼ 21	255/205	UKT 4¾ 20	245/194		99.51-103.29	N.A.
BOUY 5½ 26	136/126	UKT 5 25	137/127		99.32-100.37	N.A.

Key

- *Security* – shows the Bloomberg ticker, coupon and maturity

- *Bid/ask Spr* – shows the yield spread over the benchmark gilt

- *Bench* – shows which gilts the bond is benchmarked over

- *ZSP* – The "Z Spread"; a more complex measure of spread over the curve, favoured by many market professionals

- *PX Price* – the actual price at the time of dispatch of the email

- *Mdy* – the Moody's rating

This process may seem to many investors to be over-complicated. Why not simply quote the price, as is done in equities or futures markets?

The reason is that there are many more bonds than there are equities, and any individual issue may not trade from day to day. Thus, the market maker will establish what he considers to be fair value for a given credit and "spread it up" over gilts.

For example, "Acme Motors trades at 50bp over gilts, therefore I [the trader] will pay 55bp over gilts for the 5% Oct 2020 issue and offer the same at 45bp over gilts". The trader may have several Acme Motors issues of different maturities on his books and he will adjust this spread accordingly with supply, demand and events.

To make things even more complicated, the whole basket of bonds will rise and fall with the ebb and flow of the underlying gilt market. Thus, the final dealing price on liquid bonds will be agreed at the point of trade. Illiquid and high-yield bonds tend to trade more like equities and are discussed in price terms. This is also the case for most ORB-traded retail bonds.

The screenshot (below) from **www.fixedincomeinvestor.co.uk** gives a good idea of how the yields of corporate bonds are distributed over the yield curve. The corporate bonds can be viewed as "floating" over the surface of the gilt yield curve, and as this surface rises, or changes in shape, the yields on corporate bonds will also rise and fall, subject to adjustment of supply and demand in the individual bonds.

Chart 15.1: Sterling corporate bond yield curve

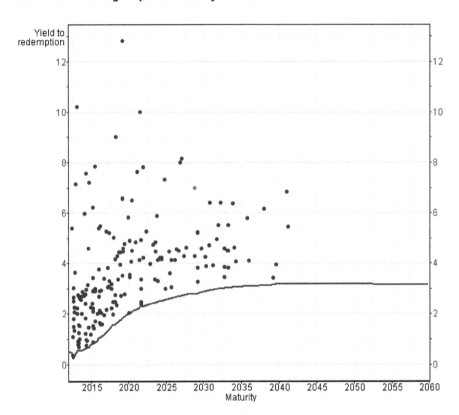

Key – the solid line represents the gilt yield curve. The dots show where the corporate bonds are positioned in yield terms relative to this yield curve.

For private investors in the UK, there is a move towards more transparent and centralised execution. The following platforms are coming to the fore.

Bondscape

The Bondscape platform was started in 1990 by Barclays Capital and Winterflood securities in order to offer private client stockbrokers and other smaller-sized operators in the bond markets a system to see competing quotes from the participating market makers, these being Winterfloods, Barcap and HSBC. The system (which is only open to brokers) offers execution in gilts and sterling corporate bonds, focusing on liquid GBP bonds and, importantly, those available in the smaller denominations favoured by private investors (most institutionally targeted bonds are now launched with minimum investment sizes of £50 or £100 thousand).

As of 2010 the system was turning over 94,000 trades a year with a value of £1.5 billion. This places the average ticket size for a private investor in the region of £15,000.

The universe of Bondscape GBP bonds as republished on **www.fixedincomeinvestor.co.uk** can be found in the appendix.

The LSE ORB

Launched in 2010, the London Stock Exchange's ORB (Order Book for Retail Bonds) is a new venture to build a retail-friendly, exchange-based market for bonds in the UK. I asked Michael Dyson, MD at Evolution Securities and a major player on this new market to outline how this works:

> "From the standpoint of the private investor, price-driven and market-maker systems have one intrinsic drawback, this being the degree or layers of intermediation. In a perfect world, investor A would be able to match his bargain against investor B and a fair price would be enjoyed by all, with little in the way of bid-offer spreads and commission to pay.
>
> Such peer-to-peer systems do exist, and private investors who have DMA (Direct Market Access) on SETS stocks on the LSE have been able to directly input their own bids and offers for some time.
>
> Of course, there are drawbacks to this system. If investors were wholly reliant on matching bargains with other investors, they might have to wait for some time. There is also the matter of size – seller A has 800 to go, buyer B only wants 750; how to match? For these and several other reasons, market-making remains a feature of most stock exchanges and execution platforms.
>
> Whilst equities have, for many years, been on a transparent and widely available platform, bonds have not. Other systems such as Bondscape.net went some way towards this but pre and post trade transparency is only partial and, importantly, the prices quoted are purely those produced by the member market makers (currently three).
>
> The ORB, however, provides firm bids, and firm offers, throughout the trading day and any LSE member firm can register as a market maker

or any member firm can add a specific bid or offer if the market maker quotes are not to their choosing. Once traded the price and size is reported immediately on publicly available screens.

This gives a number of options – firstly the home-based execution-only investor should be able to click and trade from home, exactly as they have been doing shares for many years. Secondly, through their stockbroker they can leave limit orders or challenge the market price by submitting their own buy or sell orders, perhaps between the screen bid/offer spread.

Alongside the ORB sits the RSP network. This is a system whereby market makers offer to improve on the best price available on the ORB. Therefore, where best execution is accepted as being the best bid or offer available on the order book – stockbrokers can achieve better than best execution by getting an RSP price improver. The RSP enables the market maker to offer or bid at the best possible price where they are particularly keen to clear a position.

The LSE ORB allows customers (investors) to see the bond market in one place and, additionally, all the info they need is available online. For instance, all issues admitted to ORB are backed by a full prospectus which can be read on the LSE website and are settleable in Crest and Euroclear.

For the investment adviser, managing client portfolios, or advising clients on bonds, the platform should afford a high level of critical information and confidence that previously had been hard to achieve and, frequently, directed investors toward unitised products which are very good for liquidity, risk diversification, and exposure to an asset class, but fail to give the fixed returns that are so useful as a financial planning tool.

The ORB platform is modelled on the successful electronic Italian government and corporate bond retail trading platform, MOT, operated by Borsa Italiana, part of the LSE Group. First launched in 1994 as DomesticMOT, offering Italian government and corporate bonds, it was followed, in 2000, by EuroMOT offering Eurobonds and ABS product. Annual turnover in Italy was in excess of €215 billion in 2010.

Importantly, all the components are now in place to grow a new issues market, specifically targeted at retail investors. This will encompass smaller bond denominations at the point of issue to encourage retail participation (currently often £50,000 minimum in accordance with the EU Directive) and again for comparison the MOT platform included over 360 corporate listings at the end of 2009."

A steady start

This is certainly a welcome development. However it is only through participation that a market thrives and becomes genuinely useful. At present, the LSE's ORB is at an early stage of the game.

It is worth bearing in mind that even with equities, the majority of the execution-only brokers do not deal directly with the exchange, but prefer to route their orders through RSPs (Retail Service Providers).

The next few years will be the test of the ORB. The flow of new issuance onto the platform is certainly very encouraging.

In time, it may also prove to be the perfect platform for higher yielding papers such as PIBS. Such instruments trade on a price basis and participants can simply put their orders into the market (e.g. "I am a seller of 10,000 Manchester Building Society 8% PIBS at 102"). This offer can then remain workable until a buyer comes along.

Arguably, the order-driven model is less suitable for on the run bonds – for instance a liquid high-quality corporate. Such bonds trade on a spread over gilts and are typically priced as such rather than simply being offered at price X.

The project still has some way to go, but anything that improves transparency, liquidity and access to the bond markets should be encouraged. Certainly, the ORB market is proving successful in attracting new issues on to the platform, and this bodes well for the future. The real break-through will occur when the brokers start inputting bids and offers directly into the markets, in the manner of DMA (direct market access) on SETS stocks. At this point, the liquidity and price picture will be self-feeding.

The screenshot shown below is from the ORB and reflects the bids, offers and underlying depth and size of the market in the Provident Financial 7% 2018 bond.

Figure 15.1: screenshot of ORB quote screen

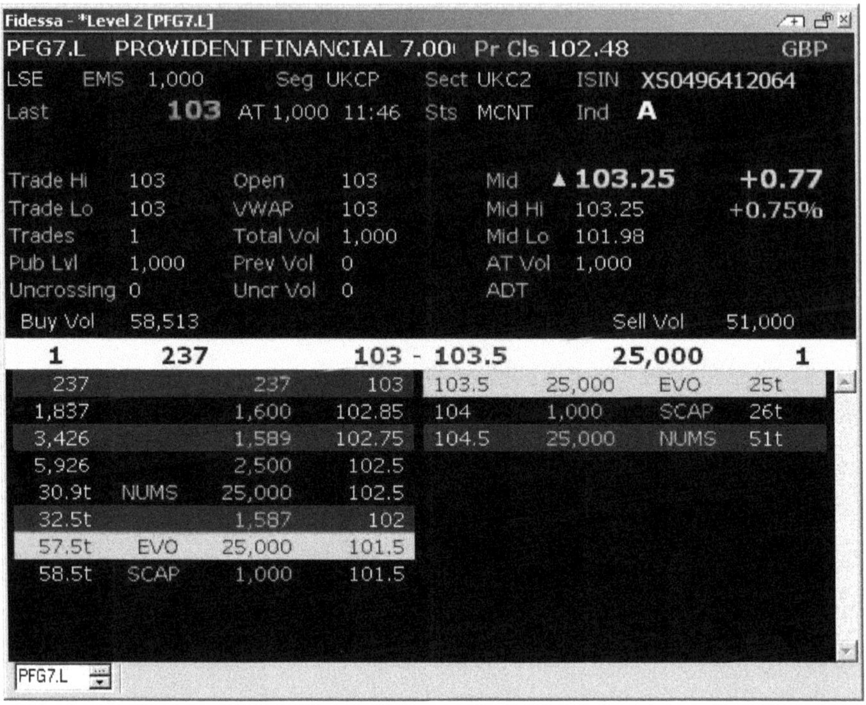

To clarify; the yellow strip shows the best bid & offer (103 bid and 103.5 offered). The bid works in just £237, whilst £25,000 is available on the offer. Below these bids and offers on the respective left and right hand columns one can see the depth of the market with substantial bids of up to 25,000 in place on the left column, albeit at slightly lower prices. A similar picture can be seen on the offer side with a larger offers of £25,000 from Numis at 104.5.

In this instance, the order-driven model is functioning well. In addition to the market maker quotes provided by Numis (NUMS), Evolution (EVO) and Shore Capital (SCAP), the unnamed bid entries on the left-hand side show broker orders pitching in to complete the price picture.

3. Custody and delivery

Hopefully, a good stockbroker should take care of all custody and delivery problems for you, but an informed investor will need to be aware of the basics.

The majority of bonds will settle via Euroclear (EC), and the ideal situation is to have a broker who is able to offer EC custody.

Often, the broker will sub-contract the custodian function to a bank or other organisation and as part of the due diligence process, it is worth checking who the custodian is.

Some of the execution-only brokers in the UK do not offer Euroclear settlement for bonds, but accept delivery through the domestic Crest system via Crest Depository Interests (CDIs). This system is adequate for most run-of-the mill purchases of bonds or gilts, although problems can sometimes be encountered with SDRT (see chapter on taxation). Recent issues admitted to the ORB market are usually settled via Crest.

More ambitious bond investors should seek a broker offering Euroclear and DTC settlement (the US Depository Trust Clearing Corporation) through a well-established custodian.

4. Choosing a broker

It would be easy to say that investors should choose the cheapest broker – however, the lowest commission charge is not necessarily the best value. When choosing a broker, consider the following:

1. Who am I dealing with? Is the broker well-capitalised or backed by a large parent? Whilst client money is invariably ring-fenced within broker accounts, it is always better to be dealing with someone who will still be around in a few years time.

2. Will this broker be able to offer me access to the bond markets? Try checking a couple of quotes to find out.

3. Will the broker be offering me advice or expertise? This may well be valuable.

4. Can the broker offer SIPP, ISA accounts etc?

5. Can the broker offer multi-currency accounts?

6. Custody and settlement (see above).

7. What are the charges? Add them up and compare.

It is worth bearing in mind that many investors utlise more than one broker; perhaps a low cost execution-only or "X-O" broker for trading simple listed instruments and a more sophisticated full service broker for dealing in more complex instruments such as illiquid bonds, or derivatives. Often it is also useful to open an additional account if dealing in overseas securities, with the US brokers offering highly competitive access to their domestic market.

The multi-broker approach also has the advantage of spreading one's assets across two or more counterparties. Whilst this creates more paperwork, it is sound practice, particularly if financial assets and the income thereof make up a large part of your portfolio.

Note: Brokers are often considered to have a true agency role when dealing for their customers. However, most private investors will also use their brokers as custodian, and at this point the relationship is blurred. Recent failures amongst brokers and in particular the complications in unwinding pooled custody of assets suggest that when push comes to shove, there is a degree of counterparty risk.

A list of brokers offering dealing and advisory services for private investors is published in the appendix.

Establishing value

I have covered the concepts of both duration (i.e interest rate related) and credit risk in earlier chapters, but as we work towards the next chapter (portfolio construction), it is worth recapping how we will identify value in individual bonds.

The most obvious method of identifying value is to buy the bond with the highest yield. At times, this approach has some merit. However, for a balanced portfolio consider the following:

1. Take a look at the yield curve. Where is the sweet spot in terms of yield. It may be that short bonds can be excluded due to very low yields, or long-dated maturities due to high volatility.

2. Having established some maturity guidelines, think about credit. Will the portfolio be AAA, high yield or a mixture? Within each credit group identify issuers that you like, and rule out those with which you are less comfortable.

Once you have identified a suitable bond or bonds, it's time to look at the relative value. The best tool is to compare the spread over gilts. This can be done simply by comparing the YTM of the bond with the YTM of a gilt of an equivalent maturity. You can use a yield calculator to do this but most dealers would use a function on the Bloomberg terminal called YAS, which offers a wide range of yield and value measures, both in terms of absolute value (yield to maturity) and relative value (spread to benchmark or curve).

The screenshot (below) shows the YAS page, which enables the dealer to input the market price and then make multiple yield and relative value calculations against gilts, swaps and other reference rates. See the key for more details.

Figure 15.2: screenshot of sample Bloomberg YAS page

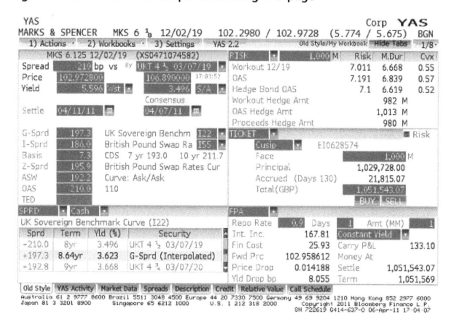

Some notes on the Bloomberg YAS screen:

- Price – market price (usually a composite from several quotations). Alternatively, manual input.

- Yield – YTM shown; 5.596%.

- Benchmark – the underlying gilt (a benchmark gilt of roughly the same maturity). The UKT4.5% 03/07/2019 is displayed towards the top of the left-hand half of the page.

- G-Sprd – shows yield margin over the gilt curve. The screen shows a value of 193 (i.e. 1.93%).

- Right hand side of screen – shows calculations for ticket writing.

So how much margin is enough?

Many novice investors assume that corporate bonds will yield considerably more than gilts. For instance, if a ten-year gilt yields 4%, they would expect the corporate bond to yield 8%. Unfortunately this is not generally the case. In the world of investment-grade bonds, where default is a rare event, the risk is efficiently priced. Very high quality bonds such as AAA-rated issues may yield only 20-30bp more than gilts. In 2011, the average non-government bond in the sterling market yielded roughly 70bp over gilts, although wider spreads can certainly be found, particularly in the post credit-crunch world.

As the chart below shows, this relationship will move around with investor confidence and economic conditions.

Chart 15.2: average corporate bond yields compared to gilts

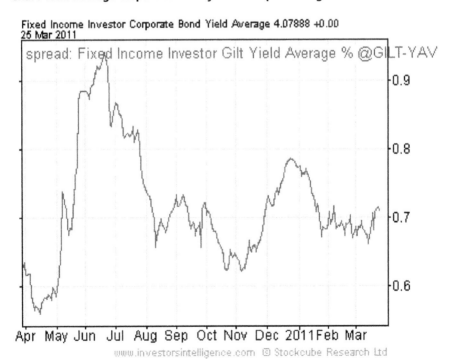

The above chart shows the relationship between the yield offered by sterling corporate bonds and the yield offered by gilts. The universe of corporate bonds is taken from the **www.fixedincomeinvestor.co.uk** website and is across all maturities.

The Y axis shows the incremental yield offered by corporate bonds (of all qualities and maturities) when compared to gilts. Note that the range is between 0.6% and 1%. This margin is perhaps less than one might expect, but consider that the corporate bond universe will contain a considerable number of issues from AAA rated organisations such as the EIB, whose yield will be fairly close to that seen on gilts.

Spread over gilts or spread over swaps?

Comparing corporate bond yields to those available on gilts is a logical process for benchmarking value. However, many professional bond dealers look at bond yields relative to the swap curve. A swap yield is the level at which banks and other credit worthy institutions exchange fixed rate for floating rate cash flows. Effectively the swap curve is a private sector forward interest rate curve whilst the gilt market is a public sector curve.

In many ways it is logical for investment firms to use the swaps curve for relative valuation because their cost of funding will be closely related to swap rates. However, in the interest of simplicity, most private investors will be better off using the spread over gilts.

Trend of spread

Establishing the relative value of a bond is one thing, but the next thing to consider is the trend of the credit spread. Is it getting better or worse? Whilst there is a case for bottom-fishing wide spreads, many investors prefer to buy improving credits. This is reasonably good sense, trends in financial markets tend to persist. The same rule of thumb is often seen in the equity markets where many investors prefer to buy a stock showing positive momentum, rather than one that is simply cheap.

Relative spreads are easy to plot over time – just compare the time series data of the yield with a gilt of roughly the same maturity.

The chart below shows a plot of the Roche 5.5% 2015 against the UK gilt 4.75% 2015.

Chart 15.3: trend of relative spread for Roche 5.5% 2015

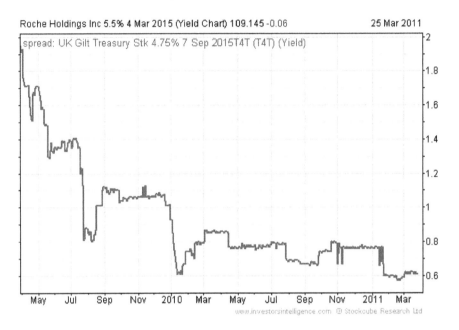

Note the initial tightening of the bond from Apr 2009 to Jan 2010, followed by range trading between 60bp and 80bp over gilts.

Finally, the cheapest bond on the list is not always the best performing. A liquid issue from a well-respected issuer can often outperform a smaller, higher-yielding bond from a second-rate name. Consider not only your own view of the investment, but that of others when assessing likely secondary market performance.

Chapter 16
Building a bond portfolio

The previous chapter covered dealing in individual bonds, but most investors will look to build up a portfolio. A well-structured portfolio holds many advantages over a single security holding, offering:

1. assets selected to present a suitable level of potential risk & reward for the investor,

2. diversification across sectors and classes,

3. regular income flows, and

4. typically, lower volatility than its individual components.

Before embarking on the construction of a bond portfolio, an investor should consider what he or she wishes to achieve, and indeed, what he wishes to avoid! The issues an investor must consider are:

1. **Risk**

   In an uncertain economic environment, investors who require security of the return of capital should stick to gilts and bonds issued by high-quality sovereigns and their agencies (such as the World Bank and the European Investment Bank). More risk-positive investors may wish to lock in the higher yields available from bank, corporate and other bonds.

2. **Time horizon**

   How long will the money be invested? If the funds are required for a specific purpose, such as childrens' school fees, the maturities of the holdings can be tailored to these dates. Alternatively, retirees may wish to lock in income for the years to come and will swing their portfolio towards longer-dated issues.

3. **Income**

   Is the portfolio for income, or will the cash flows be re-invested? Suitable selections should be made to ensure both the amount and the periodicity of the coupon payments (typically annual for corporate bonds, semi-annual for gilts).

4. **Tax**

   Bond portfolios held within ISAs or SIPPs are generally free of taxes, but investors should review their own personal situation.

This chapter will look at the following four topics:

1. Diversification

2. Ladder structure

3. When to sell

4. Two sample portfolios

1. Diversification

Diversification is a Good Thing. A diversified portfolio will spread the risk across a number of bonds enabling the investor to enjoy his return without worrying about losing his money in one isolated incident (which are many and increasing in nature, including earthquakes, industrial disaster, punitive legal action etc etc).

When building a gilt portfolio, or a portfolio of very high-quality bonds, the need for diversification is somewhat diminished. Given the absolute risk of default in such bonds is low, a reasonable portfolio of gilts can be constructed with just two or three holdings.

When buying corporate bonds, there is obviously a need to diversify across a range of different industries. This is not always easy. Bond markets, particularly the sterling markets, tend to have a high degree of issuance from the financial sector, particularly banks. Here's the breakdown of the holdings of the iShares SLXX, an ETF which tracks the iBOXX GBP Liquid Bond Index.

Table 16.1: sector breakdown of the iShares iBoxx GBP Corporate [SLXX] (Mar 2011)

Sector	Weight %
Banking	38.98
Consumer Non Cyclical	16.04
Communications	10.23
Electric	7.26
Energy	7.18
Consumer Cyclical	5.34
Natural Gas	5.09
Foreign Agencies	3.95
Finance Companies	2.43
Insurance	2.01
Other Utility	1.50

Thus, it is sometimes hard to pick up the holding needed for true diversification across industry groups.

Diversification of bond portfolios, and the resulting effect, is somewhat different to that which is practiced in equities. We will deal with diversification by maturity in the next section, but first of all let's look at credit. I would offer the following observations:

1. Equity portfolios need to be tight (i.e. a small number of stocks) to perform well. A very broad portfolio will simply perform in line with the index. This is not the case in bonds where there are many more issues to pick from.

2. Bonds have fairly high correlation with each other. Most AA-rated bonds will rise and fall together (usually in line with gilts). Thus for true diversification, a selection of government bonds, investment grade and high-yield debt should be considered. The latter typically correlates with equity markets.

Costs

Too many small holdings will push up transaction costs (and will be difficult to monitor), thus a happy medium must be found

So how much is enough?

Ten positions is a fairly basic minimum for a credit portfolio. I'd probably aim to run most of my bond portfolios with between ten and twenty positions. With larger funds, greater diversification is possible. However, most bond fund mangers would draw the line at 100 positions. Above that number, it's hard to keep track.

A good rule of thumb is to scale by risk. Each position in senior investment grade positions can be perhaps 10% of a portfolio. For more risky or subordinated holdings, a 5% exposure per instrument is a more comfortable level.

2. Ladder structure

Perhaps the simplest form of bond portfolio construction would be a fixed-maturity basket. For an investor requiring return of capital in five years time, a selection of 5-year bonds can be purchased. The maturity and duration of this portfolio will roll down over time.

A more usual construction would be a rolling maturity portfolio. In such a portfolio no defined exit date is planned. Instead, the portfolio is intended to continue for many years with the proceeds of maturing short-end bonds re-invested into longer-dated bonds.

This is an excellent system, offering a degree of immunisation against future interest rate moves. For example, if a portfolio of ten bonds is so structured to have a maturity every year, and these proceeds are then re-invested into a new ten-year bond on each redemption, the portfolio will gradually average in to prevailing rates as they change over time.

The ladder structure is always my default setting for structuring a portfolio. It is worth mentioning another advantage; with holdings structured so that one position is maturing every year, the investor is assured of some liquidity coming back into the portfolio, even in adverse market circumstances where market bids may be thin or not available. As such, it is also a useful portfolio structure for high yield and illiquid debt.

The following table shows the structure of a ladder portfolio. Bonds at the shorter end will mature, creating cash. This money can then be re-invested into the longer end of the portfolio. The process then repeats every year.

Table 16.2: ladder structure of a rolling maturity portfolio

Portfolio
1 year maturity
2 years to maturity
3 years to maturity
4 years to maturity
5 years to maturity
6 years to maturity
7 years to maturity
8 years to maturity
9 years to maturity
New 10-year bond

Surfing the yield curve

One of the most powerful features of a bond is the effect of rolling down the curve. Consider this; bond markets generally exhibit positive yield curves. The market is priced to reflect the incremental risk of lending money for longer periods. This is perfectly logical, reflecting both the uncertainties of future levels of interest rates and/or inflation and the future unknowns of the issuer's credit quality.

The effect to holders of bonds is a positive one. An eight-year gilt yields 3.25% at the time of writing. Five-year gilts yield 2.5%. All things being equal, and assuming the shape of the yield curve remains broadly unchanged, a buyer of that eight-year bond will see the yield drop by 0.75% over a three-year holding period as the bond shortens and the market re-prices the security in line with its peers. Thus a notional 3.25 % coupon eight year bond issued at par will rise in price terms by 2.3% over the holding period.

Of course, there are many variables. By the time we get to three years down the road, shorter-term rates may well have risen (and a steep yield curve implies this probability). Nevertheless, the curve effect gives most portfolios a gentle following wind.

3. When to sell

In an ideal world, bond investors should not have to sell. They will simply hold the security until redemption, enjoying the coupon until realising their asset with a commission-free final payment. There will, of course, be times when it is advisable to sell, and here are a few suggestions:

1. When **relative value is negative**. Individual bonds are often subject to squeezes of one kind or another, and the price of individual bonds can become overvalued. When this happens, you may wish to switch into a similar (or the same) credit with a higher yield.

2. **Extension trades**. A portfolio will naturally get shorter as time rolls on. You may wish to sell short-term bonds and pick up yield further out on the curve.

3. **Events** – credit deterioration or other bad news. However, try not to panic. The vast majority of bonds pay out.

4. **Over-par**? Many investors like to take profits on bonds that are well over par in order to preserve capital (remember that they will roll down to par at redemption). This is perhaps more a psychological twitch than sound reasoning, but I have to admit I do it myself.

5. **Tax reasons**.

4. Two sample portfolios

This section takes a look some bond portfolios. The first is the Model Portfolio that I have run in conjunction with the **www.fixedincomeinvestor.co.uk** website for some years. This is a portfolio that will be fairly easy to replicate for most private investors, with 13 positions, the sizes of which are between £5,000 and £10,000. Such a portfolio could be easily operated within a SIPP or ISA structure. All of the bonds are relatively well-known UK names which can be traded through most UK stockbrokers.

The second portfolio shows the breakdown of a large professionally-run fund operated by Invesco. This multi-billion pound portfolio has a much greater diversification in terms of the number of holdings. It would not be practical for a private investor to replicate such a portfolio (the dealing costs would be prohibitive), but it is instructive to see the breakdown across industry types and credit ratings.

1. Model Bond Portfolio

The model portfolio from the **www.fixedincomeinvestor.co.uk** website as of March 2011.

The Model Bond Portfolio presented here is a roll-up portfolio aiming to generate capital growth through re-investment of income. The portfolio was launched with an initial sum of £100,00 in 2007.

Table 16.3: Model Bond Portfolio

Date of Purchase	Issue	Life (yrs)	Nominal	Purchase Price	Current Price	Value (£)
9 Jan 2008	Marks & Spencer 5.625% March 2014	3	10,000	95.82	105	10,500
16 Aug 2009	RBS "Royal Bond 5.3% 2015	4	100	100	101.2	10,120
7 Mar 2007	Segro 5.5% 20 June 2018	7	5,000	97.35	99	4,950
16 Aug 2010	Enterprise Inns 6.5% Dec 2018	7	6,000	83.5	90.5	5,430
04 Jan 2011	National Grid 2.983% 2018	7	7,000	144.71	145	10,150
04 Feb 2010	GKN 6.75% 2019	8	10,000	97.56	104	10,400
28 July 2010	RBS Royal Bond 5.1% 2020	9	5,000	96.03	91	4,550
06 May/19 Nov 2010	Goldman Sachs 5.5% Oct 2021	10	10,000	87.9	92	9,200
04 Nov 2010	RBS Inflation-Linked (3.9% min) 2022	11	5,000	100	92.4	4,620
20 Sept 2010	Yorkshire Building Society 13.5% 2025 CoCo	14	5,000	116	115	5,750
16 Sept/01 Dec 2010	Lloyds 6.5% Sept 2040	29	10,000	96.35	93.5	9,350
20 May 2010	Nat West 9% prefs (undated)	U/D	5,000	1.03	1.10	5,500
12 Dec 2010	Ecclesiastical 8.625% prefs	U/D	5,000	1.02	1.11	5,550

Table 16.4: Model Bond Portfolio valuation

Category	Amount (£)	Notes
Securities	96,070	Valuation of current holdings
Accrued	2,158	Interest accrual on above
Cash	24,738	Including interest & coupons received
Total	**122,966**	

Comments

The portfolio is very much a mixed portfolio. Whilst there is a basic ladder structure of short, medium and long dated bonds, there is also a fair exposure to undated subordinated bonds and preference shares. As such, the portfolio is somewhat of a hybrid, with investment-grade holdings combined with more speculative holdings.

From a risk point of view, I would categorise the portfolio as "medium". The inclusion of preference shares and CoCos lower the quality below that of a "pure" bond portfolio, although incremental yield is obtained by these positions.

Consider also that the portfolio holds over 50% in bank and financial-sector debt, a considerably overweight position compared to the 40% "neutral" weighting suggested by the IBOXX index in table 16.1.

The portfolio shows a fairly high cash element. At the time of this snapshot the cash was waiting to be invested in upcoming new issues, then in the subscription period.

A simple and unweighted calculation of the yield (using a guestimate for the index-linked component) gives an average YTM of 6.4% based on the valuation levels at that point in time.

2. Invesco Perpetual Corporate Bond Portfolio

A popular bond fund with a mixture of holdings. The stated aims of this fund are:

> The Invesco Perpetual Corporate Bond Fund aims to achieve a high level of overall return, with relative security of capital. It intends to invest primarily in fixed interest securities. In pursuing this objective, the fund managers may include investments that they consider appropriate which include transferable securities, money market instruments, warrants, collective investment schemes, deposits and other permitted investments and transactions as detailed in Appendix 2 of the most recent Full Prospectus, although the fund will not invest in any instrument which gives rise to a stamp duty liability.

The top ten issuers in the Invesco portfolio are listed in the table below.

Table 16.5: top 10 bond issuers (allocation percentage in brackets)

Issue	Wtg(%)
Lloyds Banking Group	9.04
Barclays Bank	4.10
RBS	3.27
Santander	3.21
GE	2.58
UK Treasury	1.76
HSBC	1.72
Citigroup	1.59
Nationwide	1.52
John Lewis	1.47

The total number of holdings in the portfolio is 417, with the top ten having a weighting of 30.3%.

The breakdown of the portfolio by credit risk can be seen in the following portfolio.

Table 16.6: Invesco Perpetual Corporate Bond Portfolio breakdown by credit rating

Rating	Wtg(%)
AAA	7.01
AA	2.73
A	21.6
BBB	43.9
BB	12.1
B	1.02
CCC	0.03
CC	0.13
C	1.95
Not-Rated (High Yield)	0.41
Not-Rated (Investment Grade)	6.24
Credit Default Swaps	0.08
Future	0.06
Equities	0.40
Cash	2.51

Comments

The large size of the £5.7 billion market leader means that a greater number of bonds can be held – hence better diversification than the **www.fixedincomeinvestor.co.uk** portfolio shown above, though to my mind 400-plus holdings is rather too many to monitor. Total return three-year performance is 25.4% as of Feb 2011.

Looking at table 16.5 first, it is apparent that the top three holdings are all UK banks. Such holdings will be no doubt distributed across a number of different bonds, but exposure is concentrated towards Lloyds (9.1%), Barclays (4.1%) and RBS (3.3%). The 9.1% holding in Lloyds is a relatively high concentration for a fund manager to have in a single (non-sovereign) credit, and reflects the manager's positive stance towards the bank.

However, I would point out that most bond portfolios, particularly ones as large as this, end up with a fairly high concentration of bank credits. With billions to invest (the average position size will be £10 million plus per bond), the fund will naturally gravitate towards larger issuers such as the banks.

Turning to the table of credit ratings, it is notable that there are some AAA-rated bonds, although much of this will be accounted for by gilt holdings (typically used to fill gaps in the portfolio or to quickly add/reduce market exposure. There is very little around the AA-rated area, but over 65% of the holdings are in the single-A and BBB-rated area. It is in this category of credit that most corporate bonds can be found. A few years ago, many banks would have fielded a double-A status, but they have now generally joined the lesser mortals in the A-BBB area.

Below triple-B lies non-investment grade status. Invesco's exposure here is limited. However, I note over 6% in unrated issues, an area where the skills of the fund managers can bring some value to bear.

Note: The above data came from the Invesco website. Many bond portfolios can now be viewed on fund fact sheets, generally downloadable online. This is a great way to see how fund managers run portfolios.

Chapter 17
Trading the fixed income markets

About trading

This book is primarily written for investors, and by this I mean individuals who wish to see their money grow over medium or longer periods of time by means of the coupons paid from bonds, and the re-investment thereof. This process will be either exclusively or mostly long only, although leverage and selective hedging can be applied if required.

The business of trading is a somewhat different approach and can broadly be described as the exploitation of short-term price volatility or variations for profit. Such activity is broadly speaking speculation, although it is generally known as trading in the popular financial press. Activity can be on both the long and the short side, cross-book trades (mixed long & short trades), leverage and arbitrage.

Certainly, the fixed income markets can provide an environment where traders can profit, and bond trading desks typically provide a large proportion of most investments banks' profits (and from time to time, rather large losses!).

However, there are some key points to consider for the would-be bond trader.

- Bonds are **surprisingly volatile**, often moving 2-3 points in a day or two. However, they inhabit narrow trading ranges. Most bonds are issued at par, redeemed at par and will spend their entire trading life between 80 and 120. Thus, unlike small caps, technology or mining stocks, the bond trader is unlikely to experience the joys of an eight bagger. Even doubling one's money is relatively unusual. Thus, in order to achieve meaningful gains, a trader will generally have to employ leverage.

- Bonds pay coupons, often quite significant ones, thus, anyone **shorting** a bond will be effectively paying out this coupon. Short-side bond traders will always face this headwind which becomes more and more of a problem over time.

- **Illiquid bonds** can offer excellent opportunities for trading when the time is right. However, be very wary of entering into short-side trades in such bonds. Such instruments trade far less frequently than equities. They may prove near-impossible to cover back. Consider also that most private investors will not be able to enter into uncovered shorts, unless they have a very flexible broker.

What to trade and how

Given the above points, bond trading for the private investor is likely to fall into two possible areas:

1. long/short/curve trading in liquid benchmark futures, and

2. opportunistic long-side trades in high yield bonds.

The latter option will generally be part of a larger value-based strategy and is covered in chapter 13.

In this section we'll look at:

1. gilt futures

2. spread betting

3. credit derivative ETFs

1. Trading benchmark government futures

As I have already mentioned, leverage is a key point for investors who wish to trade the government bond markets. Professional traders are usually in and out for just a few cents, and even 1% is seen as a relatively large move in short term trading. Thus, unless a private investor has access to multi-million pound funds, leverage is the way to go, and the futures markets can provide this. The degree of leverage and margin requirement will vary from broker to broker and with market volatility but as a rule of thumb a multiple of 20x the deposited margin would be about right.

Traders looking to chop wood in the major government markets will be able to gain access to gilt futures on the LIFFE market, Bunds via the DTB and US Treasuries via the CBOT. Action in the gilt futures market is concentrated on the 10yr benchmark (although short and medium dated contracts do exist). The deeper US and German markets allow trading across a range of maturities: 2yr, 5yr, 10yr, 30yr etc, allowing curve trades (more of which below).

Table 17.1: major government bond futures contracts

Contract	Exchange	Contract size	Currency	Value of 1pt	Tick size
2-year T-Note	CBOT	200,000	USD	$2,000	1/128 ($15.62)
5-Year T-Note	CBOT	100,000	USD	$1,000	1/128 ($7.8125)
10-Year T-note	CBOT	100,000	USD	$1,000	1/32 ($31.25)
T-Bond (20yr)	CBOT	100,000	USD	$1,000	1/32 ($31.25)
Medium Gilt Future	LIFFE	100,000	GBP	£1,000	1p (£10)
Long Gilt Future (10yr)	LIFFE	100,000	GBP	£1,000	1p (£10)
Euro BOBL	DTB	100,000	EUR	€1,000	1 cent (€10)
Euro Bund	DTB	100,000	EUR	€1,000	1 cent (€10)
Euro Buxl	DTB	100,000	EUR	€1,000	1 cent (€10)
JGB	TSE	100,000	JPY	Y1,000,000	1 sen (Y10,000)

Government bond contracts can also be found for most major markets, including Canada, Australia, etc. Contracts are generally based on 100,000 nominal (USD, GBP, etc.) of the underlying security and the bulk of the turnover will be concentrated in the front contract (i.e the next 3-month deliverable). Thus traders operating in January will be focusing on the March contract. Positions left open to the delivery date will need to be either rolled into the next contract or closed out. Physical delivery is possible in most contracts, but is unusual.

> **Tip**: whilst bonds trade clean with the interest accrual element stripped out of the price, bond futures trade dirty. Interest accrues up in the price as time marches on. Short-side traders should be aware of this.

Most futures brokers will be able to deal directly on the exchanges on their client's behalf. The markets are highly liquid and it is possible to achieve very tight bid-offer spreads – as I write, the quote for the gilt future on LIFFE is 120.48 to 120.49.

2. Spread betting

An easy access route for private investors looking to trade the bond markets or add hedges or gearing to their portfolios is via spread betting. This mechanism was developed by IG Index in the mid-seventies, originally to allow private investors and speculators to put on positions in gold. The platform was widened to include equities and equity indices and by the 1990s the majority of major financial instruments were available on the platform.

Customers are able to trade on such platforms with considerable leverage across a good variety of instruments. Spread betters offer pricing based off several well known bond futures (not the underlying bond). Compared to buying or selling the underlying future, smaller-sized positions can usually be entered – a very useful attribute for traders who may wish to average in and average out of moving markets.

IG Index offers the following contracts in the bond space, all of which are based on futures contracts:

- Short Sterling: Front, 3 month forward, 6 months forward, 9 month forward, 1 year forward and 15 months.

- Short, medium and long gilts: front contracts.

- US & North American bonds: 3-month Eurodollar contract series, 2yr Note, 5yr Note, 10 yr Note and the Treasury Bond (aka the Long Bond).

- Short, medium and long-dated German Government bonds.

- Asia: Euroyen, 10yr JGB, and Australian 30-Day Rate.

3. Credit derivative ETFs

The professional market makes heavy use of credit derivatives. Broadly speaking the growth of this market has followed the path laid down by so many other derivative markets, such as index or interest rate futures, and it is often in the credit derivative markets that moves are first seen – effectively the tail wagging the dog.

What are credit derivatives?

Simply a bilateral contract, conforming to market standards, where one counterparty agrees to pay out a sum in the event of a default from a third party. The value of such a contract will rise and fall with the perceived creditworthness of that third party (and to a certain extent general risk-premiums and optionality considerations).

There are limited choices for the private investor who wishes to speculate in this area. The growing ETF market is providing some route into this area through instruments linked to baskets of Credit Default Swaps. The best known of these is the Deutsche Bank ITRAXX ETFs, which can be traded on various baskets of credits both on the long and the short side. Such products can be used for both speculation and hedging.

The most popular of these instruments is the ITRAXX Crossover 5-year TR Index ETF (XTXC). This tracks the CDS on 50 high-yield European credits. As such the ETF will have a trading pattern that correlates with high-yield corporate bonds (although inverse tracker vehicles are available). The ETF is traded on the German exchange and is denominated in Euros (see chart below).

Chart 17.1: dbx iTraxx Crossover ETF

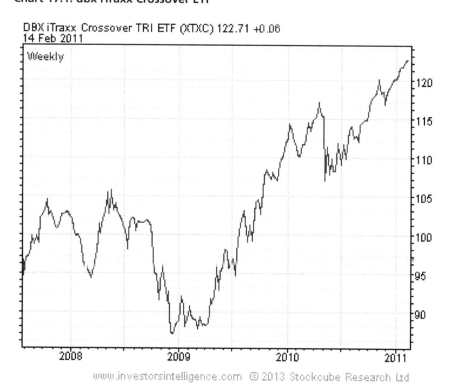

The XTXC ETF shows a good rally from early 2009 onwards. The ETF reflects the return that might be experienced by an investor selling a basket of credit protection contracts. As market confidence returned after the credit crunch (and defaults proved to be lower than some expectations), the price of the underlying index and the related ETF rose.

The DB X-tracker range of products offers ETFs in:

- ITRAXX Europe
- ITRAXX Europe Senior Financials
- ITRAXX Europe Subordinated Financials
- ITRAXX HiVOL (high spread credits).

Cross-book trades amongst these issues could be used to trade big picture credit moves; for instance, short European government credits and long corporates.

But, I suspect that these instruments will only be useful for investors from time to time, perhaps to catch a big up-spike in risk in the manner that equity traders would harness the moves in implied volatility in the VIX.

Traders should also consider that ETFs provide a ready-made route for short and leveraged trades in credit baskets, credit derivatives and government bonds, but that as ever with instrument of this nature, there will be the headwind of charges and diminishing optionality premiums to contend with.

Types of trade

Long and short trades

The most obvious trades are the naked short and the naked long. I have already raised the point that bonds are intrinsically range-trading instruments, issued and redeemed at par. However, individual bonds can have very extended trending periods.

The JGB is a good example of this with a blow-off top for yields at 8% in 1990, followed by an eight-year bull market and a 13-year ranging period (to date!).

Chart 17.2: Japan 10yr bond yield

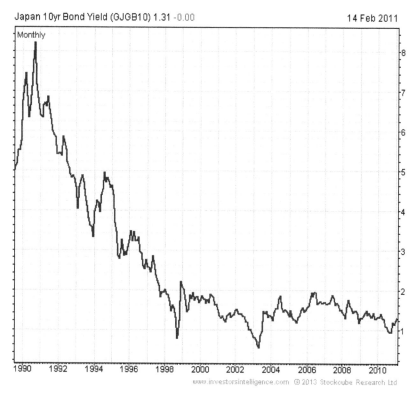

Japan 10yr Bond Yield (GJGB10) 1.31 -0.00   14 Feb 2011

Good traders will utilise these major cyclical trends and go with the flow. Bad traders will constantly attempt to place countertrend trades.

Such trades will typically be momentum driven and some tactics for entering, running and exiting trades are discussed later in the "Trading with technical analysis" section.

Curve trades

In addition to the basic long and short trades, where a trader selects a given bond or contract and buys or sells it, bond traders will frequently place curve trades, betting on the interplay of bonds of different maturities.

As discussed before, bond markets display what is known as a yield curve – pricing differentials between long-dated and short-dated securities based on a combination of future interest rate expectations, investor risk appetite and supply/demand. The normal distribution of the yield curve is positive – i.e short term bonds yield less than long-term bonds. This is an understandable state of affairs as investors will expect additional compensation for the risk of holding longer-dated maturities.

However, an economic scenario with expectations for sharply falling rates will see investors flocking to the longer end of the curve, forcing up prices and thus lowering yields. Such a scenario will result in a negative (or inverse) yield curve where short-dated bonds yield more than longer-dated issues.

The chart below shows the state of play in the US, UK and European yield curves as of February 2011. The solid plot is the gilt curve.

Chart 17.3: yield curves for UK, US and German government bonds (Feb 2011)

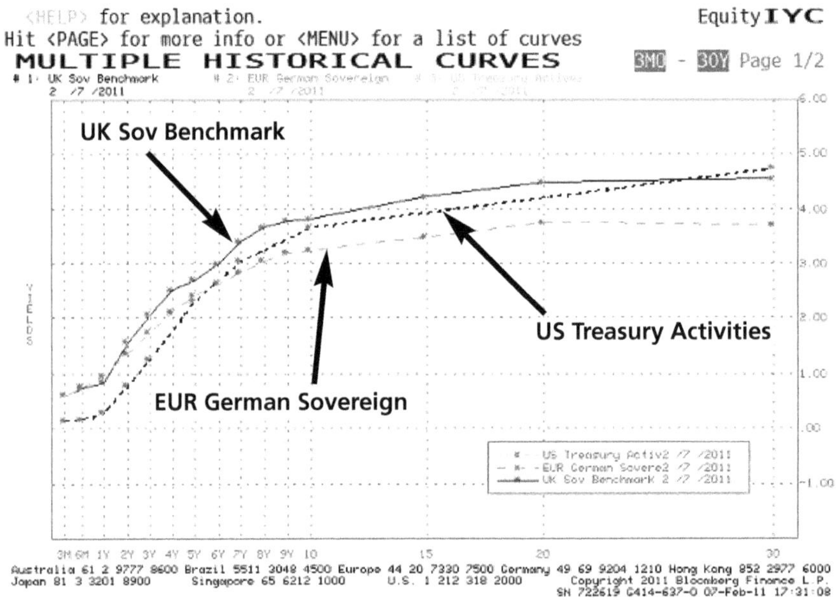

Source: Bloomberg

Yield curves are by no means static, shifting on a daily basis. The curves are particularly sensitive to economic data and can move sharply on changes in real or perceived monetary policy. Many bond market traders look to play such shifts through placing long/short pairs trades known as curve trades – typically *steepeners* or *flatteners*.

Steepener trade

A steepener is a bet that the yield curve will steepen – that long rates will push higher and that short rates will either stay the same or fall. Alternatively, long rates could stay where they are and short rates could fall. A number of economic scenarios could result in this type of market activity.

Traders who wish to bet on this move would buy the short end and sell the long end – a fairly straightforward pairs trade.

However, the duration of a ten year bond will be markedly different from that of a two year bond. Should the curve undergo a parallel shift, up or down, over the holding period of the trade, the more volatile 10yr will dominate the pair, thus, professional traders will duration-weight the trade.

Here's an example of a parallel shift of 0.25% in yield terms, using the US benchmark two-year note and ten-year note, a popular curve trade known as "two's tens". The futures will show roughly similar price behaviour:

Position	Bond	Current prices (and yields)	Duration	Prices resulting from a 0.25% upward shift in yield	Resultant price move
Long	UST 0.625% 2013	99.69 (0.79%)	1.96	99.17	0.52
Short	UST 2.625% 2020	91.43 (3.67%)	8.38	89.57	1.86

Thus, professional traders duration-weight the trades in favour of the lower duration bond. In truth, this is not an exact science because:

1. duration moves with price, and

2. the future price movement is unknown.

I would recommend any trader considering such a pair to run through several "what if" scenarios with different outcomes and then select the position size accordingly.

Flatteners

A flattener is a bet that the yield curve will flatten either by short-term yields pushing higher, long-term yields falling or a combination thereof. Traders wishing to put this on will sell the short end and buy the long end. Again the trade should be duration-weighted to hedge parallel-shifts in the curve.

Spread trades

We have looked at curve trades, which play the relationship between short-term and long-term bond yields. The curve trades we have considered compare "like with like" credits – one US government bond against another.

Another type of trade is the spread trade. This typically takes place across two different credits, and occasionally across two different currencies.

The basic theory is easy enough: if one has identified a credit that is cheap, but the outlook for rates is uncertain, a spread trade can be entered into – long the credit and short the gilt. This type of trade is popular amongst professional traders and banks, however the limited volatility of bonds and the huge size required to make such trades worthwhile generally puts such trades outside the territory of the private investor. At times they may be of interest, as the following chart of the GE 5.5 June 2021 against the 10 year gilt shows. The credit crunch is clearly visible, as the price of the General Electric corporate bond falls away sharply after July 08, whilst the price of the gilt picks up.

Chart 17.4: GE 5.5 June 2021 v 10 year gilt

Another type of trade is the cross-currency yield convergence/divergence trade – for instance buying high-yielding Portugal 10yr bonds against a lower yielding credit such as Germany.

In this example, the bet is for Portuguese spreads to tighten against the German benchmark, whilst the duration risk of the trade is largely nullified by utilising bonds of the same maturity. Such trades were enormously popular for prop traders and IBs in the run-up to European monetary union in the mid-to-late 1990s. Since that point, the money-flows have reversed, as the trend on the chart displays. Nowadays, such trades can be very volatile, as the fast-moving yield differential on the respective 10 year bonds shows.

Chart 17.5: Portugal 10yr bonds v Germany 10yr bond

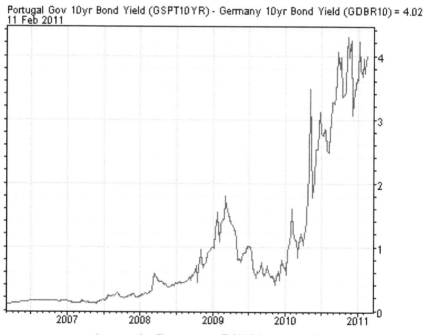

Portugal Gov 10yr Bond Yield (GSPT10YR) - Germany 10yr Bond Yield (GDBR10) = 4.02
11 Feb 2011

www.investorsintelligence.com © 2013 Stockcube Research Ltd

Short-term interest rates (STIRS)

The interbank rate is the basic building block of the money markets. Banks exchange (give and receive) deposits with each other in vast sizes on a minute-by minute basis. The agreed rate for these deposits will fluctuate in line with interest rate movements and the credit-worthiness (or otherwise) of the counterparty.

The well-known LIBOR rate is an index of the aggregated price action of these trades, fixed at 11am each morning by the British Bankers Association. Various deposit periods are tracked, but perhaps the most popular benchmark is the 3-month LIBOR rate – the annualised rate at which banks accept deposits over a 3-month period.

This benchmark has now fallen into some disrepute due to allegations of manipulation, but LIBOR (or is its successor) is and will be a vital tool for the financial markets for years to come. Thus, it is no surprise to see a futures market based on this activity. Corporate treasurers and others have an understandable need to hedge their forward borrowing and deposit rates. LIFFE have a series of contracts based on the GBP 3-month LIBOR rate. Similar contracts exist on other exchanges for the money-markets in the US, Europe, Japan etc.

The LIFFE 90-day Sterling Contract is known in the market as *Short Sterling* and is actively traded. It is a useful tool for betting on the speed and extent of future interest rate hikes and cuts. The contract size is £500,000 with a tick size of £0.01 and a tick value of £12.5, allowing for plenty of gearing for a speculator. Contracts are actively traded and spreads are tight – ideal territory for intraday traders or scalpers.

The pricing notation is "par – LIBOR", thus a 2% LIBOR rate would be expressed as 98 on the contract. A 3% LIBOR rate as 97 and so on.

An example of the Short-Sterling contract series

Contract date	Price
March 2011	99.10
June 2011	98.82
Sept 2011	98.54
Dec 2011	98.24
March 2012	97.92
Jun 2012	97.61
Sept 2012	97.31

Much longer dated contracts are also available, but liquidity may be less. Note how the positive shape of the curve is reflected in the falling Short Sterling prices further out[8].

---

[8] For readers with an interest in this important part of the money markets, I would recommend the book *STIR Futures* by Stephen Aikin [Harriman House].

Chapter 18
Trading with technical analysis

Readers of this book may be aware that I spent over a decade working for Stockcube Research, the publisher of Investors Intelligence. Thus, whilst the primary focus of this book is on value and portfolio-driven investment strategies, it would be churlish of me not to include some insights from my employer's stock-in-trade, namely technical analysis – the study of price action, and how this might be applied to the bond markets.

The first point to bear in mind when examining the technical characteristics of any instrument is to look at the long-term trend in order to identify the primary trend. It is the primary trend that should govern the majority of most trades. Successful traders trade with the trend, not against it. Indeed, I would go so far as to say that any trader constantly putting on counter-trend bets is doomed to failure, although any one trade may well succeed.

Primary trends

The situation in bonds is perhaps more complex. Primary trends certainly exist, the granddaddy of them all being the generational downtrend seen in US bonds yields from 1981 onwards (see chart).

Remember that falling yields equate to rising bond prices. This 30-year chart reflects the yields displayed by numerous 10yr benchmarks over the period. The general trend is down which will have been reflected in generally buoyant prices for the bonds, and a trend towards lower coupons with each subsequent issue.

Chart 18.1: long-term downtrend for US bond yields

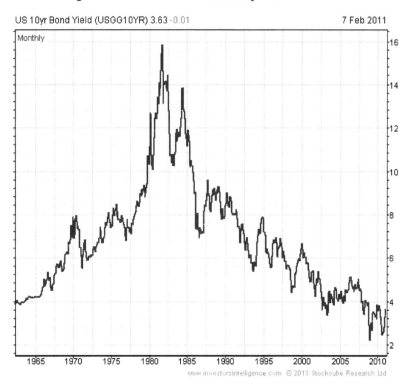

Set against this primary trend is the undeniable fact that individual bonds are issued at par, and redeemed at par, making any given bond (as opposed to indices) a range trading instrument. Thus, support, resistance and activity levels are extremely important and it is notable that bonds typically show strong reactions to such levels.

My first point of call when considering putting on a directional trade in a government bond is the long-term chart, and for this I would recommend using a yield chart.

Why?

Because price alone will not give you a true picture of investor activity. Price will be a feature of many variables of the individual bond including coupon and maturity. The yield will give a better long-term picture of investor behaviour over time and the supply/demand picture. The chart of the UK 10yr bond yield displayed below gives a good idea of the big picture in UK gilts over the last decade. Note the significant range between 4 and 5.25% and range setting up between 3 and 4%.

Chart 18.2: big picture in UK gilts

UK 10 Year Bond Yield (GUKG10) 3.82 +0.04   4 Feb 2011

www.investorsintelligence.com © 2013 Stockcube Research Ltd

Support and resistance

The theory of support and resistance is of course very simple. Investor behaviour, as displayed by price charts, typically repeats. Areas or levels that have seen previous demand or supply will reassert time and time again. The main types of support and resistance are listed below:

Sideways support and resistance – reversals occurring at identifiable prior levels.

These are the simplest types of S/R levels. The chart of the iShares 7-10yr T-Bond fund demonstrates a good example of sideways resistance. Traders will typically look to establish positions in such areas with stop levels positioned just above resistance.

Chart 18.3: iShares 7-10yr T-Bond fund

> **Tip**: old resistance levels once broken through will frequently convert to support, and visa-versa. This is not surprising given that investor activity will be triggered by the break of the level.

Sideways level corresponding to big figures

Watch out for round numbers. Bond traders are slightly less obsessed with the big, obvious round numbers than their colleagues in the equity markets, but such object fixation does occur. Perhaps more important to consider is the yield on the underlying benchmark. Three or four percent may not lie at an obvious round-number price equivalent, but the market will react. Remember that the price equivalent of the yield round number will change over time.

Fibonacci retracements.

Love him or hate him, some aspects of the work of the 13th century Italian mathematician Leonardo Fibonacci are closely followed in the bond markets. This makes Fibonacci retracement levels a virtually self-fulfilling prophecy. To draw in Fibonacci retracement levels on a chart is easy – simply identify the dominant highs and lows of the range and then slice up the gap in between these levels using the main ratios. Many systems such as Bloomberg or eSignal have the ability to do this for you, but a pocket calculator, a chart and a ruler will do the job just as well. Watch out for price reactions at the key levels of 23.6%, 38.2%, 50% and 61.8%. Here is an example of the 61.8% Fibonacci level drawn in on the US 5yr Note contract (March 2011).

Chart 18.4: price reacting to a Fibonacci level

Note how the contract encountered resistance at this 61.8% Fibonacci level (118.75) even though such a level has no obvious conventional support/resistance or activity level.

Uptrend support and resistance.

We have looked at sideways support and resistance, but perhaps more important is trend – the all-important effect of investor psychology. For an uptrend, this is manifested by a sequence of higher lows and higher highs as investors pay more for the asset, and become increasingly unwilling to sell. Such a development can be plotted as an uptrend, with a rising support line drawn in under the pattern of rising counter-trend lows.

A textbook example of an uptrend is illustrated below by the iShares High Yield Corporate Bond Fund, with investor activity printing a trail of higher highs and higher lows.

Chart 18.5: an established uptrend

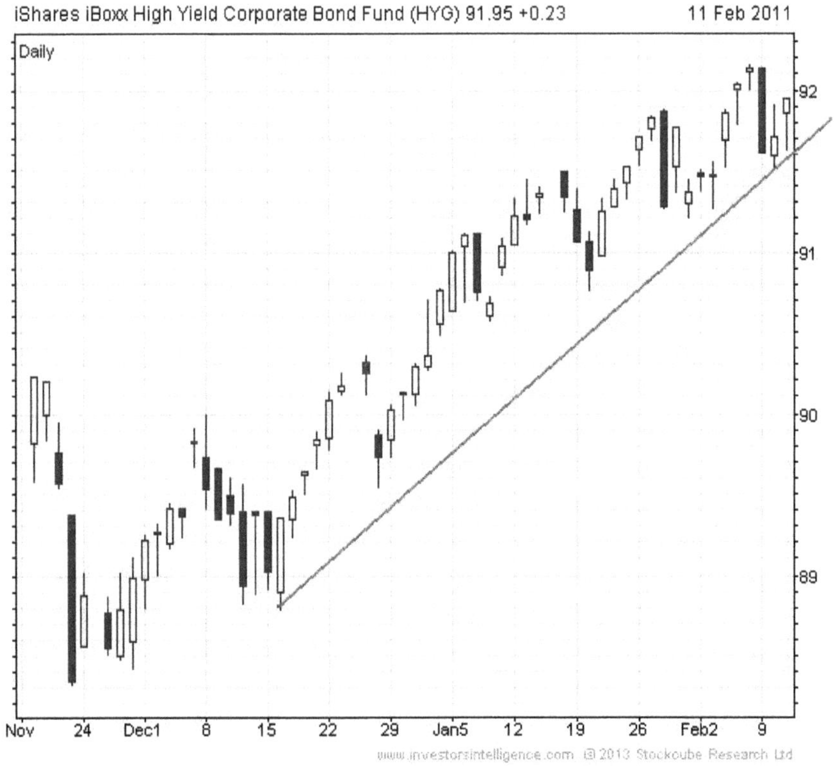
iShares iBoxx High Yield Corporate Bond Fund (HYG) 91.95 +0.23
11 Feb 2011
Daily
92
91
90
89
Nov
24
Dec1
8
15
22
29
Jan5
12
19
26
Feb2
9
www.investorsintelligence.com © 2013 Stockcube Research Ltd

The identification of such trends should be the primary task of a technical analyst. After this process of identification (which hopefully comes sooner rather than later), comes the tactical application of a trading strategy.

Tip: for good technical analysts, identification of trend is everything. Support, resistance and the application of indicators and overlays are all secondary considerations.

Breakouts and false breakouts

Do support and resistance levels last forever? No. Let's take a look at when these levels are broken, and how technically-minded traders might use such events.

It is said that traders buy low and sell high, but this is an oversimplification. As I have previous discussed, successful traders typically trade *with* the market, and will look for a signal that price action is on the move.

The simplest form of signal is the breakout. Here a trader looks to identify a move above a previous peak, or a below a previous trough. This indicates a clear change in the supply/demand picture, a situation that will typically extend.

Chart 18.6: downside break through a support level

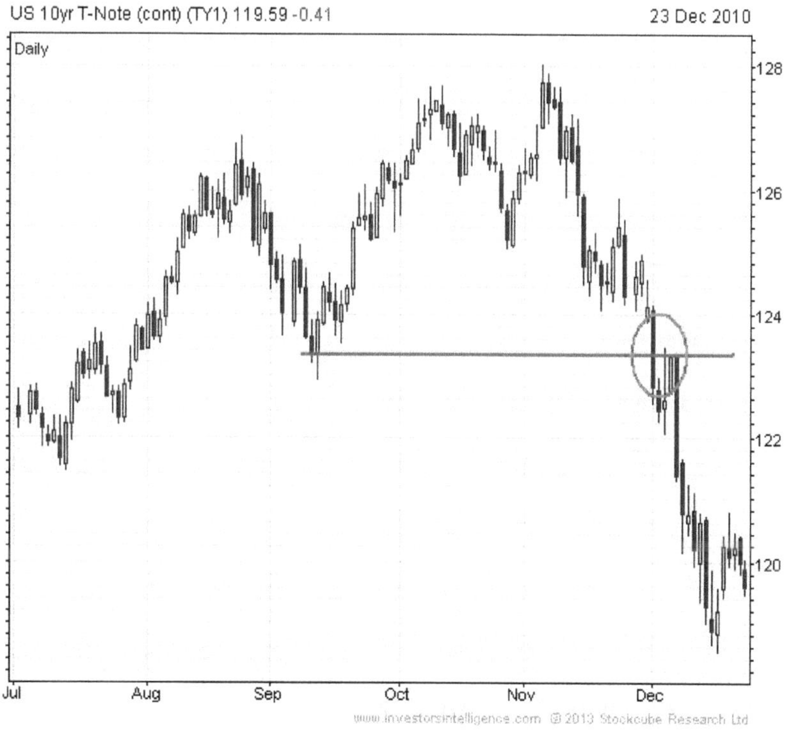
US 10yr T-Note (cont) (TY1) 119.59 -0.41
23 Dec 2010
Daily
128
126
124
122
120
Jul
Aug
Sep
Oct
Nov
Dec
www.investorsintelligence.com © 2013 Stockcube Research Ltd

The downside break of the September support in the US T-Bond contract is an excellent example of such a signal.

False breakouts

The next step to consider is what happens after the breakout, this time through resistance. Let's take a look at an upside breakout in the US 5yr Note. In the chart shown, the price has just broken the sideways resistance lying below 122. Hopefully, once the resistance is broken, follow-through will be seen. The trader will then be able to set his stop loss just below the breakout and tighten it up behind any further action.

But what should happen if the breakout is not maintained?

In the case of a failed upside breakout, new long positions will be trapped just above the resistance and these stale bulls will weigh heavily on the market. The price action seen in our chart in early November 2010 is a good example of this.

Chart 18.7: a failed breakout

The rule of thumb for failed breakouts is a retracement to the other side of the prior range.

Using moving average pairs

As I have previously mentioned, determining the trend is a crucial skill for a technical analyst. Many analysts use moving average (MA) pairs to determine this primary trend. The classic combination is the 50 and 200 day pair, although more complex combinations of three moving averages may be utilised.

By their nature, MA-based tools are lagging indicators, and thus should be viewed as a confirming indicator, rather than a trade trigger. My favourite pair for bonds is the 10 and 20-day EMA pair, shown below, again against the US 5-year Note.

Chart 18.8: moving average pair to identify trend

US 5yr T Note Futures (cont) (FV1) 120.76 -0.27   12 Nov 2010

As you can see, the crossovers make for a useful guideline – buy when the 10 day rises above the 20 day and sell when the 10-day falls below the 20.

Readers will note that the mid-September period would have rolled one in and out of the contract with very little profit, and possibly a loss. The salutary tale here is that trend-following systems work well in strongly trending markets and are unprofitable in range trading or choppy environments.

Chapter 19
Tax

It is with some trepidation that I write this short chapter on taxation. Generally I try not to get too deeply involved in tax issues when writing my *Bond of the Week* or other articles because, firstly, almost every reader will have a subtly different tax situation and, secondly, it changes all the time. But with those caveats, here goes.

The great thing about the majority of bonds is that they pay their interest gross. This is a key point – the vast majority of the long-term gains that will be achieved by running a bond portfolio will be through the coupons received. Sadly, if the government is stepping on this cash flow before it even reaches you, the chances of achieving a successful return are low. What is more, the risk reward ratio will be greatly tilted against you – basically you have all the risk and they have some of the income.

Thus, it is extremely important to run one's bond portfolio in a tax-efficient manner. This is not always easy. Investing in the UK has always been heavily biased towards equities and properties. There are numerous allowances, exceptions and wrinkles that can be utilised to minimise the impact of capital gains tax, but rather less than can be used for the income-based investor.

Fortunately, it is now easy for UK investors to tax-shelter the income flows from their fixed income investments via ISA and SIPPS (more on these below). The ready availability and falling cost of these schemes are probably the biggest single benefit for fixed income investors in the UK.

The tax treatment of bonds

Gilts

Income tax

Gilts, as with the majority of bonds, pay their coupons gross. For the majority of investors this will be a good thing – the assets can be tax-sheltered in an ISA or a SIPP. Alternatively, it may be possible to offset the income against allowances or other deductibles. However, for some investors, the gross coupon may be a nuisance. Holders of gilts who are not currently filling in a tax return many have no wish to commence this odious business. In this event, it is possible to register with the Debt Management Office's registrar and receive gilt coupons paid net of tax.

Capital gains tax

With the exception of the deep-discounted gilts strips, capital gains made on gilts are free of tax. This means that the typical private investor will favour bonds with a below par price – effectively reducing the taxable coupon element of the return and increasing the non-taxable capital gain.

Many stockbrokers and quality newspapers publish tables of gilt prices and yields with the YTM shown for investors at various tax rates. Higher rate tax payers should be cautious – in the current low interest rate environment, some high-coupon, over-par gilts are actually offering a negative return once income tax is taken into account.

Note: the current low interest rate environment is seeing gilts issued with record low coupons. In the fullness of time, and if interest rates return to more normal levels, the longer-dated, low-coupon gilts may offer higher-rate tax payers a very tax-efficient investment.

Corporate and Eurosterling bonds

The first point to consider is that, as with gilts, the vast majority of bonds pay their coupons without any withholding tax being levied. This gross income is, of course, subject to income tax unless sheltered in one of the schemes outlined below. As with gilts, the income tax element is fairly straightforward.

Unlike gilts, profits released on bonds may be subject to capital gains. However, the majority of straight bonds (i.e. bonds without unusual features) that are likely to be encountered by the private investor will be qualifying corporate bonds (QCBs). Broadly speaking, most conventional sterling bonds will qualify for the QCB status. Indeed, HMRC has been quoted as saying,

> As a general rule any non-convertible security denominated in sterling and issued on normal commercial terms will be a corporate bond.

Bonds that HMRC consider fail to meet the criteria include:

- "Deep gain securities" – ie bonds sold at a discount that will "roll up" towards redemption. This test usually applies to the coupon/discount situation at issue, as opposed to buying a bond whose price has fallen sharply in secondary trading.

- Convertibility – watch out for conversion options into equity, other securities or other currencies.

- There is also some suggestion that in order to qualify, the rate of interest paid must also reflect a "reasonable commercial rate" and should not be linked to the performance of the business or a division of the issuer.

A quirk of index-linked corporate bonds

Index-linked gilts are not subject to capital gains tax. That's a good thing, given that a spell of inflation for two decades may double the value of such bonds.

However, index-linked corporate bonds are not treated so kindly by HMRC. At the time of writing, the revenue viewed the indexation gains on the capital value to be chargeable to income. To my mind, this is a strange distortion on the tax treatment of private and public sector debt.

Preference shares

Preference shares are not bonds, they are shares, but many bond investors own fixed-interest prefs within their portfolios, attracted by the high yields that are often available on these deeply subordinated instruments.

These instruments enjoy a tax advantage over bonds when held by UK income tax payers in their own name. The dividends on preference share dividends are considered to have been paid net of basic rate income tax, so basic rate taxpayers have no more to pay. Higher rate taxpayers have to pay only the difference between the basic rate and their top rate. Effectively the treatment is the same as for equity dividends.

Tax shelters

ISAs

We know that that the profits on QCB bonds are generally considered to be free of capital gains tax. However, the majority of the return from a bond portfolio will be achieved from the income received from coupon payments. Whilst these coupon payments are paid gross, they are certainly subject to income tax.

Luckily, ISAs offer an easy method to achieve shelter from income tax – allowing the power of compound interest to roll up over the years.

To qualify for an ISA, a bond must have a maturity of five years or more at the time of purchase (including any holder put options). The bond must also be listed (or issued by a company that is itself listed). All income and capital gains achieved within an ISA are free from tax.

The allowance for ISA contributions in 2011 is £10,680 per annum. I have heard many people opine that this sum is too small for them to be bothered with. What rubbish! Even for a relatively wealthy man, tucking way £10,000 a year, and another £10,000 for his wife over a ten year period will input £200,000 into the scheme. Add some capital growth from re-investment over the period and this may rise to £300,000.

Investing this in a portfolio with a 5% average yield will bring in £15,000 a year – completely tax free. I can think of very few more tax efficient and straightforward investments. What is even better is that not only is ISA income tax-free, you do not have to declare it on your tax return – one less onerous task to perform.

Contacts in broking and wealth management tell me that there are now many "ISA millionaires" – an enviable state of affairs for these individuals.

SIPPS

The situation for Self Invested Personal Pensions (SIPPs) is even easier. Bonds of any maturity can be held within a SIPP. These can be used as a high-yielding substitute for the cash component of the portfolio, as a diversification from equity, or as an income generator during the latter years of the scheme.

The benefits of bonds are self-evident within such a wrapper and it is my opinion that as the SIPP schemes and their holders mature, we will see significant participation in the bond markets from this group of investors.

Stamp duty

In theory, bond purchases are free from stamp duty, and this will be the case within normal market settlement where the bonds are delivered into a Euroclear account. However, many private client stockbrokers use a delivery mechanism known as Crest Depository Interests (CDIs). Due to a quirk of HMRC's system of classification, some of these CDIs are attracting Stamp

Duty Reserve tax on purchases (0.5%). This generally happens on older issues. The new retail bonds that are being issued on the LSE's ORB market have all been correctly flagged as SDRT-free.

It is possible to flag such bonds to the attention of the revenue to avoid this spurious tax, however, this creates yet more admin. The easiest solution when presented with a bond that is attracting SDRT is to simply ensure that your broker accepts Euroclear delivery. Providing the broker sticks to this delivery route, the problem will not occur.

Concluding advice

Regarding tax, my rules of thumb for the private investor are:

1. Buy assets that pay gross

2. Put them in a simple tax-sheltered structure such as a SIPP or an ISA

3. If in doubt, consult a suitably experienced accountant

The Six Golden Rules of Bond Investing

Rules are dangerous thing to have in the ever-changing world of the securities market, but nevertheless here are my six golden rules for investing in bonds:

1. **Look to build a portfolio, rather than just buy one bond**. Make sure the portfolio is diversified by type of issuer and by maturity (preferably ladder structure).

2. **Don't always go for the highest yielding bond – you will end up with a portfolio of junk**. High yield does not always equal high performance.

3. **Always make sure you know what you are buying**. Read the prospectus (particularly true for complex and subordinated issues).

4. **Keep the costs down**. Make sure you are dealing efficiently and hold the bond to maturity if possible.

5. **Pick up bargains**. The vast majority of bonds pay their coupon and maturity proceeds in full, but selected issues become very oversold during periods of bad news.

6. **Don't panic during market downturns**. Remember, most bonds have fixed maturities and the price will recover.

So, keep digging through the prospectus, keep an eye out for new issues and, above all, don't forget to invest in such a manner that income and gains keep rolling up.

Beyond that, don't forget to have fun! The bond market is a fascinating place, both to work and invest in. Interest in bonds can be repaid in more ways than one.

APPENDICES

Appendix 1
Sample bond prospectus and notes

Sample prospectus

I have reprinted extracts of the document for the **Pearson Group 7% 2014** **Eurosterling** bond as an example of the sort of documentation that bond investors should study. The document is an *offering circular* and slightly shorter than some of the 100 plus page prospectuses that are often seen in the market.

The skill in reading prospectuses is knowing what to skip – much of it is legal boiler plate and can safely be ignored. The notes below highlight the salient points in this 24 page document, and this will hopefully act as a guide for the reader to decipher other prospectuses.

Note: I have summarized the most pertinent points contained within this prospectus in the notes on the following pages. However, I would recommend that readers download the full PDF document from the Harriman House website and familiarise themselves with these types of documents.

(incorporated with limited liability in England and Wales under the Companies Act 1862-1893)

£250,000,000

7 per cent. Bonds due 2014

Issue price: 98.79 per cent.

The £250,000,000 7 per cent. Bonds due 2014 (the "Bonds") will bear interest from 27 October 1999 payable annually in arrear on 27 October in each year.

Application has been made for the Bonds to be admitted to the Official List of the London Stock Exchange Limited (the "London Stock Exchange").

The Bonds may not be redeemed prior to 27 October, 2014 except as mentioned below. Pearson plc (the "Issuer") may, at its option, redeem all, but not some only, of the Bonds at any time after 27 October 2002 at the higher of par and an amount calculated by reference to yields on United Kingdom government stock, together with accrued interest. The Issuer may also, at its option, redeem all, but not some only, of the Bonds at any time at their principal amount (plus accrued interest) if the Issuer becomes obliged to pay certain additional amounts as described under "Terms and Conditions of the Bonds - Redemption and Purchase".

Copies of this document, which comprises listing particulars in respect of the Bonds required by the listing rules made under Part IV of the Financial Services Act 1986, have been delivered to the Registrar of Companies in England and Wales for registration in accordance with Section 149 of that Act.

The Bonds are expected, on issue, to be rated Baa1 by Moody's Investors Service Limited ("Moody's") and BBB+ by Standard & Poor's Ratings Services, a division of the McGraw Hill Companies Inc. ("Standard & Poor's").

The Bonds will initially be represented by a Temporary Global Bond in bearer form without interest coupons (the "Temporary Global Bond") which will be deposited with a depositary common to Morgan Guaranty Trust Company of New York, Brussels office, as operator of the Euroclear System ("Euroclear") and Cedelbank on or about 27 October 1999. The Temporary Global Bond will be exchangeable for a Permanent Global Bond in bearer form without interest coupons (the "Permanent Global Bond" and, together with the Temporary Global Bond, the "Global Bonds") on or after a date which is expected to be 6 December 1999, upon customary certification as to non-U.S. beneficial ownership. The Permanent Global Bond will be exchangeable (in whole but not in part) for definitive Bonds in bearer form with interest coupons and, where applicable, one talon attached in the denominations of £1,000, £10,000 and £100,000 only in the limited circumstances set out therein and described in "Summary of provisions relating to the Bonds while represented by the Global Bonds".

Barclays Capital	**Warburg Dillon Read**
Cazenove & Co.	**Greenwich NatWest**
HSBC	**J.P. Morgan Securities Ltd.**
RBC DS Global Markets	**The Royal Bank of Scotland plc**

The date of this Offering Circular is 25 October 1999.

To download the full copy of the Pearson 7% 2014 bond, go to
www.harriman-house.com/sterlingbonds

Notes

Page 1

The basic details of the bond (see page reproduced). Who is issuing it, coupon and redemption date plus the size of the issue. Basic details on the form of the security and listing, plus expected credit ratings. List of the lead managers and group.

Page 2

Not much here for us. As usual, there are instructions that the bond must not be sold into the United States. This is standard for Eurobonds.

Page 3

Index of contents.

Page 4 and onwards

The terms and conditions. This is the important bit. Look out for:

1. Form and denominations

Private investors need small minimum denominations – a minimum dealing size (or piece) of perhaps £100 or £1,000. Many institutionally-targeted bonds nowadays have £100,000 minimum.

The prospectus states:

> The Bonds are in bearer form, serially numbered, in denominations of £1,000, £10,000 and £100,000 each with Coupons and one Talon attached, and title thereto and to the Coupons will pass by delivery. Bonds of one denomination may not be exchanged for Bonds of another denomination.

2. Status of the bonds

This is very important. Senior or subordinated? This prospectus tells us:

> The Bonds and the Coupons are direct, unconditional, unsubordinated and (subject to the provisions of Condition 3) unsecured obligations of the Issuer and rank and will rank pan passu among themselves and (save for certain obligations required to be preferred by law) equally

with all other unsecured obligations (other than subordinated obligations, if any) of the Issuer, from time to time outstanding.

3. Negative pledge

An issuer-friendly clause to prevent the borrower launching bonds that effectively subordinate the existing claims.

> So long as any of the Bonds remains outstanding (as defined in the Trust Deed), the Issuer will not create or permit to arise or subsist any Quoted Indebtedness or grant or permit to subsist any guarantee of any QuotedIndebtedness, which Quoted Indebtedness or guarantee of Quoted Indebtedness is secured by any mortgage, pledge or other charge upon any of the present or future assets or revenues (including uncalled capital) of the Issuer, unless in any such case as aforesaid simultaneously with, or prior to, the creation of such security, there shall be taken any and all action necessary to procure that such security is extended equally and rateably to all amounts payable in respect of the Bonds, the Coupons and under the Trust Deed to the satisfaction of the Trustee, or such other security is provided as the Trustee shall in its absolute discretion deem not materially less beneficial to the interests of the Bondholders or as shall be approved by an Extraordinary Resolution (as defined in the Trust Deed) of the Bondholders.

4. Interest

Yes please. Is it annual or semi annual? Can the coupon be suspended (usually not on senior debt).

> The Bonds bear interest from (and including) 27 October 1999 at the rate of 7 per cent. per annum, payable annually in arrear on 27 October in each year, commencing on 27 October 2000. The Bonds will cease to bear interest from the due date for redemption unless, upon due presentation, payment of principal or premium (if any) is improperly withheld or refused, in which event interest on such principal amount shall continue to accrue as provided in the Trust Deed. If interest is to be calculated for a period of less than one year, it shall be calculated on the basis of a 360-day year consisting of 12 months of 30 days each and in the case of an incomplete month, the number of days elapsed.

5. Payments

I should certainly hope so!

6. Redemption

Again, this is important. In addition to the fixed redemption date, there may be puts and calls. This bond has a *tax call* and another call option by which the issuer can redeem the bonds at a yield flat to gilts (i.e. at a premium to natural value). This is common and is not a negative point for investors. (N.B. tax calls are very rarely instigated.) From the prospectus:

> Redemption for tax reasons
>
> The Bonds (other than Bonds in respect of which the Issuer shall have given notice of redemption pursuant to Condition 6(c)) may be redeemed at the option of the Issuer in whole, but not in part, at any time on giving not less than 30 nor more than 60 days' notice to the Trustee and the Principal Paying Agent and, in accordance with Condition 13, the Bondholders (which notice shall be irrevocable), if:
>
> (i)   on the occasion of the next payment due under the Bonds, the Issuer satisfies the Trustee that it has or will become obliged to pay additional amounts as provided or referred to in Condition 7 as a result of any change in, or amendment to, the laws or regulations of the United Kingdom or any political subdivision of, or any authority in, or of, the United Kingdom having power to tax, or any change in the application or official interpretation of such laws or regulations, which change or amendment becomes effective on or after 27 October 1999; and
>
> (ii)   such obligation cannot be avoided by the Issuer taking reasonable measures available to it,
>
> provided that no such notice of redemption shall be given earlier than 90 days prior to the earliest date on which the Issuer would be obliged to pay such additional amounts were a payment in respect of the Bonds then due.
>
> Prior to the publication of any notice of redemption pursuant to this Condition, the Issuer shall deliver to the Trustee a certificate signed by two Directors of the Issuer stating that the Issuer is entitled to effect

such redemption and setting forth a statement of facts showing that the conditions precedent to the right of the Issuers to redeem have occurred. Bonds redeemed pursuant to this Condition 6(b) will be redeemed at their principal amount together with interest accrued to (but excluding) the date of such redemption.

The bond can also be called by the issuer *at the higher of* par or the yield on the equivalent gilts. This is a clause that enables the issuer to redeem the bond if it really needs to, but only at a level that would be advantageous to the holder. It would be unusual for a borrower to buy back its bonds flat to gilts, but such things are not unknown during corporate restructurings.

7. Taxation

The bond is a Eurosterling bond and pays gross. The prospectus states:

All payments of principal and interest in respect of the Bonds and the Coupons by or on behalf of the Issuer will be made without withholding or deduction for or on account of any present or future taxes, duties, assessments or governmental charges of whatever nature imposed or levied by or on behalf of the United Kingdom or any political subdivision thereof or any authority thereof or therein having power to tax unless such withholding or deduction is required by law. In such event, the Issuer will pay such additional amounts as shall be necessary in order that the net amounts received by the holders of the Bonds and the Coupons after such withholding or deduction shall equal the respective amounts of principal and interest which would otherwise have been receivable in respect of the Bonds or the Coupons, as the case may be, in the absence of such withholding or deduction; except that no such additional amounts shall be payable with respect to any Bond or Coupon presented for payment:

(i)   in the United Kingdom;

(ii) by or on behalf of a holder who is liable to such taxes, duties, assessments or governmental charges in respect of such Bond or Coupon by reason of his having some connection with the United Kingdom other than the mere holding of such Bond or Coupon; or

(iii) more than 30 days after the Relevant Date (as defined below) except to the extent that the holder thereof would have been entitled to an additional amount on presenting the same for payment on such thirtieth day assuming that day to have been a Business Day in the place where the relevant Bond or Coupon is presented for payment and in London.

8. Prescription

Largely a matter for custodians.

9. Events of default

Define what constitutes a default.

Of course, the document is much longer than this. Page 12 onwards goes on to describe Pearson, shows the company's balance sheet, talks about the use of the proceeds, etc. Beyond that is more info about settlement, listing, the subscription process and so on. As stated above, the document can be downloaded online.

Features generally to watch out for with bonds

1. **Various covenants**. In the bond above we have seen an example of a *negative pledge*. Watch out also for *event risk* clauses which may give the holder the right to put the bonds under certain circumstances – usually a leveraged takeover. There are also *gearing covenants*, intended to prevent the issuer from swamping the company in fresh debt. Strong covenants are positive for investors.

2. **Cross default** – a default on one class of debt triggers a default on all.

3. **Pari-Passu** – bondholders are on an equal footing.

4. **Puts and calls**. Puts are a positive feature for investors but may make the bond more expensive. Calls are a positive feature for the issuer, but present re-investment risk for the investor.

5. **Sinking funds** – the issuer will buy back an agreed amount of the issue over the life of the bond. This helps keep the secondary price up, but ironically can dry up liquidity!

Appendix 2
Bond maths

This book is not about the minutia of financial calculations. In the professional arena, where deals run in the billions, finding a tiny advantage of a few cents in yield will be the making or breaking of a career. However, for the private investor, a decent understanding of the concepts and a few rough and ready formulae will do the job.

Much of this territory has already been covered in the previous chapters of the book but I thought it worthwhile to collect the various yield calculations in one place as a handy reference tool.

Price & yield

The key to understanding the return on all fixed income instruments is to view a bond as a series of discounted cashflows. At the start of the period, the investor pays out cash to purchase the bond. Over the course of the bond's life, the investor will then receive several payments, usually one or two a year from interest payments, known as coupons, and a final repayment at the end of the bond's life-span, known as redemption. In this respect, bonds differ fundamentally from equities, where the future cashflows are unknown.

Given that the future cashflows are known quantities, the relationship between the price of a bond and the yield received by an investor is governed by mathematical formulae. We are going to look at three methods of analysing a bond's yield:

1. income yield,

2. simple yield, and

3. yield to maturity (YTM), also known as Gross Redemption Yield (GRY).

1. Income yield

Sometimes known as running yield, or flat yield.

Let's take an example of a gilt, the UK Treasury 5% 2014. This bond pays a 5% coupon (divided into two semi-annual payments) and matures on 7 September 2014. Thus, if we were able to buy the bond at the face value of

100% (or par), we know that we would receive an income of 5% per annum on our investment until maturity.

But what would happen if we paid less than par for the bond?

Let us assume that we purchase the bond for 95% of face value. Our income yield would be:

> par/purchase price x coupon = income yield
>
> 100/95 x 5% = 5.26% per annum

At the time of writing this article, the UK Treasury 5% 2014 is trading at a price of 110. This premium to par has the effect of reducing the bond's income yield as follows:

> 100/110 * 5 = 4.5% per annum

The income or running yield does not take into account any profit or loss made by holding the bond to redemption, and simply assumes that the investor will be able to sell the bond at the same price that he or she purchased it for. For a more accurate measure of yield, we must turn to the yield to maturity, the standard calculation employed by market professionals.

Before we turn to the more complex (and more accurate) yield to maturity, it is worth considering the *simple yield*. This is a good rough guide to the return available on a bond, and can often be worked out in one's head.

2. Simple yield

Let us take a theoretical bond with one year left to run until redemption. The bond has a 4% coupon and we have purchased it in the market for 97%. Our return will consist of two factors, the running yield over the 12-month period and the profit made on maturity. Let us assume that we invest £1,000. Thus, for our initial investment of £970, we will receive the following:

> £40 coupon payment (our running yield)
>
> £1000 redemption payment (a £30 profit)

Our return over the twelve month period is £70 on £970, or 7.2%. From the point of view of the private investor, this type of calculation is perfectly adequate for assessing the return on a bond. Known as the *simple yield*, the formula can be expressed as follows:

simple yield = (100/P x C) + (100-P)/t

where,

C = coupon
P = current bond price
t = life to maturity of bond (years)

3. Yield to maturity (YTM)

With longer dated bonds, the same theory applies, but to gain a more accurate measure, we must discount each future cash flow according to when it will be paid. The formula used to calculate this is known as the *yield to maturity* (YTM) and is effectively the internal rate of return on the investment, allowing for each and every cash flow. The calculation assumes that the interest payments received on the bond can be re-invested at the same rate, although this may not be the case in real life.

The formula for this calculation is somewhat of a handful, and certainly not one for mental arithmetic. For readers who enjoy a challenge, it can be expressed as:

$$\text{Price} = \text{Coupon} \times \frac{1}{r}\left[1-\frac{1}{(1+r)^n}\right] + \frac{\text{Redemption}}{(1+r)^n}$$

where,

r is YTM

Note: For all yield to maturity calculations, allow for calls, puts and other events. The golden rule is to calculate *yield to worst* (i.e. the worse case scenario).

Duration

Duration is effectively a more sophisticated measure of the bond's maturity – effectively an average life of cash flows balancing coupons and maturity.

Note that the higher the duration of the bond the greater the price move shown per change in yield. Duration is governed by the length of time to maturity and the size of the coupon, in effect, the average period of all cash flows, with values weighted for time. A long bond with a low coupon will have the greatest duration, a short bond with a high coupon will have the lowest duration. Investors looking to benefit from falling yields should look to add duration to their bond portfolios, defensive investors, or those envisioning a rising interest rate scenario, will look to reduce.

The most popular calculation for duration is the *Macauly's Duration.*

There are various methods of expressing this mathematically, one such is:

n = number of cash flows

t = time to maturity

C = cash flow

i = required yield

M = maturity (par) value

P = bond price

Modified Duration is also commonly used, this being a more sophisticated derivative of the Macauly Duration shown above.

Accrued interest

If an investor buys a bond on its first day of issue, or just after the last coupon payment, the price seen on the screen will be the full price. However, when buying a bond half-way through its coupon period (for instance 6 months after the last coupon payment for an annual bond), there will be an adjustment for the income that has *accrued* to the bond. This is standard practice in the bond market and strikes a fair balance between buyers and sellers, as well as neatly differentiating between cash flows from income and those from capital gains.

With the majority of non-gilt bonds, the basis of this accrued interest is calculated on a "30/360" basis. This assumes that each month has 30 days, and each year has 360 days.

Thus, to calculate the accrued interest on a bond, take the number of days from the last coupon to the settlement date (use the 30/360 notation for

Eurobonds) and divide by the number of days in the year. Multiply the result by the coupon, and divide by 100. This factor can then be applied to the nominal amount of the bond. So, the formula is:

> accrued = number of days since last coupon/360 x coupon/100 x nominal value of bond

For gilts, use an actual/actual day count basis.

Note: remember, some bonds pay coupons semi-annually.

Floating Rate Note calculations

It is not possible to calculate a yield to maturity for an FRN, due to the unknown future coupon flows. Market practitioners instead use the *discounted margin* calculation to assess the yearly income from the bond compared to that available in the money markets. This calculation compares the sum of the income received from the bond's coupon with capital gain (or loss) created by holding the bond to maturity, discounted at current money-market rates.

Private investors, who have no need of single basis point accuracy, can use the rather more straightforward *simple margin* calculation, as follows:

> simple margin = 100/price * quoted margin + (100-price/years to maturity)

Index-linked calculations

As mentioned in the chapters on index-linked gilts and index-linked corporate bonds, calculating a yield on such instruments involves assumptions of the future rate of inflation. However, it is possible to calculate the *real yield*, i.e. the incremental yield above (or below) the rate of inflation.

The formula for calculating this is complex, and beyond the scope of this book. However, for readers that enjoy a challenge, the ever-helpful Debt Management Office has an excellent guide on their website at **www.dmo.gov.uk**.

Real yields are published on the FT's website and the aforementioned DMO website.

Calculating current par

Another useful ready reckoner for the private investor is the use of the current par methodology. When an inflation-linked bond is launched as a new issue, it is easy to see if the bond is rich or cheap to its intended real yield (the coupon). Over the first few months if the price drops below par – the spread has clearly become wider.

But, a few years down the road, the increase in the RPI as the bond moves towards maturity will mean that, logically, par should be above 100. This is known as *current par* and can be considered to be roughly the equivalent of net asset value in an equity or investment trust.

To calculate current par on a standard 8-month lag linker, take the orginal reference rate of RPI and compare this with recent data (allowing for an 8-month lag). For mid-period settlement dates, interpolate between the two recent RPI levels.

Appendix 3
Resources for investors

Sadly, it is still the case that resources for the fixed income private investor are limited compared to those available in the equity market. In the latter, the growth of the internet has created an almost level playing field between private and institutional investors with, RNS, live prices and research easily available (often for free).

The bond market is a little more exclusive. The main disadvantage that the private investor will face is the lack of a Bloomberg terminal – a system that is effectively the engine room of the bond market. However, a little digging around can reap dividends. The list below gives a few ideas on what resources are available, either at low cost or for free.

Books

There are many books on bonds, but the problem for UK investors is that most of these are written by, and for, US market professionals and may be of limited application to the UK investor.

The following books are either good, or have a good reputation. I have included the publisher's description (my notes follow in italics).

First Steps in Bonds, by Peter Temple

"One of the great mysteries of the investment world is why more private investors don't trade in bonds. First Steps in Bonds introduces readers to the key issues revolving around the bond markets. It covers in detail each of the main segments of the market – government bonds, corporate bonds, Eurobonds and other types. Supported by illustrative stories, trading scenarios and worked examples, it will lead investors through the concepts whilst always keeping one eye on the reality of the markets."

A good introduction.

An Introduction to the Bond Markets, by Patrick Brown

"This book gives an introduction to the bond markets to readers who have an interest in understanding what they are, how they work, and how they can be used, but do not want to be intimidated by mathematical formulae."

A useful book, although slightly more technical than the blurb above suggests.

An Introduction to Bond Markets, by Moorad Choudhry

"The bond markets are a vital part of the world economy. The fourth edition of Professor Moorad Choudhry's benchmark reference text brings readers up to date with latest developments and market practice, including the impact of the financial crisis and issues of relevance for investors. This book offers a detailed yet accessible look at bond instruments, and is aimed specifically at newcomers to the market or those unfamiliar with modern fixed income products."

Another good book. Very thorough.

The Handbook of Fixed Income Securities, by Frank Fabozzi

"This is the world's most trusted fixed income resource for more than two decades, now substantially revised and updated. Institutional and individual investors have learned to rely on the handbook for its scope and detail, along with the unquestioned global authority and expertise of its contributors."

Frank Fabozzi is a well known educator in the bond markets. The content is US-centric.

Inside the New Gilt Edged Market, by Patrick Phillips

A great old book that may well now be out of print. Note, "new" is a relative expression; I bought my copy in 1987. It cost £25 – a lot of money in those days.

Liar's Poker, by Michael Lewis

"From mere trainee to lowly geek, to triumphal Big Swinging Dick: that was Michael Lewis' pell-mell progress through the dealing rooms of Salomon Brothers in New York and London during the heady mid-1980s when they were probably the world's most powerful and profitable merchant bank. A true-life Bonfire of the Vanities, funny, frightening, breathless and heartless, his is a tale of hysterical greed and ambition set in an obsessed, enclosed world."

The bond market in the 1980s. Well worth a read to get the feel of a dealing room.

Software and systems

The Bloomberg Terminal claims to be the premier resource for all bond traders. Indeed, one could say that with 300,000 users worldwide, Bloomberg is the bond market. The system has around 2 million bonds (and most other financial instruments on its system). Charts, news, prospectus, live prices, yield and spread calculations. Individual subscriptions are in the region of £12,000 per annum. There are a limited number of Bloomberg terminals with public access (or quasi-public access). Some university libraries have Bloomberg Terminals, and Bloomberg occasionally install a terminal for PR or marketing purposes in airports (London City Airport, for instance). See **www.bloomberg.com** for more info.

Calculators

Considered old-school my many, but I would greatly recommend the purchase of a bond calculator. Consider the following:

- **Apps for iPhones**

  There are numerous financial calculators available. I use Financial Calculator v2.1 by Joaquin Greech which works just fine. Apps of this nature can easily be downloaded and cost just a few dollars.

- **Hewlett Packard 17b (ii)**

  A 1990s calculator that still sits on my desk. Menu-driven and easy to use. Comes with a great instruction book that teaches one a lot about discounted cash flows. Still available to buy on the internet from specialist retailers, or try eBay.

- **Hewlett Packard 12c**

  The benchmark for financial calculators. In continuous production since 1981. Ownership of one of these is a right of passage in the bond market. Available on Amazon.

Websites

URL	Description
www.bankofengland.co.uk	The central bank of the United Kingdom. A great website for economic statistics.
www.bondscape.net	Bondscape provides brokers and other professional investment advisers with the ability to trade bonds in smaller size, breaking down the barriers to entry for private client advisors by offering equity-style online dealing capabilities with multiple market makers. The service, delivered free of charge, is live in over 100 institutions within the UK, servicing the needs of over 700 dealers and portfolio managers.
www.bondvigilantes.co.uk	An informative blog from the fixed income fund management team at M&G.
www.bloomberg.com	Bloomberg's 11 international web sites provide an up-to-the-minute mix of data, news and tools related to financial markets, economics, politics, personal finance and lifestyle.
www.bba.org.uk	The BBA is the leading association for the UK banking and financial services sector, speaking for 228 banking members from 60 countries on the full range of UK or international banking issues and engaging with 35 associated professional firms.
www.bondmarketprices.com	A very useful website offering private investors access to the TRAX database of bond prices and other information produced by international bond dealers. This website has data on both sterling denominated and foreign currency bonds trading in the international capital markets.
www.bsa.org.uk	The UK Building Societies' website. Useful info from the association of this group of organisations, which remain frequent issuers in the bond and PIBS market.
www.cmavision.com/market-data	A useful website showing the biggest movers in Credit Default Swaps (CDS). Useful to see what is on the move, up and down, both amongst sovereign credits and corporate.
www.dmo.gov.uk	The UK Government Debt Management Office. A host of useful information on gilts and Index Linked gilts for the private investor. Full prospectuses of gilt issues can be downloaded from here.
www.eib.org/investor_info/markets/gbp-bond-market.htm	The European Investment Bank is one of the major issuers in the sterling bond markets and encourages retail participation. Link goes straight to the sterling bond page.

URL	Description
www.fixedincomeinvestor.co.uk	My own website. Prices, yields and data on the sterling retail bond market plus "Bond of the Week" and the model portfolio.
www.fixedincomeinvestments.org.uk	A website run by an enthusiast of subordinated sterling debt. Also, some strong investor activism.
www.investorschronicle.co.uk	The UK's best selling weekly investment publication. Broad coverage of the UK market and fair bit of fixed income stuff.
www.lloydsbankinggroup.com/investors/ debt_investors.asp	Useful IR section of Lloyds bank website with details of the various Lloyds' bonds and preference shares.
www.londonstockexchange.com/exchange /prices-and-news/retail-bonds/retail-bonds-search.html	The London Stock Exchange Retail Bond platform, shows prices and trades in selected gilts and corporate bonds. An increasingly important resource.
www.marketprices.ft.com	Link goes straight to the FT's international bond data page.
www.moodys.com	Register to gain access to credit ratings on over 170,000 corporate, government, and structured finance securities. Free to private users.
http://boards.fool.co.uk/Messages.asp?bid =50085	The Motley Fool's bulletin board for bonds and gilts.
http://boards.fool.co.uk/banking-sector-50033.aspx	The Motley Fool's bulletin board for the banking sector – a useful place for news and views on prefs, PIBS etc.
http://www.statistics.gov.uk/default.asp	Office for National Statistics – RPI, CPI, average earnings etc.
www.reuters.com	The leading international news agency. Coverage of international markets and related issues.
www.standardandpoors.com	Provider of credit ratings assessing the risk of default associated with different bond issues. Standard & Poor's offers the public access to current ratings information. Viewers must register (free) to view data.
http://www.swap-rates.com	A useful website with data on money market, swaps and other wholesale market rates.
www.yahoo.com	The Yahoo Finance UK bond page. Daily updates on market moves and macro-economic developments. Link goes straight to bond page.

Note: for more information on individual bond issues, try the IR section of the issuing company's website as the first port of call.

Training

- **CISI**

  The Chartered Institute for Securities & Investment offer a Bond & Fixed Interest Markets exam. This, combined with other exams, will lead to the CISI's diploma.

- **ICMA**

  The International Capital Markets Association (broadly speaking the trade body for the Eurobond market) offer both a Financial Markets Foundation Course and an International Fixed Income and Derivatives (IFID) Certificate Programme.

- **BPP**

  Professional training company offering a variety of courses including "Bond markets – Introduction". And CFA-modular courses.

Appendix 4
Brokers

The majority of private investors will buy (and sell) bonds through their stockbroker. Most stockbrokers will be able to offer a dealing service in UK gilts, but only a limited number can offer facilities in non-gilt bonds such as Eurosterling and corporate bonds. When opening an account for bond dealing, investors should consider and compare charges for both dealing and custody. Also consider what service the broker may be able to provide in terms of expertise and knowledge in the field. In many cases this will vary greatly depending on the individual account manager.

The list below features a number of brokers able to offer bond dealing services. I have used the broker's own description of their services where available.

Please note: This list is not comprehensive and it may be worth asking your existing stockbroker or wealth manager what he/she can provide.

Broker	Services provided
ADM Securities	ADM Securities (ADMS) is a specialist broking division of ADM Investor Services International Limited. ADMS offers a highly personal value added service to both Private Clients and Institutions across a broad range of markets.
Barclays Stockbrokers	Barclays Stockbrokers is the UK's number one retail stockbroker with over £10 billion assets currently under management. Barclays has been involved in banking and investment management for over 300 years and in over 60 countries.
Brewin Dolphin	Full-service wealth manager (discretionary management etc.) with fixed income research and execution capability.
City and Continental LLP	Specialists in fixed income securities with expertise in the fields of illiquid, distressed and exotic debt instruments.
Charles Stanley	Offers a comprehensive service to private clients.
Collins Stewart Wealth Management	An award-winning stockbroker committed to providing private clients with a broad array of independent wealth management services, with over £6.8bn in assets under management.
Hargreaves Lansdown	One of the UK's leading independent financial service providers and asset management specialists. HL offers customers execution in gilts and corporate bonds across a range of accounts.
IG Index	The world leader in financial spread betting. Offers trading in the major government bond contracts.
Killik & Co	Founded in 1989 Killik & Co is one of the leading advisory stockbroking firms in the UK, and offers a personal approach to doing business. Killik & Co's Personal Brokers are able to offer advice on a range of asset classes including Corporate Bonds upon which in-house research is produced. Trades can be executed either through the LSE's Order Book for Retail Bonds or manually through the Killik & Co dealers who have good relationships with most of the major counterparties.
Redmayne Bentley	A leading independent private client stockbrokers in the UK with over 30 branches nationwide. Advisory, discretionary and execution-only services available.
Selftrade	One of the UK's leading execution-only stockbrokers, offering a wide choice of account types. Online and phone trades in UK and international equities, funds and covered warrants are subject to a flat fee of £12.50. Bonds from £12.50 per deal (online) through to £40 (telephone). Dedicated fixed income dealers available.
TD Direct	TD Direct (formally TD Waterhouse) is a subsidiary of the Toronto-Dominion Bank, North America's 6th largest bank by branches. Established in 1997, TDW is the UK's second largest execution-only broker, servicing approx 200,000 customers with over £3.77 billion in customer assets under management. Customers can invest in fixed interest bonds and gilts through TD Waterhouse's Trading Account, Trading Plus Account, Trading ISA or SIPP Accounts.

Appendix 5
RPI/CPI table

The table in this appendix gives monthly figures for the RPI and CPI from 1987. Historic and current figures can be found at the website of the Office for National Statistics (**www.statistics.gov.uk**).

Some notes:

1. The current RPI was re-based in January 1987. For a longer-term measure of inflation, the ONS has data back to 1947.

2. A good measure of the devastating effect of long-term inflation is illustrated by the Barclays UK Cost of Living Index. Starting in 1899 at 100, this index stood at 6,712 in 2009.

3. Over the first 50 years, the value of money dropped by 62%. The real damage was done after the war. 1950 to 2009 saw the purchasing power of one pound drop to 4p.

Date	RPI (All Items)	CPI (All Items)	Date	RPI (All Items)	CPI (All Items)
1987 01	100		1988 12	110.3	64.8
1987 02	100.4		1989 01	111	65
1987 03	100.6		1989 02	111.8	65.2
1987 04	101.8		1989 03	112.3	65.5
1987 05	101.9		1989 04	114.3	66.4
1987 06	101.9		1989 05	115	66.7
1987 07	101.8		1989 06	115.4	67
1987 08	102.1		1989 07	115.5	66.9
1987 09	102.4		1989 08	115.8	67
1987 10	102.9		1989 09	116.6	67.5
1987 11	103.4		1989 10	117.5	68
1987 12	103.3		1989 11	118.5	68.2
1988 01	103.3	61.9	1989 12	118.8	68.3
1988 02	103.7	62.1	1990 01	119.5	68.6
1988 03	104.1	62.3	1990 02	120.2	69
1988 04	105.8	63.1	1990 03	121.4	69.4
1988 05	106.2	63.4	1990 04	125.1	70.6
1988 06	106.6	63.6	1990 05	126.2	71.3
1988 07	106.7	63.6	1990 06	126.7	71.6
1988 08	107.9	63.8	1990 07	126.8	71.4
1988 09	108.4	64.1	1990 08	128.1	72.2
1988 10	109.5	64.4	1990 09	129.3	72.9
1988 11	110	64.7	1990 10	130.3	73.5

Date	RPI (All Items)	CPI (All Items)	Date	RPI (All Items)	CPI (All Items)
1990 11	130	73.6	1994 07	144	83.6
1990 12	129.9	73.5	1994 08	144.7	84.1
1991 01	130.2	73.5	1994 09	145	84.2
1991 02	130.9	73.9	1994 10	145.2	84
1991 03	131.4	74.1	1994 11	145.3	84.1
1991 04	133.1	76.6	1994 12	146	84.5
1991 05	133.5	77.2	1995 01	146	84.5
1991 06	134.1	77.6	1995 02	146.9	84.9
1991 07	133.8	77.4	1995 03	147.5	85.3
1991 08	134.1	77.7	1995 04	149	85.8
1991 09	134.6	78.1	1995 05	149.6	86.2
1991 10	135.1	78.5	1995 06	149.8	86.3
1991 11	135.6	78.8	1995 07	149.1	85.8
1991 12	135.7	78.8	1995 08	149.9	86.3
1992 01	135.6	78.6	1995 09	150.6	86.7
1992 02	136.3	79	1995 10	149.8	86.5
1992 03	136.7	79.4	1995 11	149.8	86.5
1992 04	138.8	80.2	1995 12	150.7	87
1992 05	139.3	80.5	1996 01	150.2	86.8
1992 06	139.3	80.6	1996 02	150.9	87.2
1992 07	138.8	80.2	1996 03	151.5	87.5
1992 08	138.9	80.2	1996 04	152.6	88
1992 09	139.4	80.5	1996 05	152.9	88.3
1992 10	139.9	80.7	1996 06	153	88.4
1992 11	139.7	80.8	1996 07	152.4	87.8
1992 12	139.2	80.8	1996 08	153.1	88.3
1993 01	137.9	80.4	1996 09	153.8	88.7
1993 02	138.8	80.9	1996 10	153.8	88.7
1993 03	139.3	81.3	1996 11	153.9	88.7
1993 04	140.6	82.2	1996 12	154.4	89
1993 05	141.1	82.5	1997 01	154.4	88.6
1993 06	141	82.5	1997 02	155	88.8
1993 07	140.7	82.2	1997 03	155.4	89
1993 08	141.3	82.5	1997 04	156.3	89.4
1993 09	141.9	82.9	1997 05	156.9	89.6
1993 10	141.8	82.8	1997 06	157.5	89.8
1993 11	141.6	82.6	1997 07	157.5	89.5
1993 12	141.9	82.8	1997 08	158.5	90
1994 01	141.3	82.5	1997 09	159.3	90.3
1994 02	142.1	82.9	1997 10	159.5	90.3
1994 03	142.5	83.1	1997 11	159.6	90.4
1994 04	144.2	83.9	1997 12	160	90.5
1994 05	144.7	84.1	1998 01	159.5	89.9
1994 06	144.7	84.1	1998 02	160.3	90.3

Date	RPI (All Items)	CPI (All Items)	Date	RPI (All Items)	CPI (All Items)
1998 03	160.8	90.5	2001 11	173.6	94.5
1998 04	162.6	91	2001 12	173.4	94.7
1998 05	163.5	91.5	2002 01	173.3	94.4
1998 06	163.4	91.3	2002 02	173.8	94.5
1998 07	163	90.8	2002 03	174.5	94.9
1998 08	163.7	91.2	2002 04	175.7	95.3
1998 09	164.4	91.6	2002 05	176.2	95.5
1998 10	164.5	91.6	2002 06	176.2	95.5
1998 11	164.4	91.7	2002 07	175.9	95.2
1998 12	164.4	91.9	2002 08	176.4	95.5
1999 01	163.4	91.4	2002 09	177.6	95.7
1999 02	163.7	91.5	2002 10	177.9	95.9
1999 03	164.1	92	2002 11	178.2	95.9
1999 04	165.2	92.4	2002 12	178.5	96.3
1999 05	165.6	92.7	2003 01	178.4	95.7
1999 06	165.6	92.6	2003 02	179.3	96
1999 07	165.1	92	2003 03	179.9	96.3
1999 08	165.5	92.3	2003 04	181.2	96.7
1999 09	166.2	92.7	2003 05	181.5	96.7
1999 10	166.5	92.6	2003 06	181.3	96.5
1999 11	166.7	92.7	2003 07	181.3	96.5
1999 12	167.3	93	2003 08	181.6	96.8
2000 01	166.6	92.1	2003 09	182.5	97.1
2000 02	167.5	92.4	2003 10	182.6	97.2
2000 03	168.4	92.6	2003 11	182.7	97.2
2000 04	170.1	92.9	2003 12	183.5	97.5
2000 05	170.7	93.2	2004 01	183.1	97
2000 06	171.1	93.3	2004 02	183.8	97.2
2000 07	170.5	92.8	2004 03	184.6	97.4
2000 08	170.5	92.8	2004 04	185.7	97.8
2000 09	171.7	93.6	2004 05	186.5	98.1
2000 10	171.6	93.5	2004 06	186.8	98.1
2000 11	172.1	93.7	2004 07	186.8	97.8
2000 12	172.2	93.7	2004 08	187.4	98.1
2001 01	171.1	92.9	2004 09	188.1	98.2
2001 02	172	93.1	2004 10	188.6	98.4
2001 03	172.2	93.4	2004 11	189	98.6
2001 04	173.1	94	2004 12	189.9	99.1
2001 05	174.2	94.7	2005 01	188.9	98.6
2001 06	174.4	94.9	2005 02	189.6	98.8
2001 07	173.3	94.2	2005 03	190.5	99.3
2001 08	174	94.5	2005 04	191.6	99.7
2001 09	174.6	94.8	2005 05	192	100
2001 10	174.3	94.7	2005 06	192.2	100

Date	RPI (All Items)	CPI (All Items)	Date	RPI (All Items)	CPI (All Items)
2005 07	192.2	100.1	2008 07	216.5	109
2005 08	192.6	100.4	2008 08	217.2	109.7
2005 09	193.1	100.6	2008 09	218.4	110.3
2005 10	193.3	100.7	2008 10	217.7	110
2005 11	193.6	100.7	2008 11	216	109.9
2005 12	194.1	101	2008 12	212.9	109.5
2006 01	193.4	100.5	2009 01	210.1	108.7
2006 02	194.2	100.9	2009 02	211.4	109.6
2006 03	195	101.1	2009 03	211.3	109.8
2006 04	196.5	101.7	2009 04	211.5	110.1
2006 05	197.7	102.2	2009 05	212.8	110.7
2006 06	198.5	102.5	2009 06	213.4	111
2006 07	198.5	102.5	2009 07	213.4	110.9
2006 08	199.2	102.5	2009 08	214.4	111.4
2006 09	200.1	102.9	2009 09	215.3	111.5
2006 10	200.4	103	2009 10	216	111.7
2006 11	201.1	103.2	2009 11	216.6	112
2006 12	202.7	103.4	2009 12	218	112.6
2007 01	201.6	104	2010 01	217.9	112.4
2007 02	203.1	103.7	2010 02	219.2	112.9
2007 03	204.4	104.2	2010 03	220.7	113.5
2007 04	205.4	104.5	2010 04	222.8	114.2
2007 05	206.2	104.8	2010 05	223.6	114.4
2007 06	207.3	105	2010 06	224.1	114.6
2007 07	206.1	104.4	2010 07	223.6	114.3
2007 08	207.3	104.7	2010 08	224.5	114.9
2007 09	208	104.8	2010 09	225.3	114.9
2007 10	208.9	105.3	2010 10	225.8	115.2
2007 11	209.7	105.6	2010 11	226.8	115.6
2007 12	210.9	106.2	2010 12	228.4	116.8
2008 01	209.8	105.5	2011 01	229	116.9
2008 02	211.4	106.3	2011 02	231.3	117.8
2008 03	212.1	106.7	2011 03	232.5	118.1
2008 04	214	107.7	2011 04	234.4	119.3
2008 05	215.1	108.3	2011 05	235.2	119.5
2008 06	216.8	109			

Appendix 6
Gilt Edged Market Makers

The Bank of England issues licenses for Gilt Edged Market Makers (or "GEMMS"); there are 18 firms operating as such at present.

Barclays Capital 5 The North Colonnade Canary Wharf London E14 4BB **www.barcap.com**	Goldman Sachs International Limited Peterborough Court 133 Fleet Street London EC4A 2BB **www.gs.com**
BNP Paribas (London Branch) 10 Harewood Avenue London NW1 6AA **www.bnpparibas.com**	HSBC Bank PLC 8 Canada Square London E14 5HQ **www.hsbcgroup.com**
Citigroup Global Markets Limited Citigroup Centre 33 Canada Square London E14 5LB **www.citigroup.com**	Jefferies International Limited Vintners Place 68 Upper Thames Street London EC4V 3BJ **www.jefferies.com**
Credit Suisse Securities One Cabot Square London E14 4QJ **www.credit-suisse.com**	JP Morgan Securities Limited 125 London Wall London EC2Y 5AJ **www.jpmorgan.com**
Deutsche Bank AG (London Branch) Winchester House 1 Great Winchester Street London EC2N 2DB **https://gm-secure.db.com**	Merrill Lynch International Merrill Lynch Financial Centre 2 King Edward Street London EC1A 1HQ **www.ml.com**

Morgan Stanley & Co. International plc 20 Cabot Square Canary Wharf London E14 4QW **www.morganstanley.com**	Société Généralé Corporate & Investment Banking SG House 41 Tower Hill London EC3N 4SG **www.sgcib.com**
Nomura International plc One Angel Lane London EC4R 3AB **www.nomura.com**	The Toronto-Dominion Bank (London Branch) Triton Court 14/18 Finsbury Square London EC2A 1DB **www.td.com**
Royal Bank of Canada Europe Limited Thames Court One Queenhithe London EC4V 4DE **www.rbccm.com**	UBS Limited 1 Finsbury Avenue London EC2M 2PP **www.ubs.com/investmentbank/**
Royal Bank of Scotland 135 Bishopsgate London EC2M 3UR **www.rbsmarkets.com**	Winterflood Securities Limited The Atrium Building Cannon Bridge 25 Dowgate Hill London EC4R 2GA **www.wins.co.uk**
Santander Global Banking & Markets UK 2 Triton Square Regent's Place London NW1 3AN **www.santandergbm.com**	

Appendix 7

GBP corporate bond prices and yields

The table below shows a selection of actively traded sterling denominated bonds as displayed on the **www.fixedincomeinvestor.co.uk** website as of 22 May 2012. The 180 bonds shown are selected by the market makers participating in the Bondscape platform and represent a good selection (but by no means the whole universe) of those bonds which are available in smaller minimum dealing sizes. The selection includes some of the new retail bonds that are now being issued for listing on the London Stock Exchange's ORB market.

Issuer	ISIN	Coupon	Maturity	Price	Yield
GE	XS0328406805	5.875	1 Nov 2012	101.95	1.37
Centrica PLC	XS0137672381	5.875	2 Nov 2012	101.8	1.72
Dixons Group Plc	XS0157632562	6.125	15 Nov 2012	100.35	5.21
KFW International Finance	XS0212069115	4.75	7 Dec 2012	102.15	0.72
Kommunalbanken AS	XS0158814706	4.875	10 Dec 2012	102.7	-0.06
Carrefour Sa	XS0155152951	5.375	19 Dec 2012	101.8	2.14
European Investment Bank	XS0160908249	4.5	14 Jan 2013	102.45	0.66
KFW International Finance	XS0255658600	4.875	15 Jan 2013	102.675	0.7
Total Capital SA	XS0284605036	5.5	29 Jan 2013	103.1	0.92
Wal-mart Stores	XS0160673264	4.75	29 Jan 2013	102.7	0.76
JTI (UK) Finance PLC	XS0161361828	5.75	6 Feb 2013	103.2	1.15
Eurofima	XS0162167554	4.375	11 Feb 2013	102.4	1
Carlsberg	XS0084333219	7.0	26 Feb 2013	103.55	2.19
GE	XS0357123131	6.0	11 Apr 2013	103.95	1.45
CIBA UK Plc	XS0085895935	6.5	24 Apr 2013	103.65	2.42
RWE Finance Bv	XS0147048259	6.375	3 Jun 2013	104.75	1.66
Deut Tel IF	XS0261792039	5.625	19 Jul 2013	104.35	1.77
Next Plc	XS0169287124	5.25	30 Sep 2013	103.8	2.34

Issuer	ISIN	Coupon	Maturity	Price	Yield
Morgan Stanley & Co Inc	US617446HS12	5.375	14 Nov 2013	102.15	3.86
BAT Intl Finance Plc	XS0171812547	5.75	9 Dec 2013	106.15	1.67
BAA Plc	XS0472751055	2.625	10 Dec 2013	102.3	1.11
General Elec Cap Corp	XS0167497881	5.25	10 Dec 2013	105.45	1.64
Nedwbk 2.375 10 Dec 2013 MTN	XS0496515973	2.375	10 Dec 2013	101.65	1.28
GUS plc	XS0162820228	5.625	12 Dec 2013	105.6	1.91
World Bank	XS0121646615	5.375	15 Jan 2014	107.85	0.56
Halifax Plc	GB0004037171	11.0	17 Jan 2014	108.1	5.59
John Lewis	GB0005140958	10.5	23 Jan 2014	112.6	2.62
KFW International Finance	XS0197066565	5.375	29 Jan 2014	107.6	0.81
KTW	XS0414238898	3.25	24 Feb 2014	104.3	0.77
Marks &Spencer Plc	XS0188430721	5.625	24 Mar 2014	105.55	2.47
European Investment Bank	XS0103080544	6.25	15 Apr 2014	109.35	1.22
Italy (Republic of)	GB0004601430	10.5	28 Apr 2014	108.55	5.6
Lloyds Tsb Bank Plc	XS0149620691	5.875	20 Jun 2014	101.125	5.21
European Bk Recon & Dev	XS0115314741	5.875	4 Aug 2014	110.85	0.86
Safeway Plc	XS0100362911	6.5	5 Aug 2014	109.75	1.91
Pearson Plc	XS0102793642	7.0	27 Oct 2014	112	1.88
Compass Group PLC	XS0100559037	7.0	8 Dec 2014	112.8	1.78
Severn Trent Wtr Util Fin	XS0176529583	5.25	8 Dec 2014	109.45	1.43
GE Capital Uk Funding	XS0191374817	5.625	12 Dec 2014	109.3	1.85
Merrill Lynch & Co Inc	XS0191960896	5.75	12 Dec 2014	105.05	3.6
Kingfisher Plc	XS0178322474	5.625	15 Dec 2014	106.95	2.75
Nordic Investment Bank	XS0105219553	5.75	16 Dec 2014	112.675	0.73
Unilever	XS0418570130	4.0	19 Dec 2014	107.6	0.99
BP	XS0436300247	4.0	29 Dec 2014	106.45	1.44

Issuer	ISIN	Coupon	Maturity	Price	Yield
Bank Nederland Gemeenten	XS0241013472	4.375	19 Jan 2015	107.3	1.54
Pacific Life Funding LLC	XS0209922714	5.125	20 Jan 2015	104.75	3.2
GE Capital Uk Funding	XS0213823619	5.125	3 Mar 2015	108.5	1.94
Roche Holdings Inc	XS0415625283	5.5	4 Mar 2015	111.5	1.26
Heineken	XS0416081296	7.25	10 Mar 2015	113.65	2.15
Lloyds Tsb Bank Plc	XS0109722990	6.625	30 Mar 2015	101.35	6
European Investment Bank	XS0223923870	4.375	8 Jul 2015	108.05	1.7
Lloyds TSB	XS0517466198	5.375	7 Sep 2015	103.95	4.08
Rabobank	XS0451037062	4.0	10 Sep 2015	105.45	2.25
Segro PLC	XS0093802055	6.25	30 Sep 2015	109.55	3.17
Anglian Water Services Fin	XS0211684831	5.25	30 Oct 2015	111.8	1.67
Neder Waterschapsbank	XS0092411916	5.625	17 Nov 2015	113.45	1.61
Land A2BR 5.292 28 Nov 2015 MTN	XS0204776446	5.292	28 Nov 2015	103.85	2.67
Kreditanstalt fuer Wiederaufbau	XS0138034631	5.5	7 Dec 2015	114.8	1.19
Goldman Sachs Group Inc	XS0212249014	5.25	15 Dec 2015	103.6	4.09
GE Capital Uk Funding	XS0241042141	4.625	18 Jan 2016	107.85	2.34
BOC Group Ltd.	XS0123544529	6.5	29 Jan 2016	117.1	1.66
Bank Nederland Gemeenten	XS0288626798	5.25	26 Feb 2016	112.05	1.89
Rolls-royce Plc	XS0112487482	7.375	14 Jun 2016	122.15	1.67
Smiths Industries	XS0111725049	7.25	30 Jun 2016	115	3.25
European Investment Bank	XS0274987873	4.875	7 Sep 2016	112.025	1.92
Lloyds TSB	XS0604804194	5.5	25 Sep 2016	104.05	4.46
British Telecommunications PLC	XS0123682758	8.75	7 Dec 2016	123.1	3.17
La Poste (France)	FR0000482770	5.625	19 Dec 2016	109.75	3.26

Issuer	ISIN	Coupon	Maturity	Price	Yield
Safeway	XS0140144204	6.0	10 Jan 2017	115	2.51
Goldman Sachs Group Inc	XS0142963445	6.125	14 Feb 2017	105.05	4.84
Scottish Power UK Plc	XS0073359548	8.375	20 Feb 2017	124	2.86
BG Transco Plc	XS0141704725	6.0	7 Jun 2017	118	2.18
Unilever	XS0434423926	4.75	16 Jun 2017	114.6	1.71
Anheuser-Busch InBev NV	BE6000183549	6.5	23 Jun 2017	119.9	2.29
European Investment Bank	XS0055498413	8.75	25 Aug 2017	131.5	2.3
Kreditanstalt fuer Wiederaufbau	XS0138036099	5.625	25 Aug 2017	120.45	1.53
Co-operative Bank	XS0542823892	5.125	20 Sep 2017	101.3	4.84
European Investment Bank	XS0434040167	4.125	7 Dec 2017	109.5	2.26
Total	XS0430265693	4.25	8 Dec 2017	110.825	2.14
General Elec Cap Corp	XS0148124588	6.25	15 Dec 2017	115.2	3.19
Société Généralé	XS0161798417	5.4	30 Jan 2018	86	8.43
Bank Nederlandse Gemeenten	XS0162957012	4.5	20 Feb 2018	111.2	2.37
Hsbc Holdings Plc	XS0043041879	9.875	8 Apr 2018	106	2.79
United Utilities Water PLC	XS0168054673	5.375	14 May 2018	114.75	2.65
Segro PLC	XS0221323693	5.5	20 Jun 2018	108.1	3.93
GE Capital Uk Funding	XS0381559979	6.75	6 Aug 2018	117.85	3.47
Tesco Personal Finance	XS0591029409	5.2	24 Aug 2018	104.15	4.43
European Investment Bank	XS0160386875	4.75	15 Oct 2018	112.95	2.51
Enterprise Inns Plc	XS0163019143	6.5	6 Dec 2018	79.7	10.93
Dailyml 5.75 07 Dec 2018	XS0170485204	5.75	7 Dec 2018	103	5.12
Citigroup Inc	XS0173603969	5.125	12 Dec 2018	96.6	5.68
Safeway	XS0093004736	6.125	17 Dec 2018	120	2.73

Issuer	ISIN	Coupon	Maturity	Price	Yield
First Group PLC	XS0181013607	6.125	18 Jan 2019	106.7	4.86
Eni Coordination Centre	BE0119012905	5.0	27 Jan 2019	107.75	3.63
European Investment Bank	XS0302736219	5.375	7 Mar 2019	117.45	2.53
GE Capital Uk Funding	XS0297507773	5.625	25 Apr 2019	110.2	3.88
GKN	XS0103214762	6.75	28 Oct 2019	108.85	5.2
Nordic Investment Bank	XS0104228845	5.25	26 Nov 2019	125.35	1.63
Mark & Spencer	XS0471074582	6.125	2 Dec 2019	110.55	4.39
BAT Intl Finance Plc	XS0182188366	6.375	12 Dec 2019	122.2	3.01
Tesco Plc	XS0159013068	5.5	13 Dec 2019	113.55	3.4
Cdc Ixis capital Markets	XS0107813452	5.875	24 Feb 2020	111.2	4.11
British Telecommunications PLC	XS0052067583	8.625	26 Mar 2020	132.2	3.76
Provident Financial	XS0496412064	7.0	14 Apr 2020	106.15	6.01
GE	XS0118106243	6.25	29 Sep 2020	116.05	3.91
AXA SA	XS0122028904	7.125	15 Dec 2020	97.95	7.31
RWE Finance Bv	XS0127992336	6.5	20 Apr 2021	121.95	3.55
Halifax Plc	XS0066120915	9.375	15 May 2021	98.275	9.45
General Elec Cap Corp	XS0092499077	5.5	7 Jun 2021	109.85	4.13
IBRD	XS0091139914	5.4	7 Jun 2021	128	1.97
Bank Nederland Gemeenten	XS0092607497	5.375	7 Jun 2021	117.9	3.05
European Investment Bank	XS0091457027	5.375	7 Jun 2021	118.45	2.99
Inter-American Development Bank	XS0121569957	5.25	7 Jun 2021	124.3	2.24
National Grid Plc 1.25 06 Oct 2021 MTN	XS0678522490	1.25	6 Oct 2021	102.06	4.32
Goldman Sachs Group Inc	XS0270349003	5.5	12 Oct 2021	89.9	6.88
Segro	XS0125077122	7.0	14 Mar 2022	116.65	4.85

Issuer	ISIN	Coupon	Maturity	Price	Yield
Scottish & Southern Energy plc	XS0095371638	5.875	22 Sep 2022	119.4	3.56
Prudential Finance	XS0083544212	6.875	20 Jan 2023	123.05	4.11
Linde Finance Bv	XS0297700006	5.875	24 Apr 2023	127.7	2.86
GE Capital Uk Funding	XS0254673964	5.125	24 May 2023	106.45	4.33
Scottish Power UK Plc	XS0087240163	6.75	29 May 2023	124.7	3.9
HSBC Bank Plc	XS0088317853	6.5	7 Jul 2023	109.2	5.31
Anglian Water Services Fin	XS0089553282	6.875	21 Aug 2023	131.25	3.44
Roche Finance	XS0175478873	5.375	29 Aug 2023	124.8	2.76
RWE Finance Bv	XS0170732738	5.625	6 Dec 2023	116.55	3.79
National Grid Co Plc	XS0094073672	5.875	2 Feb 2024	120.45	3.65
Severn Trent Wtr Util Fin	XS0094475802	6.125	26 Feb 2024	121.95	3.74
Citigroup Inc	XS0195612592	5.875	1 Jul 2024	95.25	6.35
KFW International Finance	XS0200320579	5.0	10 Sep 2024	122.45	2.79
United Utilities	XS0058209106	8.5	31 Mar 2025	143	4.08
European Investment Bank	XS0110373569	5.5	15 Apr 2025	121.65	3.37
Kreditanstalt fuer Wiederaufbau	XS0138036842	5.5	18 Jun 2025	129.1	2.79
Transco	XS0058343251	8.75	27 Jun 2025	151.4	3.68
Vodafone	XS0181816652	5.625	4 Dec 2025	119.9	3.69
United Utilities Electricity plc	XS0058957316	8.875	25 Mar 2026	149.15	4.09
National Air Traffic	XS0174424902	5.25	31 Mar 2026		nan
EDF	XS0169169355	5.5	5 Jun 2026	114.4	4.09
Barclays Bank Plc	XS0134886067	5.75	14 Sep 2026	79.45	8.08
Aviva Plc	XS0138717441	6.125	16 Nov 2026	79.95	8.41
Sncf 5.375 18 Mar 2027	XS0144628053	5.375	18 Mar 2027	110.7	4.33
EDF	XS0148889420	6.125	7 Jun 2027	119.65	4.27

Issuer	ISIN	Coupon	Maturity	Price	Yield
National Grid Co Plc	XS0132735373	6.5	27 Jul 2028	129.6	3.94
Italy (Republic of)	XS0089572316	6.0	4 Aug 2028	80.1	8.1
Kreditanstalt fuer Wiederaufbau	XS0138037733	6.0	7 Dec 2028	137.05	3.08
European Investment Bank	XS0085727559	6.0	7 Dec 2028	126.85	3.75
British Telecommunications PLC	XS0097283096	5.75	7 Dec 2028	110.35	4.77
General Elec Cap Corp	XS0096298822	5.25	7 Dec 2028	106.95	4.58
Severn Trent Wtr Util Fin	XS0097777253	6.25	7 Jun 2029	126.25	4.04
Tesco Plc	XS0105244585	6.0	14 Dec 2029	117.1	4.51
Procter & Gamble Co	XS0106655235	6.25	31 Jan 2030	134.25	3.57
RWE Finance Bv	XS0147048762	6.25	3 Jun 2030	122.1	4.39
Citigroup Inc	XS0116066449	6.5	16 Aug 2030	110.55	5.49
Wal-mart Stores	XS0121617517	5.75	19 Dec 2030	126.55	3.75
Electricite De France	XS0132424614	5.875	18 Jul 2031	108.15	5.13
GE	XS0154681737	5.625	16 Sep 2031	107.75	4.93
Prudential Finance Bv	XS0140198044	6.125	19 Dec 2031	99.05	6.11
European Investment Bank	XS0114126294	5.625	7 Jun 2032	122.95	3.91
E.ON International Finance	XS0148579666	6.375	7 Jun 2032	125.7	4.37
KFW	XS0138038624	5.75	7 Jun 2032	136.65	3.21
Vodafone Group PLC	XS0158715713	5.9	26 Nov 2032	120.7	4.31
Tesco Plc	XS0159013142	5.5	13 Jan 2033	110.45	4.64
GE	XS0340495216	5.875	18 Jan 2033	111.2	4.03
Proctor & Gamble	XS0158603083	5.25	19 Jan 2033	121.85	3.68
HSBC Bank Plc	XS0174470764	5.375	22 Aug 2033	88.8	6.25
Wessex Water Services	XS0178489844	5.75	14 Oct 2033	117.7	4.4

Issuer	ISIN	Coupon	Maturity	Price	Yield
Glaxosmithkline Cap Plc	XS0140516864	5.25	19 Dec 2033	119.55	3.9
Segro PLC	XS0221324154	5.75	20 Jun 2035	99.2	5.73
Walmart	XS0202077953	5.25	28 Sep 2035	118.9	4
General Elec Cap Corp	XS0229561831	4.875	18 Sep 2037	87.25	5.77
Lcr Financial Plc	XS0094835278	4.5	7 Dec 2038	119.4	3.39
European Investment Bank	XS0096499057	5.0	15 Apr 2039	114.05	4.08
Lloyds TSB	XS0543369184	6.5	17 Sep 2040	95.25	6.77
GE	XS0182703743	5.375	18 Dec 2040	101.9	5.18
Hsbc Capital Funding Lp	XS0110560165	8.208		101.8	7.39
Barclays Bank Plc	XS0118932366	7.125		87.3	9.15
Barclays Bank Plc	XS0120327571	6.875		90.15	10.08
Abbey National Plc	XS0124569566	7.037		71.45	10.9
Standard Chartered Bank	XS0129229141	8.103		102	7.36

The above table is drawn from the **www.fixedincomeinvestor.co.uk** website, with prices and yields sourced from **www.bondscape.com**.

Appendix 8
Glossary

Term	Description
ABS	Asset backed securities. A bond backed by financial assets such as credit card receipts, loans, leases etc.
accrued Interest	The theoretical (ie not yet paid) amount of interest that the bond has earned since the last coupon payment.
basis Point (BP)	One-hundredth of one percent. Used to describe small increments of yield and price. For instance, a quarter of 1% would be expressed as 25 basis points (or 25bp). Generally used for yield.
bulldog	A sterling bond issued by an overseas borrower into the UK domestic bond market. Now rare.
Bund	German government bonds.
call	A feature where the issuer has the option to redeem the bond early.
cap	A maximum coupon.
CD	Certificate of Deposit. A short-term note issued by a bank.
CDI	Crest Depositary Interest – a virtual certificate representing a security in Crest.
CDS	Credit Default Swaps: a contract offering protection against the default of a given issuer. The premium charged will be closely related to the spread on the bond and is a measure of perceived risk.
CGT	Capital Gains Tax.
Clearstream	The Deutsche Borse settlement and custody system.
CMO	Collateralised Mortgage Obligation.
CoCo's	Contingent Convertibles – subordinated bonds with mandatory conversion to equity in certain circumstances. Also known as ECNs.
collar	A combination of minimum and maximum coupon features.
convertible	A bond that may be converted into equity (or another asset).
convexity	The rate of change of a bond's duration over price shifts.
coupon	The annual (or other) regular interest payment from a bond.
CPI	UK Consumer Price Index – a measure of inflation. See also RPI
credit rating	The creditworthiness of a bond, as determined by several credit rating agencies.
Crest	The central securities depository for UK and Irish markets. Certain bonds can be settled in Crest.
cross default	An issuer failing to pay one debt may be often viewed as in default on all outstanding debt.

debentures	A bond issued with security on real assets (UK definition).
default	The issuer failing to pay a coupon or redemption payment. See also cross default.
dirty price	The price of a bond plus any accrued interest outstanding.
discount	Where the price of a security is below its principal amount. Large amounts are known as deep discounts.
discounted margin	Calculation used by market professionals to establish the spread over LIBOR for an FRN. Also known as DM.
DMO	The UK's Debt Management Office.
DTC	Depository Trust & Clearing – US clearing & settlement system.
duration	The weighted average of a bond's cash flows. Used as a measure of the bond's sensitivity to interest rate shifts.
ECNs	Enhanced Capital Notes. Subordinated mandatory convertibles, sometime known as CoCos.
Eurobond	A bond issued into the international capital markets, may be denominated in any currency.
Euroclear	Large custodian used by all professional traders for holding Eurobonds and other securities.
Eurodollar	Refers to either the offshore deposit rate for the USD or the international (i.e. non-domestic) USD bond market.
FIPS	Fixed Income Preference Shares.
floor	A minimum coupon.
FRN	Floating Rate Note.
FSA	The UK Financial Service Authority.
GEMMS	Gilt Edged Market Makers.
Gilt	British government bonds.
Global	A bond tradable on both the US and the international markets.
investment grade	Bonds rated above BBB.
ICMA	The International Capital Markets Association – the trade body for bond dealers.
immunisation	A technique for structuring a portfolio to negate the impact of future interest rate shifts.
ISA	Individual Savings Account.
ISIN	International Security Identifier Number.
JGB	Japanese government bond.
junk bond	A bond rated below investment grade. Generally BBB- or lower.
lead manager	An investment bank running a new issue.
LIBOR	The London Interbank Offered Rate – the wholesale lending rate.
maturity	The redemption date of the bond.

MBS	Morgage backed securities – bonds backed by mortgage loans.
Moody's	Major international credit rating agency.
MTN	Medium Term Note.
nominal	The face value of the bond.
OAT	French government bond.
ORB	The LSE's Order Book for Retail Bonds.
perpetuals	Bonds with no fixed maturity date.
PIBS	Permanent Interest Bearing Securities. Issued by many UK Building Societies.
preference (shares)	A type of equity, often bearing a fixed coupon; taxed as shares and subject to stamp duty.
premium	When the price of a security is greater than its principal amount (see discount).
prepayment	A feature on MBOs and some asset-backed instruments allowing for full or partial early redemption.
prospectus	The documentation, released at issue, of a bond's terms and conditions.
put	A feature allowing the bondholder to redeem the bond ahead of maturity at a specified date or dates.
QCB	Qualifying Corporate Bond. See tax section.
redemption	The maturity date of the bond.
Retail Bond	A bond issued to private investors, wealth managers etc. Low minimum dealing size and increments.
RPI	UK Retail Price Index – a measure of inflation. See also CPI.
running yield	The coupon payment adjusted for the price. Sometimes known as the income yield.
S&P	Standard & Poor's, a major credit rating agency.
seasoned	Certain US accounts may not purchase a bond until it is trading freely in the secondary market or "seasoned".
senior debt	The highest ranked obligation of a company (although below secured assets).
Short Sterling	The LIFFE 3-month interest rate futures contract.
simple margin	Simple calculation used to establish the spread over LIBOR for an FRN.
simple yield	An easy-to-use yield calculation allowing for both income and capital gain/loss. See also running yield and YTM.
sinking fund	Where the issuer has an obligation to repurchase a given number of outstanding bonds.
SIPP	Self Invested Personal Pension.
spread	The difference between the yield of a bond (typically corporate) and the yield of a benchmark such as a UK Gilt.
strip	A component of a bond such as a coupon or redemption payment which trades independently from the bond.

sub-investment grade	Bonds with ratings below BBB-. Some times known as junk bonds.
subordinated	Debt ranked below senior debt in the balance sheet.
swap	A financial transaction where cash flows are exchanged (e.g. swapping fixed income from a bond to a floating rate).
Talon	The stub of a bearer bond representing the final redemption payment.
TIPS	Treasury Inflation Protected Securities (US).
tranche	Bonds may be issued in several blocks, known as tranches.
yield curve	The relationship between yield and maturity. Shows the market's future expectation of rates.
yield to worst	The yield allowing for the potential exercise of any issuer options.
YTM	Yield to maturity. The standard yield calculation used in the industry. Discounts all cash flows.
zero (coupon)	Bond without coupon, generally issued at discount.

Index

Z